STAGES OF LIFE

T0294630

STAGES OF LIFE

Transcultural Performance & Identity in U.S. Latina Theater

Alberto Sandoval-Sánchez
Nancy Saporta Sternbach

THE UNIVERSITY OF ARIZONA PRESS   TUCSON

The University of Arizona Press
© 2001 The Arizona Board of Regents
First Printing

⊛ This book is printed on acid-free, archival-quality paper.
Manufactured in the United States of America

06   05   04   03   02   01   6   5   4   3   2   1

Library of Congress Cataloging-in-Publication Data
Sandoval-Sánchez, Alberto.
Stages of life : transcultural performance and identity in U.S. Latina
theater / Alberto Sandoval-Sánchez, Nancy Saporta Sternbach.
p. cm.
Includes bibliographical references and index.
ISBN 0-8165-1828-9 (cloth : alk. paper)
ISBN 0-8165-1829-7 (pbk. : alk. paper)
1. Hispanic American theater.   2. Women in the theater—United States.
3. One-person shows (Performing arts)—United States.
4. Hispanic American drama (Spanish)—History and criticism.
I. Sternbach, Nancy Saporta. II. Title.
PN2270.H57 S267 2001
792'.089'68073—dc21   2001001830

British Library Cataloguing-in-Publication Data
A catalogue record for this book is available from the British Library.

Research and publication of this project were partially funded by a grant from the National
Endowment for the Humanities, a federal agency.

A nuestras madres, hermanas, y sobrinas
con nuestro amor y agradecimiento:

María Monserrate Sánchez
Milagros Sandoval
Manuela Rivera Sánchez, in memoriam
Laura Estrada
&
Claire Saporta Sternbach
Joni Saporta Sternbach
Zoë Sternbach-Taubman
Jane Sternbach

CONTENTS

List of Illustrations viii
Acknowledgments ix
Introduction 3

1. Rehearsing Transculturation:
    A Theory for U.S. Latina Theater and Solo Performance 13

2. Setting the Stage: Un teatro de mujeres 41

3. Latina Theater: Stages of Life 57

4. Theater Matters: Foundational Feminist Practices 75

5. The Performance of Their Lives:
    A Hybrid Genre for Transcultural Identities 95

6. From Molcajete to Microwave:
    Agency and Empowerment in Chicana "Dinner" Theater 127

7. Homing the Stage:
    Staging the Discourses of Home in U.S. Latina Theater 153

Notes 191
Bibliography of Latina Playwrights 207
Critical Works Cited and Secondary Sources 221
Index 253

ILLUSTRATIONS

1. Showbill for Cherríe Moraga's *Heart of the Earth: A Popol Vuh Story* 45

2. Josefina López's *Real Women Have Curves* 51

3. Poster for Milcha Sánchez-Scott's *Roosters* 53

4. *Women of Ill Repute* 64

5. Video photograph of Bibi Ramahatulla in Dolores Prida's *Beautiful Señoritas* 89

6. Advertisement for Carmelita Tropicana's *Milk of Amnesia* 105

7. Poster for Monica Palacios's *Greetings from a Queer Señorita* 114

8. Poster for Marga Gomez's *Marga Gomez Is Pretty, Witty, and Gay* and *Memory Tricks* 119

9. Poster for Marga Gomez's *A Line around the Block* 121

10. Alicia Mena's *Las nuevas tamaleras* 140

11. Elaine Romero's *The Fat-Free Chicana* 144

12. Advertisement for Migdalia Cruz's *The Have-Little* 160

13. Playbill for Migdalia Cruz's *Another Part of the House* 165

14. Elaine Romero's *Walking Home* 186

ACKNOWLEDGMENTS

Our first thanks go to the countless Latina playwrights and performers who so generously shared their works and time with us. To them, we owe everything in this book. Thank you, a todas y a cada una, for sending us your manuscripts, for being willing to talk to us, for helping us contact each other, for being patient and forbearing, and, most of all, for producing all of your wonderful work, without which this book would not exist.

Our families near and far sustained us by helping us to get to plays by Latinas, by accompanying us to them, by taking countless phone messages, by being willing to do without us while we devoted ourselves to this project. Thank you especially to John and David, Rafael and Tobias, Claire and Joni, Robert and Margaret.

Our friends and colleagues have generously and patiently listened to us talk about this topic for longer than the normal call of friendship requires or even hopes to expect. We thank Janie Vanpée, Rosetta Cohen, Patricia González, Marina Kaplan, Reyes Lázaro, Lourdes Rojas, Sheila Ortiz Taylor, Susan Bourque, Susan Van Dyne, Marilyn Schuster, Gail Hornstein, Karen Remmler, Michelle Joffroy, Rick Millington, Cornelia Pearsall, Ranu Samantrai, Janice Dewey, Awam Amkpa, Maria Cristina Donnadieu, Mary Heyer, Ruth Smith, and Joan Dwight. Likewise, we thank the Founding Collective of *Meridians* for believing in this project.

To the community of critical readers and practitioners of Latina theater and performance whose dialogue has engaged and continues to engage us, we want to extend our thanks. Your presence and support at our many public and academic speaking venues made this book stronger and more theoretically informed. Gracias a María Teresa Marrero, Yolanda Flores, Diana Taylor, Tiffany López, Diana Rebolledo, Teresa Delgadillo, Lillian Manzor, Antonia Castañeda, Ellen McCracken, Silvia Spitta, José Muñoz, Len Berkman, Beatriz Rizk, David Román, and Deborah Paredez for helping create the dialogue.

Our institutions have offered us generous support in the measure that they were able. We thank John Connolly, provost/dean of the faculty at Smith College, for his unswerving enthusiasm and support. Special thanks to Sandy Doucett at the Office of Advancement at Smith College, who generously read grant proposals at a crucial time in our writing process. We also gratefully acknowledge the support of President Elizabeth T. Kennan and President Joanne V. Creighton, Dean of the Faculty Peter Berek and Dean of the Faculty Donal O'Shea, and Associate Dean of the Faculty Sarah Sutherland at Mount Holyoke College.

We have had research assistants extraordinarias, some of whom have now graduated. Thank you to Odilia Rivera, Monica Dacumos, Rosario Swanson, Alexis Pott, Meredith Field, Diana Archuleta, and Nita Bhasin for all your help. Thank you also to Jo Cannon and Laura Wickware for your technical support during moments of disaster.

From the moment she heard about this project, Joanne O'Hare provided continued and sustained interest, recognizing its urgency and timeliness. We owe our thanks for her vision.

We also thank the anonymous readers at the National Endowment for the Humanities for saying yes to this project and for giving us the needed time to finish it. Likewise, we wish to thank Annie Barva for her careful copyediting.

Finally, we wish to acknowledge all our students, who have patiently listened in classes while we worked out theories of transculturation in the teaching process. Muchas gracias.

STAGES OF LIFE

INTRODUCTION

Uncharted Territories

When in 1992 we perceived that a new phenomenon was underfoot, a new way of looking at and articulating Latina identity through the performing arts, we began to contact Latina playwrights and performers with the idea of editing a volume of their plays and solo performances. At that point, we envisioned an anthology of six or seven plays with our scholarly introduction. We had no clue at that time what we were about to discover: that more than one hundred women were working in all aspects of Latina theater, that at least sixty of them were playwrights or solo performers, and that publications representing this phenomenon were not nearly commensurate with the enormous vital energy being expended in the theater.

As we received manuscripts, it became clear that in order to do justice to this incremental emergence of new voices, we would be compiling a very, very large book. Finally, when the work could no longer be contained in a single volume, we saw that our "scholarly introduction" was in fact the outline for the present book, which now serves as a companion to the anthology of the literature we compiled and called *Puro Teatro: A Latina Anthology* (2000). Our desire to do justice to the many new voices in Latina theater also influenced our decision to include two separate bibliographies in this companion volume: one strictly devoted to the works of Latina playwrights and the other listing the scholarly works we cite in articulating our theories about these works, as well as the secondary sources we recommend to readers. We thought it would be a shame to bury Latina creative works in an overall "works cited and secondary sources" bibliography. Our "Bibliography of Latina Playwrights" is an incredible testament to the astounding creativity of Latina playwrights in the past thirty years.

As new plays arrived in our mailboxes and as others were published in a variety of new venues, we discovered a need to develop a theoretical model that would serve as a way to examine, understand, and contextualize Latina theater as a genre in its own right. Tracing the genealogy of theater (produced, but not necessarily published) by Latinas became a necessary first step in generating this model. Given the absence and invisibility of Latinas in the preestablished and existing paradigm of Latino theater in the U.S., an archeological project emerged. We found ourselves in the situation of having to write the history of Latina theater and solo performance not as a linear, historical trajectory, but rather as synchronic bursts of energy and commitment throughout the country. Although it is important to establish a chronology and development of the emergence of Latina theater, we discovered that if we approached the plays synchronically, our critical reading would locate a unique dialogic relationship. Our study reveals that Latina playwrights (perhaps unknown to each other and at different locations in their careers, in their geography, and in history) have created a corpus of works that has surprising results when read together. These cultural productions, so dissimilar in so many ways, nevertheless seem to share commonalities and similar dramatic structures—that is, a poetics of their own.

This book is possible because Latina theater and solo performance have emerged in the last decade as vibrant, energetic new genres. Visible in a multitude of ways throughout the country, their practitioners range from teenagers to grandmothers, from individual to collective playwrights, and from ethnic groupings to political affiliations. In the East and the West, the Midwest and the Southwest, these performances have ranged from the solo to the grandiose, from the comic to the tragic, and from the serious to the camp. Such heterogeneity and diversity indicate that we are indeed at a historic crossroads for Latina theater and solo performance. Examining the ensemble of such work suggested a way to theorize the historic emergence of Latinas on stage. And understanding these theatrical productions in given historical conjunctures clearly called for a theory born in Latin America, but applicable to U.S. Latinas—namely, Latin American theories of transculturation.

As we immersed ourselves in our project of collecting manuscripts from far and wide, our first theoretic challenges were the absence of any established history of a poetics of Latina theater and solo performance and the paucity of criticism.[1] Through theories of transculturation, however, we have been able to locate these works in given synchronic moments and processes that show how they build on politics of representation, identity, location, and affinity.

By *politics of representation,* we mean the double-pronged conscious process whereby playwrights dismantle and undo dominant stereotypical representations at the same time that they revise and rearticulate new ways of seeing. How Dolores Prida, for example, undergoes this process of deconstruction is manifest in her play *Beautiful Señoritas.*

A *politics of identity* is the process by which a speaking subject constitutes herself in given social relations of power and discursive formations, while at the same time positioning herself in the dialectical "give and take" of a subjectivity-in-process—known as "toma y daca" in theories of transculturation. In the plays *Giving Up the Ghost* by Cherríe Moraga and *Simply Maria or The American Dream* by Josefina López, spectators witness the trials and tribulations of the young protagonists in their agonizing struggles to construct a transcultural mestiza identity. These protagonists confront their Chicana identities in the face of a politics that previously essentialized them in nationalist, patriarchal, heterosexist models.

A *politics of location* situates a subject in a given geopolitical space, acknowledging the relations of power within that space and the identity formations that emerge from it. The tolerance of difference sets the stage for a recognition of more than one way of doing theater, especially in lesbian representation. Mutual respect, activist politics, and everyday acts of intervention, for instance, showed through the urban experience during the Reagan-Bush years and beyond that community action and coalition building provided a much needed epicenter for an emerging politics of affinity and survival.

A *politics of affinity*—embracing Chela Sandoval's theorization of "oppositional consciousness" (1991:11)—recognizes difference without attempting to erase uncomfortable and painful issues such as homophobia, racism, class boundaries, and AIDS. A firmly placed politics of affinity enables the protagonists of *Heroes and Saints* by Cherríe Moraga, *I'll Be Home para la Navidad* by Janis Astor del Valle, and *Milk of Amnesia* by Carmelita Tropicana to derive strength from their communities and their agencies.

Given that theater is a creative space where a politics of identity can manifest itself with the greatest resonance, it functions as a model of and for the urgency of social action through which audiences can witness alternative or dominant paradigms. Taking in consideration that in their own process of reception, all individuals in the audience will react in particular ways according to their own experiences and politico-ideological points of view, Michel Pêcheux's model of subject formation (1982) is applicable here. He proposes three mechanisms through which subjecthood is constituted: identification, counteridentification, and disidentification. For our purposes, audiences can identify, counteridentify, and disidentify with the protagonists and with the dramatic action as imaginary social constructions of reality are staged. Identification occurs when the spectator, a "good subject," feels comfortable and goes to see a play or performance to confirm her or his own horizon of expectations, ideologies, and identity enacted or performed. At the other side of the spectrum is counteridentification, which is oppositional by nature. In this case, the "bad subject" rejects both dominant ideology and those positions claimed by the "good subject." As for disidentification, Diane Macdonell has further developed Pêcheux's theoretical apparatus: a disidentified subject works " 'on and against' prevailing practices of ideological subjection" (1986:40; citing Pêcheux 1982:159, 215). She adds: "Disidentification, by contrast [to counteridentification], comes from another position, one existing antagonistically, with the effect that the identity and identifications set up in dominant ideology, though never escaped entirely, are transformed and displaced" (40). In *Disidentifications: Queers of Color and the Performance of Politics,* Latino cultural critic José Esteban Muñoz takes Pêcheux's project a step further by exploring disidentification as a "strategy of survival or resistence" (1999:5) for minority subjects.

For those who inhabit the margin or border—spiritually, physically, or metaphysically—disidentification signifies flexibility, straddling, oscillation, and liminality in a constant juggling of identities as a "survival strateg[y]" (Muñoz 1999:5) within the dislocations and contradictions of the subjects' cultural presence.

Many of the protagonists in the plays and solo performances we analyze inhabit the space of a disidentified subject in a transcultural identity, which is why they can claim their own agency in all its hybridity. Never should we assume that this hybridity is a given; rather, it is constructed as a process whereby protagonists (and audiences) problematize the multiple strands of their identity simultaneously. For this reason, once these hybrid, transcultural identities are staged, their newness exposes their function as a dialectic pedagogical model. This is to say that both protagonists and audiences leave the play or performance with a sense of being, becoming, and belonging. They learn a new grammar of ontology at the same time that they begin to unlearn racism.

Before the 1960s and the "Chicano Renaissance," when Latinos/as had little control or power over self-representations and instead saw themselves through the prism of the dominant gaze, it is no surprise that a literature would emerge whose very core insisted on a politics of resistance. Centering on theater in their own image and on the deconstruction of stereotypes, practitioners of Latino theater saw the genre as a way both to create new dramatic models and in the process to educate audiences on political issues that affected their everyday lives. To a large extent, that pedagogical project, legacy of the Teatro Campesino and others like it that followed, is still intact today. Although the immediacy of the political issues continually changes, the model to deal with them remains.[2]

The pedagogical function of the plays and performances we examine is crucial because at given historical moments of cultural transformation identities are always fluid and in the making; that function is especially crucial when applied to transcultural subjects. The dramatic action in these works typically moves from crisis to negotiation, from incertitude to affirmation, from meandering to anchoring, from confrontation to accommodation, from ambivalence to reconciliation. As new protagonists stage moments of all of these dramatic situations, they articulate and develop a sense of self in the world; this is to say that *who they are* and *where they are located* are inextricably linked. These subject positionalities place them in social contexts that constantly demand the enunciation of an ever-evolving self within shifting identity formations. Given that the protagonists in Latina plays and performances deploy the theater as the means by which these transitions can occur, we decided to center our own work on these selected paradigmatic moments when identity in all its provisionality and cultural transformation is questioned. While viewing the tensions surrounding these transitions, audiences can experience the full range of the existential and ontological processes that we outline within the theories of transculturation discussed in chapter 1.

The present project is the result of our having read a vast number of plays and solo performances by Latinas, in both published and manuscript form. Some of these names are widely known nationally and internationally, such as Cherríe Moraga, Maria Irene Fornes, Milcha Sánchez-Scott, Dolores Prida, Marga Gomez, and Carmelita Tropicana. We are not the first critics to group them together in an attempt to establish a genre called Latina theater and solo performance. Although some of our effort was historical, other parts of it became archeological. In that regard, we found ourselves tracing and mapping these works in dialogue with each other. The first part of the book outlines our methodology, a model by which to approach Latina theatricality through the theory of transculturation; it is followed by a historical introduction that also includes our attempt to define, organize, and theorize a poetics of Latina theater and solo performance. The ideal way to trace the genealogy of Latina theater, we realized, was to read seemingly disparate pieces simultaneously. In a dialogic strategy, we decided to group works thematically, chronologically, and ideologically. Given the disconnected, sporadic, and episodic spurts of early Latina theater, our insistence on this approach helped us to identify specific historic formations. In particular, our chapter "Theater Matters: Foundational Feminist Practices," discusses these germinal moments in detail by pointing to feminist political agendas through which it is possible to speak of a genealogy of Latina theater and of what we call its foundational discursive sites.

Once we compiled and categorized Latina theatrical works, it became obvious that solo performance was capturing audiences nationwide and merited its own chapter. Many of the Latina solo performers discussed in this book and published in *Puro Teatro* began their careers in acting companies such as El Teatro Campesino, Teatro de la Esperanza, Culture Clash, and Latins Anonymous. Latina solo performance, like Latina theater, does not exist in a vacuum. It has its own history, properties, structure, and poetics, all of which share in and digress from more traditional modes of Latina theater. Solo performance and traditional theater complement and enhance each other; each is the richer for having experienced the other; one depends and thrives on the other. Both performative models register specific moments of transculturation. If in Latina theater such a moment is made manifest in a ritualistic collective form, in solo performance the same paradigm appears from the personal, individual, and even intimate vision of the artist. In this regard, we look at the solo performances of Carmelita Tropicana, Monica Palacios, and Marga Gomez, whose complex hybrid identities as Latina lesbians constitute living examples of transculturation in the making.

In the last two chapters, our aim is to highlight the dialectical relationship between location and transcultural identity. From the vast array of congregating places, we focus on the two sites where the transculturated subject empowers herself in these plays. These two sites, the kitchen and the home, although most often read as confining spaces in a patriarchal context, acquire new currency and significance in Latina plays as protagonists gain agency within them. It is within the framework of transculturation that these women exercise their full potentiality and creativity. The dialectical relationship between a politics of identity in its intersection with a politics of location facilitates a critical reading centering on how positionality is more than a mere physical or geographic site. Rather, our work locates the subject in relation to her cultura. The interplay between these dynamic forces produces the dramatic conflict in which tradition is negotiated with new ways of seeing. As these transcultural protagonists transform these domestic spaces and rewrite tradition, they change the function of the spaces themselves. Within these dramatic discursive locations, they struggle to present alternative worlds as they simultaneously attempt to reconcile the past with the present and the future. Such moments of cultural crisis function as sites of intersection where ideologies—both previous and emergent—meet, confront, and accommodate each other.

At its core, then, this book attempts to address the transcultural dynamics of a politics of representation, identity, and location. Our critical practice argues that at specific moments of cultural crisis, identities are reevaluated, revised, reformed, and transformed. This continuous process of negotiation and revision constitutes the kernel of the dramatic action in Latina theater and solo performance: from it there will be not only other theatrical and cultural manifestations, but, more importantly, a wellspring from which hybrid, transnational, border identities can and will construct themselves in every single theatrical production.

Process of Collaboration

Colleagues from all disciplines have inquired about the nature of our collaboration in these many years of research and writing. "Do you each write a section and then give it to the other? Does one person do the research while the other concentrates on the writing? Do you argue? Are you still friends now that the project is completed? Does one person's point of view prevail? Does one person dominate the collaboration?"

No doubt, a division of labor might have cut down on the times we needed to see each other—daily, at the end of the project. But the writing aspect of our profession is sometimes a lonely endeavor. It is one thing to seal oneself off in isolation and academic pursuit when the object of the study has a historical precedent. For us, however, that approach proved to be anathema to our project; for a fledgling study like ours, finding a way to process theoretical issues and understudied texts became a necessity. We considered the fact that many other professionals work in teams with the idea that two brains function better than one. In this sense, our project was born of the notion that a collaboration suited its temperament perfectly. After all, what is theater but a collaboration of many brains, hands, bodies, hearts, and fields of expertise working collectively? Thus, in answer to the aforementioned questions, we can confirm that every aspect of the book was collaborative: we read and discussed all the plays together; we researched and discussed new theoretical practices together; and, most importantly, we wrote every single sentence together. Our success in completing such a monumental collaborative project owes much to two factors that propelled our work. The first was simply the idea of sticking to it. Despite health issues, pregnancy, the birth of a new baby, personal crises, family responsibilities, computer breakdowns, and all the other obstacles that get in the way of finishing books, we met nearly every day when we were not teaching. Some of these days turned out to be "talking" days; some were heavy theoretical days, with emphasis on the esoteric; but most were writing days, and almost all of them were intellectually stimulating and mutually fulfilling.

The satisfaction of simultaneously seeing a friend, sharing ideas, laughing together, and accomplishing our goal enriched each of us. The further pleasure of developing a thesis, applying it to a myriad of works, and seeing how texts respond to a theoretical apparatus opened new venues of inquiry and investigation. While our colleagues at our respective institutions were complaining about the isolation and loneliness of the long-distance writer, we were enjoying each other's company as well as the texts we were reading.

We are certainly not the first professionals to approach our field as a team. Physicians, attorneys, and others work in teams that enhance the output of a single individual. Academics, too, have taken up collaboration in a variety of styles. In the sciences and social sciences, it is a natural phenomenon. Though rarer in the humanities, many models of joint projects exist, especially within feminist praxis. Each of these models has its own agenda and working procedures. Nevertheless, most of them seem to privilege the notion of a division of labor whereby each partner participates by writing only a section, a fragment, a chapter, and so on. In our case, every step of the project and every word written entailed the process of collaboration. Although this procedure might not have been the most economical, it served as a sort of miniseminar in which we were the two participants.

Our common denominator was our grounding in feminist theory and in Latino/a and Latin American studies. We brought together complementary fields of expertise in our own personal critical practices, which entail revisionist and alternative modes of inquiry. When we began this project, the dominant paradigm in our field, Latino theater, continued to be male and patriarchal. The dominant paradigm within feminist theater had only just begun to recognize work by Latinas. Neither paradigm acknowledged a history, poetics, or a theoretical framework from which to approach these works archeologically, genealogically, and systematically. Thus, the project was much more monumental than we had originally anticipated, which is why collaboration became a necessary procedural strategy. And, although our experience, politics, and academic training easily conflated, our individual identities and ethnicities of diaspora and migration—a Puerto Rican and a Sefardita, male and female, gay and straight—added the mortar to the building blocks of the text we produce here.

What does this mean, when two people sit down and write every word together? Writing in collaboration means sacrificing individualism to the partnership. It means long hours of discussion until an idea consolidates, coalescing both points of view. It means negotiating not only those ideas, but also style, vocabulary, rhetoric, and even theoretical jargon. This dialogic process involves a certain fear of loss. Will one person's ideas be appropriated by the monster called "collaboration"? Will a review committee judge our collaboration a lesser effort because it contains more than one signature? Will colleagues at other institutions question our capacity to work alone: "Is so-and-so good enough?" and "Who wrote what?" Will we be so changed by the process itself that our own writing will be transformed? Will we argue about some part of the process and sacrifice the friendship to the book?

These questions defined our positions vis-à-vis each other and the project. We quickly learned who obtained the most efficacious results in each task or whose previous knowledge contributed seamlessly to the theoretical underpinnings, and we used these discoveries accordingly. As the book advanced, we found ourselves saturated with the work it engendered. At those moments of complete exasperation and exhaustion, we exchanged tasks and responsibilities. Consequently, we developed an uncanny sense of being able to recognize those unpredictable signs of frustration in each other in order to offer some relief. Although discipline and respect for the other's time kept us on track, patience with the other person's personal life enabled us to shift professional responsibilities back and forth. Day by day the process of negotiation that we had established in the writing spilled over into a process of accommodation as we recognized each other's life outside the book. It goes without saying that none of this could have happened without the deep intellectual respect that we hold for each other. If one of us had doubts about the other's ideas, this powerful sense of respect overrode those individual responses. Thus, we not only talked; we also listened. That our two discrete voices have merged into one in these pages is a product of our process of reading both the plays and the theory out loud to each other.

As the project evolved, the undeniable intellectual pleasure of sharing our newly discovered field with each other unfolded. Not only were we not working in isolation, but we had a way to bounce ideas off each other, no matter how outlandish they might have seemed. In our continual process of negotiation, we found that the subjects of our sentences often left us searching frantically for the right verb. That search, and many others of its kind, led us to paroxysms of laughter and hilarity as we played with ideas and language. To have had such fun and relief from the pressures and detachment of writing compensated for the necessary commute to each other's institutions as well as for the enormity of the project itself. Our friendship and intellectual curiosity moved us from the solitary experience of the scholarly life into a solidarity, which is the true nature of theater itself. As we disengage ourselves from the institutional role of the scholar, nos saludamos cariñosamente.

ONE

REHEARSING TRANSCULTURATION

A THEORY FOR U.S. LATINA THEATER
& SOLO PERFORMANCE

One of the first questions that confronts the scholar in Latina/o studies is the current and necessary interdisciplinarity of the field itself, for anchoring Latina/o studies to one specific academic site raises myriad questions. Its affiliations—theoretical territories coupled with the border crossings of its positionality and resistance—intersect with and have been informed by so many existing disciplines and methodologies that much confusion arises when we attempt to fix it in one specific location. Shall we place Latina theater and solo performance, a versatile and heterogeneous genre, in Latina/o studies, in Spanish, English, or theater departments, or rather in American studies, Latin American studies, women's studies, performance studies, or ethnic and Chicano studies programs? That each of these home bases sees itself as a rightful site for the genre demonstrates the intersection and cross-pollination of Latina/o studies in general and of Latina theater and solo performance in particular.

Of course, each of these programs also has a vested interest in what it sees as the most salient critical features of these performative texts according to its own scholarly, curricular, and political interests. Among the programs listed above, of vital importance to our project is the intersection of Latin American studies and American studies. That Latin America and Anglo America share a continent surely grounds scholars concerned with one and the other in similar histories, if in different situations of power. Yet each of these fields never seems to overcome the limitation imposed on it by its lack of understanding of the other.

In the past few years, in one of the most visible new moves of academia, American studies reconfigured itself to include previously marginalized U.S. cultures and their literatures. Given that Latina/o literature is produced in the

U.S. and is written in English, it is perfectly reasonable to expect that American studies—in its new version of itself as encompassing all the Americas—should discover Latinos/as and with them, of course, the border. Although Americanists' efforts to include *all* Americans is surely to be applauded, our own training emerges from Latin American studies, a field that is as historically determined by the Cold War period as postcolonial studies is connected to millennial globalization. Here, our goal is to establish a constructive dialogue of experiences and theories that could join the Americas precisely at their most dramatic encuentro, the borderlands.

It is quite fitting that American studies, in its task of reinventing itself and taking stock of its "imperial house," would also consider U.S. imperial legacies and practices, both abroad and—more controversially—at home, specifically at la frontera. Once marginalized as outposts, the borderlands are crucial now that American studies recognizes the U.S. as a site of nation and empire building; in this manner, Americanists redefine their field and its political platform by exchanging the "frontier" for la frontera, as Amy Kaplan has written: "Where the frontier implies a model of center and periphery, which confront one another most often in a one-way imposition of power, the borderlands are seen as multidimensional and transterritorial: they do not only lie at the geographic and political margins of national identity but as often traverse the center of the metropolis" (1993:16).

Such a geopolitical view, which these Americanists hold now in their new multicultural perspective, is nevertheless consistent with the longstanding Latin American and Latin Americanist position: that the U.S. is the site of overwhelming imperialism, both internally and externally. It is not insignificant or coincidental that two of Latin America's greatest thinkers of the nineteenth century, José Martí and Rubén Darío—both of whom lived transnationally and both of whose work spans the last decades of the century—were the most vociferous about the expanding and terrifying new role of the U.S. From them, we get such well-known phrases as "the belly of the beast" and "Mañana podremos ser yanquis" ("Tomorrow we may all be Yankees").[1] They knew that the U.S. had emerged as the tyrant of the hemisphere after the Mexican War, and both of them intuited what this tyranny might mean for Latin Americans. Darío's famous question, "¿Tantos millones de hombres hablaremos inglés?" ("Will millions of us be speaking English?" [1946:73]), reveals not an anxiety about bilingualism, but his chilling prescience about being "delivered to the ferocious barbarians" (73)—i.e., the U.S.

Thus, at this historical moment, it seems all the more crucial to anchor our work, a Latina studies project, in a base that not only acknowledges and reclaims the Latin American roots of what we will be calling a transcultural subjectivity,[2] but also that calls into question critical practices that tend to obliterate the Latin American component of "the Americas." Thus, in order to locate our critical reading of U.S. Latina theater and solo performance in a hemispheric theoretical framework, we purposely privilege Latin American theories of transculturation that, it seems to us, would have had more international currency had they been written in English. This move on our part is both methodological and political at the same time that it is practical: if we are going to "study" the Americas, let us do more than pay lip service to the Spanish language and to the vast critical repertoire that it contains. If we require that students graduating with degrees in Latin American studies be proficient in Spanish or Portuguese, so too should the same requirements apply to academics who have suddenly revamped American studies to include "the Americas." It is a politically dangerous moment when all circulation of texts about the "Americas" happens in English only and when the only Latin American intellectuals invited to our "multicultural" programs and "celebrations of diversity" on U.S. campuses are those proficient in English. (As a side note, our views on this subject have also influenced our decision *not* to have Spanish-language terms italicized and thus distinguished in this volume, as is common practice. We also translated Spanish terms and phrases only when there is difficulty in understanding the meaning of the whole sentence.)

Even scholars with the slightest modicum of interest in Latin America know of the long and problematic relationship the U.S. has had and continues to have with the region. Economic, political, or tourist designs on particular locations since the end of the Spanish-American War established colonial conditions through such epithets as "banana republic," "the good neighbor," "south of the border," "commonwealth," "backyard," or "Free Trade Zone." One glance at the U.S. role in the Cuban war of independence, the invasion of Puerto Rico, the Mexican annexation, or subsequent interventions in the affairs of Caribbean and Central American nations surely would contest any ideas about U.S. neutrality. Indeed, each decade of the twentieth century brought a specific list of discursive constructions and agendas according to the administration in Washington, D.C. But one thing is clear: as a nation, El Norte is never, nor has it ever been, indifferent about Latin America.

At the centenary of the U.S. imperialist project (1998), a revisionist reading of Latin America took place when Americanists took stock of what Amy Kaplan calls the "absences" in U.S. recognition of its imperial self. For

Kaplan, these absences are: "the absence of culture from the history of U.S. imperialism; the absence of empire from the study of American culture; and the absence of the United States from the postcolonial study of imperialism" (1993:11).

Books such as Kaplan and Pease's *Cultures of United States Imperialism* are supremely important efforts for both the visibility and the paradigm shift, but as Silvia Spitta (n.d.) has written, only five out of twenty-six essays in that book have to do with Latin America.[3] Of those five, none addresses the unique situation of Puerto Rico's colonial status vis-à-vis U.S. imperialism. Most crucially, the U.S. relationship with Latin America should never be viewed as simply "one more" practice of U.S. imperialism: it is a unique one, for it is with Latin America, and specifically with Mexico, that the U.S. shares a 2,000-mile border. Our "other" border, the nonmilitarized 4,000-mile one we share with Canada, becomes invisible as all the attention shifts southward. It is striking to note that the low-intensity conflict of the Mexican border has required the removal of Immigration and Naturalization Service (INS) agents from our northern border to "police" our southern one. The domestic colonialism, constant migration, and increasing Latino demographics also point to a series of hegemonic maneuvers that take place not only in a political arena, but also at a cultural level. For us, it is in this domain that transculturation emerges in all of its resistance, subversion, and creativity.

Transculturation to the Second Power

Because the main theoretical lens with which we examine the phenomenon of Latina theater and solo performance is transculturation, a useful beginning is the work of Cuban anthropologist Fernando Ortiz. His 1940 book *Contrapunteo cubano del tabaco y del azúcar* (reprinted in 1973) outlines the analytical uses of the term *transculturation* and the specific application of it for Cuba and, by Ortiz's own suggestion, for the rest of America.[4] Ortiz's continental vision is not limited just to Cuba; its application has a widespread appeal: "el concepto de la transculturación es cardinal y elementalmente indispensable para comprender la historia de Cuba y, por análogas razones, la de toda la América en general" (1973:135).[5] Little did Ortiz know in 1940 just how far his proposal would reach *all* the Americas, including the U.S.

Entering into the theoretical space of transculturation shows how Latin American intellectuals have found Ortiz's anthropological framework to be instrumental and applicable not only to literature but to culture in general. Ortiz's awareness of his neologism *transculturación* constitutes an ideological intervention for his theoretical stand, in his own words, "in counterpoint" to dominant metropolitan uses of the term *acculturation*. For Ortiz, transculturation signifies the accumulation of historical processes that include the many transmigrations of a diversity of peoples to the Americas and not just the homogenizing view of the imposing Spaniard or the enslaved African. Rather, his schema includes the entire Mediterranean world: non-Spanish Europeans, Chinese, subcontinent Indians, and, of course, the indigenous peoples who were living on the island. He specifies transculturation as:

> las diferentes fases del proceso transitivo de una cultura a otra, porque éste no consiste solamente en adquirir una distinta cultura, que es lo que en rigor indica la voz anglo-americana *acculturation,* sino que el proceso implica también necesariamente la pérdida o desarraigo de una cultura precedente, lo que pudiera decirse una parcial *desculturación,* y además significa la consiguiente creación de nuevos fenómenos culturales que pudieran denominarse de *neo-culturación.* (1973:134−35)[6]

Significantly, it is precisely the relations of power constructed between the dominated and the dominator that have given rise to the processes of transculturation, processes that would never have taken place without these transmigrations.

Although Ortiz's theory of transculturation was disseminated by Angel Rama's widely read *Transculturación narrativa en América Latina* (1982), it is noteworthy that neither Rama nor any of the critics familiar with his or Ortiz's work have paid much attention to Cuban poet Nancy Morejón's contribution to this vital discussion. Unlike Rama, Morejón's analysis complicates the issue by expanding Ortiz's categories of race, class, ethnicity, and nationality, and suggestively introducing the term *nueva sexualidad* (1982:26). As Morejón maps the experience of conquest and colonization of the Americas with special attention focused on the Caribbean, she underscores Ortiz's point about the hetereogeneity of what she calls the "immigrants" from Spain and Africa within their own cultures even before the colonizing moment. Neither Spanish nor African forebears of contemporary denizens of Cuba were a monolithic ethnic unit, but rather represented a cornucopia of races, languages, ethnicities, and even sexualities. For Morejón, the concept of mestizaje and self-fashioning mestiza/o identities cannot be excised from the historical processes—particularly the ones that gave rise to slavery and the plantation economy—that brought these immigrants to Cuba in the first place.

We cannot here delve into the entire genealogy of mestizaje, a long and complicated cultural polemic in Latin America. Suffice it to say that mestizaje is a sociohistorical reality, a "performance of identity," with different ideological meanings and functions in given conjunctures of Latin American political and regional history. If at one time and place it was an ideological classification imposed by the metropolitan apparatus of power, later on, after independence as each discrete country defined itself ethnically and nationally, the formation of a criollo identity insisted on constructions such as mestizaje in order to preserve their whiteness. In Peru, for example, mestizaje was most certainly cross-referenced with the indigenous population, as it was in Mexico. But in the Caribbean, Morejón argues, the genocide of the indigenous populations gave rise to a new unequivocal meaning of mestizaje: it must move away from the mythical invocations of Indians to include the Caribbean reality of slavocracy. Therefore, if at first *mestizaje* was an imposed term, a currency coined for Spanish and criollo convenience and privilege, later on it became an act of reclamation, intervention, and self-definition. When we finally arrive at Gloria Anzaldúa's 1987 Chicana definition of mestizaje, we have come a long way from the days of Spanish colonial rule and Caribbean slave-owning plantations.

Mestizaje, then, must be understood as a social construct, whether that construct benefits the subaltern subject (as in self-definition) or the imperial hierarchy and caste (as in the famous Spanish pyramid of power); in both cases, mestizaje is a racial categorization that may lean more heavily in some cases on race, in others on culture, and in others on nation. For this reason, seeing mestizaje only in cultural terms erases African presence and history. Therefore, when Cuban cultural critic Roberto Fernández Retamar claims that raza is an "irrevelante hecho biológico" ("irrelevant biological fact" [1972:97, note 2]), we question his position: Is he complicit in the erasure of African presence and history? Does he merely see mestizaje as another historico-cultural ideological construct? Or does he intuit José Vasconcelos's interesting and problematic thesis of the "raza cósmica" (1942)?[7] Retamar quotes Vasconcelos's concept, which states that Latin America would be the place where the ultimate new (mestizo) race would be "forged." Little could either Vasconcelos (1920s) or Fernández Retamar (1972) in their historic moments envision that the real test of mestizaje would not actually be in Latin America, but rather on the frontera and "transfrontera" (Saldívar 1997:13−14), as the new mestiza/o identities have constructed themselves both literally and figuratively in Tijuana/San Diego, El Paso/Juárez, as well as in New York, Miami, and Los Angeles. Even Martí and Darío, who intuited the future with uncanny accuracy, did not foresee that mestizaje's main stage would actually be in "las entrañas del monstruo" (in the belly of the beast).

Returning to Morejón's crucial discourse on the nuances of transculturation, we can see how her work coincides with Rama's and with the postcolonial theory of the late 1980s that emerged from English-speaking theorists. For Morejón, the term *transculturation*

> significa interacción constante, trasmutación entre dos o más componentes culturales cuya finalidad inconsciente crea un tercer conjunto cultural—es decir, cultura—nuevo e independendiente, aunque sus bases, sus raíces descansen sobre los elementos precedentes. La influencia recíproca es aquí determinante. Ningún elemento se sobrepone a otro; por el contrario, uno se torna otro hasta convertirse en un tercero. Ninguno permanece inmutable. Todos cambian para crecerse en un 'toma y daca' que engendrará una novísima textura.(1982:23)[8]

Morejón's vision—her early use of such terms as *subaltern, Eurocentric, identity, nueva sexualidad,* and *third space*—surely deserves more attention than the shelf life her book receives in remote libraries. As Morejón theorized from the margin, her own positionality as a woman—an Afro-Cuban one at that—an American, and a poet reproduced in theory what had already taken place in fiction: writers of the Latin literary boom of the 1960s and 1970s, almost all of whom were men, had already relegated women fiction writers to the margin. These male writers, revolutionary in their politics but sometimes reactionary and chauvinistic in their sociopolitical patriarchal praxis, considered "subalterns" such as Morejón and her theories marginal and inconsequential. Furthermore, the process of decolonization, as Morejón reminds us, is never a swift one. In their cultural resistance and revision of Caribbean history, the new transcultural subaltern subjects to whom Morejón's book listens echo through time as they "toman la lengua del conquistador y la viran al revés" ("take the language of the conquistador and turn it back on him" [1982:318]). In such terms, Fernández Retamar also reenacts Calibán as the symbol of the Cuban, Marxist revolutionary subject and reminds us of Calibán's prophetic words: "You taught me language, and my profit on't / Is, I know how to curse" (*The Tempest* I.ii; Fernández Retamar 1972:12).

Morejón's contribution augured a new theoretical framework that is applicable to what later became known as "the new politics of ethnicity and diaspora" in British cultural studies. Although her thesis is that the concept of nation—specifically the Cuban nation—cannot be understood without considering the process of transculturation, her real purpose is much more ambitious. In it, Nicolás Guillén's poetry serves as an anthropological case study with which she formulates a new politics of identity for the Caribbean. For Morejón, transculturation must be taken into account with the politics of class struggle and with a history of violence, slavery, and the slave trade. That history is the history of mestizaje, which, for Morejón, is the common, everyday name for transculturation (1982:165–66). Morejón's visionary outlook predates many postcolonial theoreticians who complicate issues of race and ethnicity, as she says: "la doble condición de explotación que sufre el ciudadano cubano negro: es un trabajador cuya situación, en la vida social del país, está 'limitada' por el color de su raza" (1982:201).[9]

Brilliant though he was, Latin America's preeminent literary critic Angel Rama did not make a point of including race or gender in his widely disseminated theory of transculturation, *Transculturación narrativa en América Latina,* published in 1982 but developed as an article in 1974. In his analysis, Rama relates literature to the process of modernity and centers his discussion on the ever-constant preoccupation of Latin American intellectuals with Latin American identity formation. Rama's interdisciplinary approach allows readers to see literature as an integral part of a cultural process that cannot be dissociated from the political and social praxis of the intellectual. Specifically, he uses transculturation to explain the intricate relationship as well as the discrepancies between Latin American regional autochthonous literary expressions and cosmopolitan avant-garde literature that derives from European models. The emergent literature is the creation of a new literary expression that both recovers and preserves American languages (such as Quechua), oral traditions, and ways of seeing in a bicultural/bilingual world. Neil Larsen succinctly summarizes Rama's theory when he describes transculturation as the "mediatory agency whereby the Latin-American work of art actively transforms and regrounds the modernism of the metropolis by prompting a synthesis of the metropolis's antirationalism with the prerationalization of rural peasant and indigenous tribal cultures" (1990:xxxvi).

Like Ortiz, Rama sees these acts of transculturation as processes that include such notions as *deculturation* and *neoculturation,* both of which speak to the condition of transformation, fusion, and hybridity. Thus, even if such a process incurs loss, it also is simultaneously overcome with the capacity for selection from elements of both cultures from which it draws, bringing about a new moment of rediscovery. Most important, though, is the notion that the positionality of transculturation is about resistance and subversion, and not about passivity and assimilation. Aware that transculturation implies a fractured and bifocal condition, "mestiza y original" (1982:173), Rama instead focuses on the possibility of creativity and renovation in a counterattack against deculturation. It is this dimension of resistance that allows for the agency of the counterhegemonic subject to decolonize the mind and that speaks directly to the projects of U.S. border writers such as Gloria Anzaldúa and José David Saldívar or to Latina playwrights, which is our main focus.

Before we proceed, it is important to place all three theorists—Ortiz, Morejón, and Rama—in their ideological and historical spheres within Latin American cultural history. Specifically, each speaks from her or his historic location as a Latin American subject in a determined national context. That they represent three defining moments in Latin American history places their theoretical apparatus in a situation that is at once both national and transnational, contestatory and political, but in all three cases counterhegemonic in their implicit or explicit dialogue or quarrel with U.S. imperialism in Latin America.

Significantly, Ortiz's book was published in 1940 (translated in 1947) precisely at the moment the U.S. set its Good Neighbor Policy into action in Latin America. In a revealing introduction to the book, Bronislaw Malinowski tells us: "la interdependencia [entre Cuba y los Estados Unidos] es mutua. Cuba, junto a México, es el más próximo de esos pueblos latinoamericanos donde la 'política del buen vecino debería ser establecida con toda inteligencia, previsión y generosidad de que son ocasionalmente capaces los estadistas y hasta los magnates financieros de los Estados Unidos' " (1973:13–14).[10]

Malinowski's precise allusion is to the new relationship with the south that Franklin Roosevelt himself initiated in an attempt to minimize nearly a century of interventions in Latin America. Roosevelt said: "In the field of world policy I would dedicate this Nation to the policy of the good neighbor—the neighbor who resolutely respects himself and, because he does so, respects the rights of others—the neighbor who respects his obligations and respects the sanctity of his agreements in and with a world of neighbors"

(Roosevelt 1938–50:14). Although Roosevelt's ideological platform depended on and validated the political, economic, and cultural crusade against the Axis and potential Nazi penetration of the Americas, he also knew that he had to secure a hemispheric alliance, a Pan-American unity, which he negotiated through diplomacy, economic policies, strategic military agreements, and cultural exchanges. However, Ortiz's position is neither simple, docile, nor facile, nor is it simply a response to Roosevelt and the Good Neighbor Policy. According to Gustavo Pérez-Firmat, every instance of Ortiz's theory is grounded in his resistance to assimilation and imperialism with the persistent neologisms that pervade his text. Pérez-Firmat brilliantly argues that Ortiz's use of such terminology is neither casual nor ideology-free. Instead, Ortiz emblematizes resistance, "an anti-colonial gesture" (Pérez-Firmat 1989:26–29, 32) to the Good Neighbor Policy, by Cubanizing his own vocabulary.

Nancy Morejón, on the other hand, embodies in the flesh the possibility of social and national transformation after the revolution. Her argument, which incorporates the Other, constitutes a project that redefines Cuban nationhood in all its transcultural condition by problematizing how the nation changes when race and gender constitute categories of analysis. Thus, while Ortiz's theory is a first formulation of transculturation, Morejón and the Cuban Revolution represent a second one.

The third application is inaugurated with Rama's complicated project—begun as his 1974 article "Los procesos de transculturación en la narrativa latinoamericana," which entails a myriad of social, political, theoretical, and literary agendas. Several points must be acknowledged at the start: (1) this article appears at the apogee of the Latin American literary boom; (2) Latin American intellectuals were exiled from the region in mass numbers during these years because of military dictatorships and the repression that they brought; (3) Rama's decade-long project sought to establish a new paradigm in theoretical approaches to Latin American literature—approaches that, in turn, would also articulate and contribute to a continental definition of "nuestra América"; and (4) his inclusion of marginal, regional literatures established a dialogue between the metropolitan and the regional, the dominant and the periphery.

Accounting for all these factors, we can see that Rama's project on transculturation was actually much more ambitious than even Rama himself anticipated. Shortly before his death in 1983, in a letter to Jean Franco, he expressed his disappointment that his theory of transculturation had not reached a wider readership and acceptance.[11] Significantly, although he intuited his book's importance, what he could not have anticipated was the application of his theory for minority writers outside of or descended from Latin America and for the entirety of the postcolonial theoretical framework that emerged in the 1990s.

Rama's attempt to include the Other speaks to and of his own subject positionality as a transcultural critic at the site where theory and practice intersect. In 1973, Europeans were devouring García Márquez, Vargas Llosa, Fuentes, Donoso, and other writers of the boom who were avidly published in Barcelona. Simultaneously, Rama turns his gaze inward to the region and specifically to José María Arguedas, whose work epitomizes the transcultural subjectivity that Rama endeavors to theorize. That this work is set in indigenous Peru places it apart from the magical realism of the boom club,[12] whose gaze (and, in some cases, whose residence) is firmly placed on/in Europe. 1973 is nothing short of a turning point in the annals of Latin American history, for the series of military dictatorships and coups that swept the continent would have a chilling and reverberating effect on the intellectuals who opposed them.

Rama's critical practice also contains a canonical dimension in that it negotiates between official and emerging canons. His first task was to question the traditional Eurocentric canon defined by imported literary models. The second was the formulation of a new Latin American canon that would include an indigenous, transcultural subjectivity in opposition to the commodifying commercialism devoted to the boom. Finally, the third was a creation of a new canon in all its Latin American, mestizo, heterogeneous transculturalism, one that did not fully materialize until 1992, when the question of European colonialism in America rose again to the forefront of international attention.

Without first problematizing the year 1992, discussion of the theories of transculturation and their current application remain stagnant. While quincentenary celebrations were held in Europe on the five hundredth anniversary of "Discovery," Native Americans from Canada to Patagonia made their resistance more vocal, more political, and in some cases more violent. Rigoberta Menchú, for example, initiated her walk for peace throughout the region; artist Guillermo Gómez-Peña responded with the performance piece *1992* and Coco Fusco with the video *The Couple in the Cage.* Las Hermanas Colorado performed *1992: Blood Speaks,*[13] a work indicating that the end of the Reagan-Bush years coincided imperially with Native Americans' outrage about their living conditions, an outrage that transcended national borders and individual tribal affiliations.

1992 is also the year the academy began to rethink Latin American colonial literature, infusing it with the new theories that postcolonial studies had developed since the 1980s. One such book, Mary Louise Pratt's *Imperial Eyes: Travel Writing and Transculturation,* is an example of the way Latin Americanists began to expand on Rama's theory of transculturation by conflating disciplines in a new postcolonial moment. Pratt's contribution to the theory of transculturation is her concept the "contact zone," which she defines as "the space of colonial encounters, the space in which peoples geographically and historically separated come into contact with each other and establish ongoing relations, usually involving conditions of coercion, radical inequality, and intractable conflict" (1992:6). Just as the contact zone is not an ideology-free location, and just as there are power relations in colonial and postcolonial encounters, we concur with Pratt that "[t]ransculturation is a phenomenon of the contact zone" (1992:6). That the Zapatista uprising (January 1, 1994) and the awarding of the Nobel Peace Prize to Rigoberta Menchú (1992) should occur within this same time frame reveals to us and the world the continuing (post)colonial and neocolonial condition of Latin America.

To sum up, we have just looked at the many ways in which transculturation affects certain moments of Latin American history and the peoples and cultures who inhabit Latin American spaces. But in order for transculturation to work as a theory for scholars of Latina/o studies, we must make both the geopolitical leap from Latin America to la transfrontera as well as a theoretical leap from the literature and theories of the Good Neighbor Policy, the Cuban Revolution, and the boom/dictatorships. The book that accomplishes this transnational transition is Silvia Spitta's *Between Two Waters* (1995). This text is informed by the theories of postcolonialism that bring us to our fourth moment of transculturation, the current one, the one we call transculturation to the second power. Spitta's book differs from previous transculturation theoretical treatises for various reasons. In the first place, Spitta resists reading a transcultural subjectivity as a single moment; rather, she sees this identity as constantly evolving and in process, from the first moment of contact of the conquest to the contemporary situation of U.S. Latinos/as. Spitta's transnational sweep reminds us that all discussions of transculturation must start at the initial moment of violence, for a transcultural subject is a resisting one. Thus, her work unites in one location the many discursive sites of the processes of transculturation and acknowledges them to be "consciously or unconsciously situated between at least two worlds, two cultures, two languages, and two definitions of subjectivity . . . who constantly mediate between them all—or . . . whose 'here' is problematic and perhaps undefinable" (1995:24).

That the Latin American bicultural subject could serve as a model for the Latina/o bicultural subject helps us to understand why the aforementioned theories of transculturation serve as models of resistance and contestation within the U.S. Spitta's analysis of subjectivity, where the subject is split and always in process and flux, also leads to an evaluation of mestizaje—previously read as part of a nationalist agenda, but seen now as a continuum rather than as a unified "finished" (1995:4) product. Mestizaje, whether in Latin America or the U.S., has to be redefined according to "specific cultural contexts and geopolitical situations" (1995:12). As Spitta closes her book, she refers to the U.S.–Mexico border as both an internationalized space and a war zone that "systematizes the consciousness of displacement" (1995:213). In so doing, she targets the exact locus of concern in a new global order, the redrawing of maps, the metaphorical, literal, and symbolic crossing of borders (and the study of these migrations) that define our age of globalization—a euphemism, no doubt, for neoimperialism.

Charting the positionality and articulation of U.S. Latina/o transcultural identity requires questioning the postcolonial theoretical apparatus that emerged from English-speaking locations. Certainly, the most widely used definitions of postcolonialism equate it with the end of colonial rule and with a "dismantling of colonialism" (Williams and Chrisman 1994:1) in order to examine imperialism with "different maps, chronologies, narratives, and political agendas" (Williams and Chrisman 1994:5) as well as to question the "process of the production of knowledge of the Other" (Williams and Chrisman 1994:8). One theorist reminds us that postcolonialism may very well be "a polite way of saying not-white, not-Europe" (Ahmad 1995:30). As long as the focus is on nonwhite and non-European peoples, Latin Americans surely qualify as postcolonials. But the other side of postcolonial studies, as Robert Young reminds us, is not merely "a specialized activity only for minorities or for historians of imperialism and colonialism, but itself forms the point of questioning of Western knowledge's categories and assumptions" (1990:11).

The circumstances surrounding a postcolonial subjectivity, although sharing many conditions of the peoples of the Americas, is rooted in a historicity far more contemporary than the one to which we draw attention. That is to say, although theoretical arguments of postcoloniality are useful in analyzing the situation of Latinas/os and Latin Americans—given the geopolitical and historical realities of the signal dates 1492, 1848, and 1898, which signify conquest, violence, and colonization both by Spain and the U.S.—the dates of contemporary English-speaking postcolonial theory, beginning with Frantz Fanon in the 1960s, are less relevant in our analysis. Postcolonial theory draws on sources as wide as Fanon, Stuart Hall, and Homi Bhabha, but a major form of its development resulted from a transmigration of intellectuals from the subcontinent to metropolitan sites from which this theory was able to contest a particularly British model of colonialism. This is not to imply that such a model has no significance for or does not share qualities of Spanish and U.S. colonialism, but rather that whatever forms of colonialism are universal, each form has also its own specificity, historicity, and geography. Addressing the specificity of Spanish and Anglo-American colonialism must concern us here. Latin America as well as the U.S.–Mexico border are perfect examples of the truism uttered by Masao Miyoshi that "Ours . . . is not an age of *post*colonialism, but of intensified colonialism, even though it is under an unfamiliar guise" (1993:750).

In recognition of Ortiz, our "counterpoint" dialogue with postcolonial discourse differs in two crucial areas. In the first, we must acknowledge that the third world did not suddenly materialize into the first. Rather, there is a centuries-long and complicated history of this implosion. Needless to say, that history must be addressed as a "domestic colonization," identified as early as 1983 in the introduction to *Cuentos: Stories by Latinas* (Gómez et al. 1983). Such a terminology precedes what Jameson calls "an *internal* Third World" (1990:49, emphasis in original). The second difference resides in the continuous migratory patterns of Latin American and Caribbean populations to the U.S., particularly in the latter half of the twentieth century. Not to understand these migrations as part of a larger pattern of colonialism and its effects is to minimize a paradigmatic example of Miyoshi's thesis of globalization and the politics of transnational movements. Both postcolonial studies and Chicano studies agree that the third world is at the center of the first world. However, although London is called the "postcolonial city *par excellence*" as the former "capital of the world's largest colonial empire" (Ahmad 1995:31), for our purposes that "privileged" location belongs to New York, Miami, and Los Angeles.

In order to place a theory of transculturation in a transnational context, it is essential to recognize the contrapuntual properties of transculturation, a quality that enables it to be the provenance of more than one culture or nationality. Phyliss Peres, for example, who applies the term to Luso-African narrative, notes, "it opposes the framework explicit in acculturation that assumes a static tension between indigenous cultural discourse and the presumedly superior metropolitan mode. . . . Transculturation assumes a fluidity . . . that functions in both directions. . . . This fluidity . . . counters . . . colonial constructs of nation" (1997:10).

When we consider transculturation in Latin America or among Latin Americans, three issues and patterns of migration concern us. The first is, of course, the colonial encounter, the contact zone between Europe and the Americas, so well theorized by Pratt and others. The second consists of the internal migrations within Latin American countries from rural to urban settings as a result of technology, demographics, agribusiness, multinationals, and other imperializing factors or survival tactics. Finally, the subsequent migrations of these Latin American populations to the U.S. also triggers another moment of transculturation. We must understand, in Rama's terms, that an internal initial transculturation had already occurred in Latin America's great "lettered" cities, the ports, the industrialized centers.[14] In the postwar period onward, this movement was galvanized as multinational corporations sought to expand and intensify their operations in Latin America, especially during the 1960s.[15]

It is the third, more recent pattern of migration to the U.S. in discrete historical moments and in varying political circumstances that most concerns us: the legal and "illegal," the elite and the impoverished, the bourgeois and the peasant, the educated and the uneducated; they all, in the words of a pop star, "come to America." Not to understand those circumstances—be they class based, as in devastated economies, or politically motivated, as in civil wars, disappearances, and dictatorships—is to underestimate and to do violence yet again to those populations. More recently, natural disasters such as hurricanes, earthquakes, and floods have motivated another wave of migration to the U.S.[16] If the first wave of this new migratory shift centered on urban-to-urban flows of population, current studies reveal that Latinos now move to smaller cities after migration, dispersing within the U.S. As this new migration settles into populated areas, another moment of transculturation takes place within the U.S., not only between these Latino groups and the Anglos with whom they must interact—as we might expect—but also between the differing Latino groups among themselves, those newly arrived in contrast to those whose home has always been in the U.S.

Such a complex cultural dynamic is not simply a matter of migrations producing varieties of displacements and transculturations. Rather, they bear witness to the worldwide phenomenon of *transnationalism* or *globalization*. Recent definitions of the first term distinguish it from the earlier renditions of *multinationalism*, which referred to American imperial entrepreneurialism in the third world. When we speak of transnationalism, we refer to the "emergence of a social process in which migrants establish social fields that cross geographic, cultural, and political borders," thus maintaining "multiple relations" that "link together their country of origin and their country or countries of settlement" (Schiller, Basch, and Blanc-Szanton 1992a:ix).

In a contemporary transnational world, an explanation of the above-mentioned deterritorializations of peoples is consistent with Masao Miyoshi's thesis on the function of a transnational corporation, which is, in his words, "adrift and mobile, ready to settle anywhere and exploit any state, including its own" (1993:736). As these transnational corporations move into new areas, they exacerbate the existing class system by establishing a hierarchy between the professionals and the workers. For Miyoshi, these patterns constitute a third industrial revolution, which, like the other two, has its underclass "of the unemployed, the underemployed, the displaced, and the homeless people" (1993:742). No industrialized region is without these changes, and, in that sense, we could argue that Latina/o migratory patterns, although specific in some contexts, are also part of the changing global demography.

To be able to apply Miyoshi's concept of globalization and the politics of transnational movements, it is helpful to draw on Arjun Appadurai's inventive neologisms concerning these demographic shifts: "ethnoscapes, mediascapes, technoscapes, finanscapes, and ideoscapes" (1990:296). These categories help explain a "new global cultural economy that cannot any longer be understood in terms of center-periphery models" (Appadurai 1990:296).[17] As Appadurai suggests, the speed of cultural, technological, and commodity flow across national and international boundaries has triggered a remarkable swiftness in deterritorialization of both people and goods, resulting in "growing disjunctures" (1990:301) between these "perspectival constructs, inflected very much by the historical, linguistic, and political situatedness" (1990:296). Among these constructs, of major interest to us is his term *ethnoscape*, defined as a "landscape of persons" (1990:297) whose ethnographies must inscribe their transnational, diasporic condition. Ethnoscapes account for complex ethnic relationships and cultural flows in a shifting disjunctured world where people are always on the move. Appadurai concludes what is obvious everywhere: that "ethnicity . . . has now become a global force, forever slipping in and through the cracks between states and borders" (1990:306).

The fact that nation and state are no longer connected by their hyphen, as he suggests, reveals why it is precisely in the interstices of the border where we may begin to look for cultural processes and models of transculturation. At this point, too, we may map a broader spectrum of border theorization as it applies specifically to Latinas/os with the work of two of its most eminent practitioners.

At first glance and given the current consumerism of postcolonial theory, it is not surprising that only two figures serve as paragons within borderland studies: Gloria Anzaldúa and Guillermo Gómez-Peña. Each one's "situatedness" in a specific national and ethnic plane demonstrates the fluidity of a gendered "border identity": Gómez-Peña is Mexican—a given national identity—who becomes a Chicano and a minority in the U.S., and Anzaldúa is a Chicana who finds a continental identity in Aztec cosmography complemented by Vasconcelos's "raza cósmica." Not only do they meet at the inevitable point of intersection—the border—as one moves north and the other south, but also they both concentrate their work on the politics, metaphors, and symbols of the border. Such a transnational articulation of identities makes both artists agents of a postmodern condition. They are simultaneously specifically Latina and Latino, and generally part of a larger world panorama of postmodern transnationalism. Their work, although giving the U.S.–Mexico border an international audience, also engages in a transnational conversation with postcolonial studies—evidenced, for example, in titles such as *Borderlands/La Frontera* and *Borderscape 2000.*

It is important to acknowledge that what is today known as Borderlands has since the early 1970s been recognized, theorized, and problematized as "Aztlán" by Chicana/o scholars and by cultural practitioners such as Alurista, Américo Paredes, Genaro Padilla, José David Saldívar, Héctor Calderón, Pat Mora, Denise Chávez, and others. Since Chicano studies emerged, as Juan Bruce-Novoa suggests, the space between two points and the interlingual code-switching that takes place there serve as yet another metaphor for theorizing about the border. In this regard, Bruce-Novoa's early recognition of the "space not the hyphen" (1990:98) between Mexican and American is substantial.[18] He correctly assesses its potential if we consider the case of Gloria Anzaldúa, who has shown how the border assisted her in carving out a personal space and identity in its full hybrid potentiality. Anzaldúa's notion of border identity is historically positioned in the conflictive politics between the north and the south: by interweaving her personal history with that of the region, she shows how the border became a business to the Anglo interlopers who had begun to usurp it, displacing and uprooting the Mexican families that lived there. Anzaldúa's critical eye perceives not only the war on immigration but also agribusiness, maquiladoras, coyotes, and the military complex. Every new business spawned by the border stands in dialectical relationship to the denizens of the 2,000-mile "implosion of the Third World into the first" (Rosaldo 1989:85).

Three years later, José David Saldívar, in recognition both of Anzaldúa's germinal work and the genealogy of Chicano cultural studies, announced, correctly, that "in the 1990s, a Border zone of conjunctures, must aspire to be regionally focused and broadly cosmopolitan, a form of life and travel in our global Borderlands" (1991b:84). If Anzaldúa materialized the border in a borderland subjectivity by making it mobile—"I am a turtle, wherever I go I carry my home on my back" (1987:21)—the "portability" of the border led Saldívar and other border theorists to the conclusion that those subjectivities in that liminal space are always in flux and always evolving, just as Spitta theorized about a transcultural subjectivity. What Saldívar calls borderland "cultural poetics" and "border aesthetics" in 1990 (178) leads him to theorize the border as "la transfrontera" in 1997, which is "the social space of subaltern encounters, the Janus-faced borderline in which peoples geopolitically forced to separate themselves now negotiate with one another and manufacture new relations, hybrid cultures, and multiple-voiced aesthetics" (1997:13–14). Crucially, the conflation of Chicano studies with postcolonial theory places us at the fulcrum of transculturation. Put another way, for more than twenty years Chicana/o studies had been developing a critical praxis that, when conflated with postcolonial studies of the early 1990s, resulted in an agenda that included the "implosion" of the third world into the first, internal colonization, diaspora and not-diaspora ("we have always been here"), cultural clashes, displaced identities, and the politics of being dark in a white-skinned place.

Theorizing about the border is not limited to poets or performance artists, however. Anthropologists, too, see the border as a legitimate space for research and theorization. As an anthropologist, a Chicano, and border dweller, Renato Rosaldo significantly called for creativity in the discussion of border theory. At the same time that he is vitally concerned with migration and mobility at those "in between" zones, his real focus tells us about this space of "cultural distinctiveness" (1989:199). In postmodernity, according to Rosaldo, the ethnoscape of individuals who constantly negotiate across "porous cultural boundaries" produces a cultural reality that is "criss-crossed by border zones, pockets, and eruptions of all kinds" (1989:207). Rosaldo moves easily between center and margin, global and local, mind and body, assimilation and trans-culturation, theory and practice. His border theory, not unlike Appadurai's globalization, focuses on the intersection of peoples, languages, identities, and cultures. In opposition to those theorists who would see these border spaces as "analytically empty transitional zones," Rosaldo instead views them "as sites of creative cultural production that require investigation" (1989:208).

For all of these border theorists, the border is not a transcendental, esoteric location, but rather a real life-and-death space, inhabited by real people in specific relations of power. It is no wonder, then, that the border has produced a myriad of metaphors and poetic evocations. Those who contem-plate it seek to understand it. Anzaldúa calls it an "herida abierta" (1987:3), and anthropologist Néstor García Canclini considers Tijuana "one of the major laboratories of postmodernity" (1992:40). Regardless of their poetic sensibil-ity or theoretical approach, both Anzaldúa and Canclini conceive the border in terms of the transcultural paradigm described above. Anzaldúa's graphic imagery moves south, noting "the Third World grat[ing] against the First and bleed[ing]. And before a scab forms it hemorrhages again, the lifeblood of two worlds merging to form a third country—a border culture" (1987:3), and contrasts with Canclini's focus on Mexico. At this moment of transnational exchanges and globalization of cultures, Canclini's theoretical apparatus—his well-known theory of hybrid cultures or "hybridization" (1995b:11)—has made him the border theorist par excellence in Latin American aca-demic circles.

Up to this point, we have emphasized Rama's theory of narrative transcul-turation, but Canclini's term *reconversion* bears much similarity to Rama's terms regarding the border and modernity. Whereas Rama's discussion focuses on a literary genre, the Latin American regional novel, Canclini does not limit himself to one genre or cultural expression. Rather, his analysis encompasses all manner of contemporary cultural "texts," such as music, performance art, journalism, television, video, and film. If Rama saw transculturation as a liter-ary cultural model, Canclini recognizes its transnational postmodernism in his understanding and definition of reconversion.[19] For Canclini, because the old ways of doing things are always in transition, "[r]econversion prolongs their existence," providing a "new system of symbolic production and communca-tion" (1992:31, 32). Here we may begin to experience Canclini's notion of cul-tural transformations, especially in places such as the border, which exemplify his theory of hybridity, where "transformations [are] generated by the horizon-tal co-existence of a number of symbolic systems" (1992:32). Undoubtedly,

Canclini's definition of reconversion is indebted to his experience and theorization of Tijuana as a place where many overlapping paradigms can coexist. Thus, we can hear in Canclini the same notions of heterogeneity and multiplicity that echo later in the work of other theorists of minority experience. This "multiplicity of simultaneous patrimonies, this process of interchange and re-utilization," for Canclini is exemplified when we see the ways "[h]igh, popular and mass art nourish each other reciprocally" (1992:32).[20]

Postcolonial theorists not only from Latin America but also from other areas of ethnic studies, such as Asian and Asian American studies—that is, those also concerned with literal or figurative borders—have concentrated their efforts on the intersecting, complicated notions of hybridity, sometimes with its corollaries of heterogeneity and multiplicity.[21] Asian American studies, for example, gained a solid theoretical grounding with Lisa Lowe's *Immigrant Acts,* which, although concentrating on Asian Americans, provides a useful framework from which to examine a vast array of "immigrant acts," also applicable to recent Latin American migrations (1996:67–68). The ways in which individuals and groups of peoples deal with the semiotics and the multiplicity of identities that emerge in border situations bring us to a discussion of hybridity. In particular, Lowe's concept of hybridization bears much resemblance to a Latin American reality; she defines it as "the uneven process through which immigrant communities encounter the violences of the U.S. state, and the capital imperatives served by the United States . . . and the process through which they survive those violences by living, inventing, and reproducing different cultural alternatives" (1996:82).[22] For Canclini, hybridity is a "liminality, a material whose existence exhibits the dual affirmation of a substance and its lack of identity, that which is in the interstices" (1995a:77). However, he clearly eschews any controversial discussion of the term *hybridity,* relegating it to a mere footnote, but it cannot be as incidental as he makes it appear because it is also the title of his book. Nevertheless, the footnote equates hybridity with the continuous construction of culture, or, as Rosaldo's introduction to the English translation of Canclini's book puts it, with "the ongoing condition of all human cultures, which contain no zones of purity because they undergo continuous processes of transculturation (two-way borrowing and lending between cultures)" (1995:xv). Therefore, if for Canclini the modern and postmodern conflate to a single experience in Mexico, the notion of hybridity is nevertheless not limited to unidirectional cultural encounters.[23] It is, if we remember Ortiz, a "toma y daca" situation, where cultures are fused, recycled, and reconverted.

Reconversion, at its very core, is a tool for resistance and reconfiguration; as an active manifestation of agency, reconversion is essential to the construction of identities in all kinds of cultural practices. Privileging reconversion—or, our preferred term, *transculturation*—calls into question the notion of a homogeneous, mononational identity. That is to say that these border identities are simultaneously constructed and deconstructed as the unitary concept of national imaginary communities disappears. Just as we saw in Rosaldo and Saldívar, the border materializes a third space that transcends national boundaries. Thus, transcultural subjectivity emerges in a border identity when the subject is hybrid and transnational in cultural and linguistic terms.[24]

Performing Transculturation

In the 1990s, Latina theater and solo performance moved from a position of marginality to one of international attention. It is not mere coincidence or even a coming of age that has triggered such a proliferation and visibility of Latinas on national stages. Rather, the particular conflation of globalization, transnational circumstances, and postmodernity are precisely the ingredients for what we have called the transcultural subjectivity of Latinas on stage. Because we argue that theater and performance are the ideal cultural locations to examine transculturation, what we outline below is a specific theoretical framework for border hybrid identity formation, whose equation would read:

SUBJECT + LOCATION + AGENCY = IDENTITY

Given that any of the components of the equation can and do change under specific historical circumstances, so too do identities. In this sense, the processual construction of identity is contingent on the dynamics of transculturation. Thus, they share many characteristics: both are complex and nonstatic, and both are constantly inventing themselves with a series of unpredictable, chaotic, and often contradictory components. According to the practices and agency of the particular subject, the fusion that results—a confusion, for purists—is the sum of all potential transcultural, discursive locations. Although a transcultural person may have *no* identity based on national or a nationalist agenda, may feel he or she belongs nowhere, and may not have a "pure" identity, that same person can very well be comfortable in many locations.

Transculturation manifests itself in a variety of ways: (1) bilingualism; (2) material culture, including the body; (3) dramatic action; (4) geographic and physical space; and (5) discursive locations (ideological and cultural). On the stage, the obvious use of bilingualism in transcultural plays by Latinas (and Latinos) is often the very first point theater critics and audiences notice. This code-switching, which, among other things, is a way to mix theory with practice, often confounds the Anglo critic to the point that it is the only comment in a transcultural play. Works such as Dolores Prida's *Coser y cantar* and Alicia Mena's *Las nuevas tamaleras* are truly bilingual texts—with no negotiation about translation—that alternate between the two languages according to a previous Latin American identity and a current transcultural one in process. A generational linguistic difference between the abuelitas (grandmas) and the young Chicanas in *Las nuevas tamaleras* (one generation speaks Spanish, the other Spanglish) bespeaks the constitution of the social and cultural imaginary (in the abuelas) bequeathed to the younger generation. As the play progresses, the protagonists accommodate each other's speech patterns: the younger generation speaks more Spanish and the older one gradually lets a few words of English slip in. Crucially, these exchanges are never translations, but rather an oral display in the process of transculturation. Here we have a bilingualism that is not code-switching (a spontaneous utilization of both languages that assumes the interlocutor is proficient in both), but rather a manifestation of transcultural linguistic politics. If Spanish is the language predominantly used at home and on the street, the younger generation oscillates between the domestic, familial sphere and the public and educational realm.

Education plays an important role for both generations: those children whose parents are Latin American immigrants of the middle class speak Spanish at home, as do those children whose parents are working class. The difference is that the children of the middle class will probably educate their own children to be *literate* in Spanish, just as they are, whereas working-class children will not have the same access to a formal education in written Spanish.[25] Those playwrights whose primary language is English and who write in English but whose social construction of reality is Latina/o assert their transcultural condition in the bilingualism of their protagonists. Even in those plays that are English dominant, when the drama heightens and the emotion spills over, the action often moves from English to Spanish. This is especially true of scenes involving holidays and moments of cultural ritual, memory, and celebration.

After this initial moment of noticing *what* is being spoken, another coordinate of transculturation has to do with *material culture:* Who is on stage performing? Whose body is seen? What aspects of the stage materialize a Latina/o cultural space? Is there an altar as in *Novena narrativas?* Are they preparing tamales as in *Las nuevas tamaleras?* Is there a mural as in *The Fat-Free Chicana?* Do we see healing herbs and remedies as in *Botánica?* Is there a pernil (roast pork) as in *I'll Be Home para la Navidad?* Such visual props embodying Latinidad are only one way to show transculturation. Far more personal is the use of the body itself as the marker and, hence, the prop, a utilization that occurs at the moment when our horizon of expectations is confirmed by what we visually see, and usually a racialized and ethnic body is the only determinant for a Latina/o identity. As the body takes on the properties of a sign, the racial, ethnic, class, and gender markers of Latinidad are fully displayed and semiotically represented. Undisputably, in these representations, the mestiza/o becomes the racialized ethnic body par excellence and is now enlisted utopically to represent all Latinas/os.

Here is the pivotal factor for the future of Latina/o plays and solo performances: the mestiza/o identity of these protagonists (which is completely tied to the historicity and community of Latinas/os) tends to be the *only* marker others take into consideration in defining Latinas/os, when in reality the Latino population is composed of so much more—i.e., mulattos, blacks, Asians, Jews, and whites. The fact that dominant white culture views Latinos only in the mestizo and mulatto categories shows us why Latina/o plays have had difficulty crossing over into the mainstream. If in the first coordinate of transculturation (bilingualism) class plays a crucial role, here in its second coordinate, the staging of bodies, class is also inscribed. Audiences expect Latina/o plays to have the barrio community and its working-class, disenfranchised denizens as a referent and as a proof of "authenticity." Once a playwright, such as Caridad Svich or Lynn Alvarez, de-essentializes her work by setting it outside those expected class locations, she may find herself at odds with the very community her writing serves.

Up to this point, we have discussed language, material culture, and the body as a prop on the stage. Now we must add another coordinate, the *dramatic action,* in which the transcultural self interacts, transacts, or negotiates its identity. We have to raise the question why identity continually commands such attention as the main theatrical paradigm in Latina theater and in our analysis. Now it becomes crucial to examine a history that has been violated, colonized, diminished, or erased, and a playwright who is part of a marginalized community and educational system. Because all these hegemonic devices constantly define such subjectivities by what they are *not,* identity is always in a constant state of transmutation. Resisting assimilation, violence, and amnesia all require myriad acts of agency and intervention. The transcultural subject who happens to be a Latina playwright or solo performer deploys the stage in a counterhegemonic gesture against that violence. The dramatic action in these plays always involves a transcultural process, a how-to that serves as a prescription for her audience. Regardless if the action is based on returning home after a formal education *(Botánica),* on constructing a Latina lesbian identity *(Greetings from a Queer Señorita* or *Giving Up the Ghost),* or on articulating Latina feminism *(Real Women Have Curves),* the ending of the play does not offer a solution, but rather an interrogative without closure. Indeed, the endings of many Latina plays reaffirm the processual nature of transculturation. Although plays and solo performances do not necessarily offer solutions, they almost always inevitably do show how the protagonists manage to arrive at their fluctuating but desired destinations. How the past is negotiated and preserved in order to make sense of the present and to embark on a way to deal with and derive meaning for future acts and identities forms the core of the dramatic action. Although the protagonists' journey may be agonizing and painful, at the play's end the protagonists are able to affirm the fact that they have learned to juggle cultural realities. Transculturation is not a placebo for assimilation. It is a medium, part of the "toma y daca," a useful tool in the dramatic action whose ultimate function is to achieve agency.

As we approach Latina transcultural identity, two more intersecting coordinates appear: *geographic* and *discursive locations.* Like language, material culture, and dramatic action, these coordinates are crucial to the development and articulation of identity. Here, lessons learned from Adrienne Rich, who gave us the marvelous term *politics of location,* come into play because location is almost always a determinant of identity, and in women that location derives from their bodies.[26] In plays and solo performances by Latinas, *location* is not limited to the places where the specific action occurs, although it certainly includes them. Rather, location encompasses a large range of spatial sites: from what is possible on the stage—kitchen, home, restaurant, altar, sweatshop, bedroom, border—to the place of one's birth (or one's parents' birth) that constitutes an ancestral homeplace (such as Cuba in Carmelita Tropicana's *Milk of Amnesia).* Clearly, the location of the theater itself is another determinant of identity: a theater in Chicago and one in the Southwest will necessarily play to discrete audiences whose expectations derive in part from their physical location. The geopolitical discourse of the border, for example, will necessarily provide a context that may be undecipherable to a barrio audience in Chicago. The vast difference in these locations reveals how identity is historically and experientially constructed. Although these plays are communal, they are not interchangeable. Regardless of where the plays are located, the local audience sees itself represented on these stages. It is here where class, race, ethnicity, and gender can be read as social constructions that constitute the Latina performative imaginary in all its transculturation.

For a hybrid subject always in the making, positionalities are continually intersecting in what we call *discursive transculturation.* By this term, we refer to cultural and ideological models with given structures of meaning and ways of seeing. In Rama's theory, discursive transculturation applies to the transformations of narrative patterns from an established set of rules and codes imposed by dominant ideologies, genres, and aesthetics to a new cultural or narrative formation. As these overlapping patterns come together in a single subjectivity, the possibilities for chaos and confusion are rife. Although there are countless examples of Latinas dealing with WASP ideology during their education, for example, these plays and performances tend to concentrate on the empowering qualities of transculturation rather than on the crisis. Whatever the potential crisis may be—a feminist dealing with uneducated, migrant parents; the dynamics of racism and how to deal with it in families; the possibility of forging a lesbian identity—all become possible in that third space we speak of as transculturation.[27]

A little-known but powerful example of discursive transculturation occurs in Silvia Gonzalez's *Alicia in Wonder Tierra,* when the dominant paradigm of the *Wizard of Oz* is redefined and recharted according to Latina racial, ethnic, and class experiences. The *Wizard of Oz* is such an overarching example to Latina playwrights who grew up in the dominant culture that it appears in no less than three plays—one Chicana, one Cuban American (Prida's *Coser y cantar*), and one Nuyorican work (Migdalia Cruz's *The Have-Little*). In chapter 3, we demonstrate how discursive transculturation in Latina plays is not the appropriation of the *Wizard of Oz* per se, but rather the restructuring of an entire genre, the bildungsroman. Here the addition and appropriation of the narrative structure within ethnic and racial parameters works on various levels. As we shall see in chapter 7, the protagonists of these plays also leave home like their male counterparts. If for the latter returning home as a self-made man fits the bildungsroman paradigm, in the Latina version the protagonist leaves in order to pursue an education. Her departure, although conflictive at the time, manages to signal a sign of hope because her eventual return to work with the collectivity and with the community that she seemingly abandoned previously is almost always assured. Significantly, as the play-wrights we analyze here shed the Aristotelian dramatic structure, they create a theater that is mainly based on vignettes in which the dramatic action does not center on a male hero. In fact, removing the male figure from these plays and subverting the logic of the dominant paradigm by doing away with the beginning, middle, and end permit a major new focus on women and their stories. This change, too, is transculturation.

Now that we have seen transculturation in action through language, material culture, dramatic action, location, and discourse, we are in a position to consider the function of ritual in the theater in general and in Latina theater specifically. Given that many plays stage the processes of identity formation and definitive rites of passage, both protagonists and audiences alike experi-ence transculturation through that ritual. As spectators witness the protago-nists' critical conditioning, the dramatic situations address possible cultural models for the spectators' own transculturated reality. For the protagonist, the dramatic action functions within the structure of a rite of passage: a crisis has occurred, forcing her into a liminal state of being; as the play develops, a series of contradictions, obstacles, and hardships lead her to a closure, which for the present time grants her a reprieve. Although the solution may be only tempo-rary, at least it allows her to progress from that liminal state of crisis to one of further transculturation. With more time now for reflection, she can see herself within a continuum of her culture, a process that allows her to experi-ence both the individual and the collective.

By the close of the play, her learning process has also been transmitted to the audience, who leaves the theater with a sense of having accompanied her on her transcultural journey, a journey that reflects and refracts their own reality and provides a sense of satisfaction and accomplishment, not to men-tion empowerment, for the time being. In this manner, the transcultural rite of passage occurs at various levels: (1) the protagonist as she constructs her own subjectivity-in-process; (2) the audience as they identify, counteridentity, dis-identify, engage, or learn to juggle transculturation; and (3) the audience as they experience their own rite of passage by entering an imaginary world. If during the theatrical representation members of that audience were separated from their own reality by failing to recognize their transcultural condition, once they reintegrate into the real world beyond the theater, they do so with a new perspective and consciousness of who they are or could be. The theatrical model has given them the means to reshape their own social construction of reality and politics of identity through a new transculturated memory. Furthermore, the theater is precisely the place where this subjectivity-in-process, or what Norma Alarcón calls an "identity-in-difference" (1996:129), can represent itself, can transculturate. Ultimately, transculturation is validated by a sense of communitas. Thus, we concur with Diana Taylor when she recognizes the "liberating potential" (1991c:71) of transculturation, for it validates, affirms, and gives impetus to these transcultural identities—at least for now.

TWO

SETTING THE STAGE

UN TEATRO DE MUJERES

I'll tell you what my dream is—one of my dreams. And I know I'll get to do it because it's a driving thing in me. . . . My dream is to be able to do a theatre piece on the phases of womanhood. It's something that has not been done yet. . . . I want to put womanhood into every form that I can express: in singing, in crying, in laughing, everything. That role is not yet there. That role has not been written. Maybe it has been written in a Shakespearean way. But I don't relate to those European images of women. . . . Women are obviously in a type of great void. They are balanced, but in terms of the way the work looks at us they've put us in this position where we've accepted the condition of doing one role instead of many. If there were some way of taking that and putting it into words that are theatrical, I would like to do that. I don't believe a man is going to write that. I don't believe that for a single minute. And I sure can't wait for Luis [Valdez] to write that role.

—Socorro Valdez (1983), actress in
El Teatro Campesino, in *Chicana Voices,* by Yolanda Broyles-González

It is as if Socorro Valdez and countless other Latinas in the theater suddenly had their dream come true in the last decade of the twentieth century. All over the country, Latinas in the theater moved from their heretofore peripheral roles backstage to occupy the limelight. Not only as playwrights and protagonists, but as actresses and performance artists, directors and producers, Latinas have become a visible presence in the theater, and their work has now attracted a wide enough following to yield both critical attention and publishing opportunities. In the festivals devoted to Latino theater that abounded throughout the country during the 1990s, women's roles became increasingly more prominent. It was their plays that were the featured performances at the major Latino theater festivals during this period.[1] Even today, everywhere we turn, a new Latina theater is emerging. Although Latina playwrights' male counterparts were long credited with the creation and survival of Latino theater in the U.S., plays and performances by women drew larger audiences and received more enthusiastic feedback at these festivals and academic conferences. As playwrights, performers, and protagonists, Latinas have gained a reputation as the most creative and dynamic aspect of Latino theater today. Consequently, these women playwrights and solo performers are increasingly being invited to participate in workshops, panels, and teaching and residency programs, and are commissioned to write new plays.

Until recently, only rarely did academics lend serious critical attention to Latina plays: those who did were usually feminists either in the Latina or Anglo community.[2] And only a fledgling corpus of works constituted what we could call Latina theater. In this recent confluence of Latina productions, we bring together the three main Latino ethnic groups, Chicanas, Cuban Americans (or Cubans), and U.S. Puerto Ricans.

Before we begin our discussion of Latina playwrights and solo performers artists, it is important to clarify our definition of *Latina* or *Latino.* For us, this term refers to all persons who ethnically, racially, nationally, and culturally identify with Latin American origins or roots and who reside permanently in geographically dispersed locations within the U.S.[3] Most Latinas/os have come to prefer this term, using it as an act of contestation to the establishment's categorization of them as *Hispanic* following the 1980 U.S. census. In more recent years, the term *Latina* or *Latino* has also come to connote an act of solidarity in which a diversified group of U.S. Latinos and Latin Americans coalesces politically as a strategy to unite themselves.[4] As an act of intervention, they insist on defining their own subjectivity, self-representations, and discursive constructions. Their identity formation is the direct production of their own agency in a politically conscious counterhegemonic stance.

The terms *Latina* and *Latino* have, in recent years, gained stronger currency by second, third, and later generations of Latinas/os who privilege it over their previously defined nomenclatures, which were based solely on nationality and ethnicity as articulated in the 1960s and 1970s (i.e., *Chicana/o* and *Puerto Rican*). *Latina/o* is adopted from the Spanish term *Latinoamérica,* which once more transgresses and challenges Anglo linguistic hegemony. Furthermore, although *"latina/o,"* like its once acceptable cousin *"hispana/o,"* is still a perfectly legitimate form of identification in Spanish, when used in English, it has different linguistic, political, and cultural definitions, connotations, and implications than the word in Spanish. Nor do we consider the English words *Latin* or *Spanish* to define U.S. Latina/o identity, although both terms are still sometimes used in certain situations, both in Latino and Anglo communities. We eschew the term *Latin* because of its Eurocentric, imperialist, exclusionary connotations, as well as its stereotypical signifiers, such as "Latin lover," "Latin bombshell," etc. Popular media such as Spanish-language television adds to the confusion by addressing its audience as we "hispanos." Native-born Latin Americans have a tendency to translate the term *hispano* into English without recognizing how politically charged such an act may be for those born in the U.S. In so doing, they relate the concept of "hispanidad"—which identifies their connection with Spain, their solidarity as Spanish-speaking countries, and their pride in their "Hispanic" heritage—to Latino communities in the U.S.[5] The use of any one of these terms, necessarily, makes a political statement by showing how, even when the speaker may claim to be apolitical, the term itself has a historical referentiality and trajectory. Thus, each and every one of these terms and the people who use them are, in our view, firmly rooted in the politics and concomitant ideologies to which they subscribe. Therefore *Latina* and *Latino* are more inclusive terms because they include transculturation—that is, the heterogeneity of cultures, ethnicities, races, and languages of Latin America. We have no doubt that the terms *Latina* and *Latino* will evolve, given that identity shifts in a fluid state that always begs for further definition, articulation, and reconfiguration in its given historic moment.[6]

From this perspective and in this context, we must also consider the unique position of white Latinas/os within two separate frameworks: those who were born in the U.S. and who identify as U.S. Latinas/os, and those who define themselves in terms of their Latin American nationality—i.e., Argentine, Chilean, Colombian, Mexican, and Puerto Rican. Although some "Latin Americans" feel culturally invisible in the U.S. and therefore identify with Latinas/os in order to recover their own cultural heritage and language, their invisibility cannot equal the oppression, marginalization, and silencing of people of color in the U.S. Some educated, white, middle-class and upper-middle-class Latin Americans—whose command of a sophisticated intellectual discourse in Spanish often intimidates U.S.–born Latinas/os—question Latina/o identity, and Latinas/os themselves often perceive this "betrayal" as crueler than the racism they experience from the dominant culture.[7]

By centering this book on Latina theater and solo performance as a whole rather than on the discrete theaters of Cubans, Puerto Ricans, or Chicanas, our critical framework and inquiry rely on a theoretical approach that places Latina playwrights and solo performers in dialogue with one another in such a way that ethnic and national divisions are mitigated by the playwrights and performers' affinity as Latinas in teatro. As we embark on this project, we seek to highlight the notion of dynamic, multiple identities, ethnicities, and trans-cultural subjectivities-in-process. Whereas a single classification (Cuban, Puerto Rican, Chicana/o) limits, potentially essentializes, and divides in na-tionalistic terms, a transcultural subjectivity takes the differences into account while at the same time facilitating a political coalescence and solidarity. How-ever, *Latina/o* does not translate as any single one of these theaters, but rather as all of them. In this sense, *Latina/o* does not replace either *Cuban, Puerto Rican,* or *Chicano,* but rather represents a processual self-definition that operates according to new identity formations of Latinas/os in the U.S., including those nationalist allegiances that usually receive less attention—i.e., Dominican, Colombian, Salvadoran, or newer emigrations.

By imagining transcultural and transnational identities, Latina playwrights and performers have reconceived Latina identity. This capacity to oscillate, commingle, fluctuate, and flow from one ethnicity and regionality to another became an identifier of Latina theater in the late 1980s and early 1990s. For this reason, Migdalia Cruz, a Puerto Rican, can write about Frida Kahlo, a Mexican; Dolores Prida, a Cuban, can write about Puerto Ricans; and Diana Sáenz, a Central American, can write about other Latin Americans.[8] Thus, Dolores Prida's play about Puerto Ricans and Cubans, *Botánica,* is as success-ful in Texas and California as it is in New York; Cherríe Moraga's play *Heart of the Earth: A Popol Vuh Story* opened to full houses in New York as well as in California, and Denise Chávez has taken her play *Women in the State of Grace* to enthusiastic audiences all around the country. Likewise, a trans-cultural moment is mitigated by Marga Gomez's visit to the Alamo when she tells her audience, "I'm not Mexican, but I was representing."[9]

For the purpose of this book, when we refer to Latina theater, we are already departing from the models established by Latino theater, which makes specific reference to the three well-known and discrete Latino groups based on their geographical location and historicity: Mexican (Chicano) in the Southwest, California, Colorado, and Chicago; Puerto Rican in New York and Chicago; and Cuban in Miami, New York, and New Jersey. As each of these groups produced its own theatrical representations and discursive practices,

SHOWBILL®

INTAR HISPANIC AMERICAN ARTS CENTER

Heart of the Earth: A POPOL VUH STORY

1. Showbill for Cherríe Moraga's *Heart of the Earth: A Popol Vuh Story* at INTAR, New York City (1995). Used by permission of Playbill®. Playbill® is a registered trademark of Playbill, Inc. All rights reserved.

male playwriting continued to be the dominant paradigm by which Latino theater evolved and was defined, both historically and critically. In general terms, we can characterize that theater in the following manner.[10]

In its very earliest days, Chicano theater developed simultaneously as political performance and social movement: El Teatro Campesino, "born in the huelga [strikes]" (Valdez 1990:10), was designed to raise consciousness among the migrant farmworkers and later inspired many other Chicano theater groups in areas with large Chicano populations in different parts of the country. Their platform, as defined by Luis Valdez in the 1970s, was to "inspire the audience to social action. Illuminate specific points about social problems. Satirize the opposition. Show or hint at a solution. Express what people are feeling" (1990:12). It was a didactic, "agit-prop" (8) way of doing theater which prided itself on not being another "imitation of the gabacho" (7). Instead, it was grounded in barrio life and held a deep political commitment to revolutionary ideologies and "social change" (8). When Teatro presence was no longer the only catalyst to ensure the survival of the Farmworkers Union, this theater moved on to other issues of concern to Chicanos, such as "Vietnam, the barrio, racial discrimination" (10). Although in its early days, given its name, the Teatro Campesino concentrated on a theater for migrant workers, in the 1980s and 1990s, a second generation of Chicano *plays* no longer followed the agit-prop theater techniques of earlier years.

In the 1990s, formally educated Latino playwrights, lesbians, gays, and, of course, Latinas questioned and in some cases reconceived the ideological platform of Teatro Campesino.[11] As Chicanos began to recognize differences among themselves, their previous signifier—*Chicano*—could no longer stand as a unified and monolithic category that could claim its roots solely in a neo-indigenous past, with Aztlán as its utopian landscape. For this reason, El Teatro Campesino found it could no longer limit itself to identity formations anchored uniquely in the values of the 1960s, particularly heterosexual, patriarchally centered ones.

A new image of Teatro Campesino emerged in the late 1980s with Luis Valdez's sudden visibility into the mainstream through his Hollywood success *La Bamba,* signaling a "crossover" from a specific Chicano culture and audience to Latinos nationwide, as well as to Anglos. Nevertheless, *La Bamba* was not Valdez's first attempt at national recognition. Teatro's play *Zoot Suit,* also written and directed by Valdez, flopped on Broadway (1979) after enjoying a great box office success at the Mark Taper Forum in Los Angeles the previous year. Furthermore, during this time, Chicano teatros sprang up in

many locations in the West and Southwest, and included a multitextured definition of chicanismo that incorporated urban experiences, class differences,
and educational aspirations as well as other Latino groups and lifestyles.[12]

The failure in New York City to recognize *Zoot Suit*'s importance registers a more deeply rooted issue: at the time, minorities were creating spaces of
their own, each with its own particular political agenda, many with separatist
politics. Under these circumstances, in the urban setting of New York City,
Puerto Ricans were the Latino majority, and they responded with their own
dynamics of imperialism and neocolonialism as applied to them specifically.
Their concerns included dysfunctional families and the crisis of patriarchy
after migration. Just as the male farmworker of the 1960s defined the paradigm of Chicano theater, the Puerto Rican working-class male from the barrio
did the same in U.S. Puerto Rican theater.[13] In this very urban, working-class,
and streetwise environment, Nuyorican plays portrayed the immediate experience of life "down these mean streets." Playwrights such as Miguel Piñero,
whose *Short Eyes* was staged off-Broadway in 1974, and Juan Shamsul Alan
depicted the raw reality of marginalization, substance abuse, imprisonment,
welfare dependency, and later AIDS. The protagonists in these plays confronted
alienation, violence, poverty, and unemployment. The men's sense of loss
contributed to a disarticulation of families, individuals, and values. Therefore,
they experienced life in the U.S. as a lack of access to the public spaces they
had enjoyed on the island. When a second generation entered the stage, the
central male figure of the plays faced a deterritorialization by having to leave
"home" yet again, this time for an education or for upward social mobility
instigated by a Protestant work ethic or by enforced assimilation (e.g., José
Rivera's *The House of Ramón Iglesia* and Edward Gallardo's *Simpson Street*).

The mere mention of the third ethnic Latino theater, Cuban, creates
further disjunctures because of the frequent interchangeablity yet marked
discrepancy between the terms *Cuban* and *Cuban American.* U.S. Puerto
Rican/Nuyorican and Chicano theaters have been bilingual since their inception, but Cuban theater in the U.S. was originally written in Spanish by Cuban
exiles. Some of them were already playwrights before they left Cuba; others,
educated in Spanish, became playwrights in the U.S. This theater—in the last
few years—has been and is being translated into English and packaged as
Cuban American.[14] At the same time that many of these playwrights consider
themselves to be a part of the canon on the island, some of them equally
recognize publishing opportunities and marketability by now calling themselves Latinos and by translating their plays into English.

A close reading of this theater reveals that the exiled playwrights prefer to depict and deploy the philosophy and techniques of the avant-garde and European theater of the absurd that they had used on the island.[15] In the 1980s, a new generation of Cuban American writers emerged: individuals who were raised in the U.S., who are truly bilingual, and who may question their parents' prerevolutionary values.[16] Confronting their parents' conservative politics, younger Cuban Americans find themselves challenging issues such as homophobia, machismo, and bourgeois ideologies—ultimately issues that deal with reconciling what is known as "the two Cubas." This new theater is exemplified in the works of Luis Santeiro, Elías Miguel Muñoz, Dolores Prida, Ofelia Fox and Rose Sánchez, and Nilo Cruz, as well as in the performances *Milk of Amnesia* (Carmelita Tropicana) and *God Smells Like a Roast Pig* (Melinda López).[17]

Migration, nostalgia, ethnic memory, transcultural identity, and home continually appear as the most outstanding constructs in discussions of the common denominators of Chicano, Puerto Rican, and Cuban theaters. Together, they articulate ideological and social perceptions of each ethnic group according to its own historical processes and experiences. For Chicanas/os, this articulation means reappropriating Aztlán, a mythical homeland that, for historical imperialist reasons, coincides geographically with the U.S. Southwest, where there is the largest concentration of Chicanas/os in the country. For Puerto Ricans, whose migration since the 1940s has set off a chain reaction entailing a myth of eternal return to the homeland of their dreams, their island has been "tropicalized" into a paradise in their imagination.[18] Cubans, because of their imposed exile, channel their nostalgia into a Cuba that no longer exists, a mythified, prerevolutionary, middle-class and upper-middle-class island fantasy of property owners. Of course, these utopias were inherited by second and subsequent generations, who wrote longingly about their parents' imagined homeland and national communities.

Indeed, the search for "home" is crucial in the process of establishing a bilingual, bicultural Latina/o identity, both for new immigrants as well as for those generations born on the mainland of the U.S.[19] Since the 1980s, in theater, as in other literary genres, the mythical return to the homeland becomes a rude awakening from those expected utopian or imaginary spaces. This painful but necessary process of returning to one's ethnic and cultural roots as well as geographical origin helps to consolidate and establish a Latina transcultural identity. U.S.-born Latinas acknowledge their past and heritage, but proclaim their difference from the ancestral homeland based on their

consciousness in Morejón's concept of mestizaje. It is not surprising to encounter this problematic in the theater, for practitioners of all Latina literature
have addressed it. In fiction, essay, and poetry, we find Lorna Dee Cervantes
calling herself a "pochaseed" while in Oaxaca; Rosario Morales needs to
return to Puerto Rico in order to discover Cambridge as her home; while in
California, Aurora Levins Morales dreams of the Puerto Rico inside her;
Cristina García "dreams in Cuban"; Gloria Anzaldúa dedicates *Borderlands* to
Mexicans on both sides of the border; and Julia Alvarez's protagonists flaunt
their U.S. feminism when visiting their Dominican cousins on the island.[20] As
new generations come to maturity in the theater, nostalgia, migration, and a
mythical home are attenuated by concerns of the 1980s, 1990s, and beyond—
such as education, social mobility, crossing over, city life, gender politics,
sexual preference, ecology, illness and healing, AIDS, and all manner of cultural
heterogeneity.

In order to understand Latina theater historically, we must problematize the role of education as it affects transcultural identity formations. New
Latina/o generations find themselves confronting, negotiating, and accom-
modating formal and nonformal education as part of their intercultural identities as Latinas/os who live in the U.S. and who are here to stay. Like their
parents before them, many Latinas/os must juggle a nonformal education
received at home with the formal one acquired in or imposed by the dominant
system. The former consists of Latino cultural, social, religious, and ethical
values, and often uses Spanish, or a bilingual version of it, as the first language.
The latter education involves the imposition of English and the subsequent
erasure of ethnic, ancestral values. For some Latina students, their first contact
with English is when they enter the public school system, which operates, in
most cases, as an instrument of the dominant culture. In this educational
environment, the use of Spanish may be prohibited; their cultural heritage is
often denigrated, denied, or both; institutional racism is frequently rampant;
and assimilation is expected. Because of these practices, separation from home
and disidentification from Latino culture and the Spanish language seem to be
the only possibilities of survival for these students.

In order to transform this self-hatred into self-esteem and confidence,
Latinas/os often learn to identify with an Anglo formulation and perception of
"Latin" culture, which disassociates them from the reality of *being* Latina/o
that they have learned in the home. In some cases, the educational experience
produces such a state of alienation that the students find themselves either
denying their roots or searching for a way to express what has been silenced in

the curriculum, organizations, classes, and residential and social life of the academic domain. What is more, the greater the educational level, the more difficult it becomes for the student to find her way back home, as expressed in a multitude of literary works by Latinas/os. The theater, often the space where issues are raised publicly, has become the ground on which parents and their educated and upwardly mobile children interact as new identities are tested. We can see these dynamics in action in many Latina/o plays, such as Dolores Prida's *Botánica,* José Rivera's *The House of Ramón Iglesia,* Luis Santeiros's *Our Lady of the Tortilla,* Josefina López's *Simply Maria, or The American Dream,* Ofelia Fox and Rose Sánchez's *Of Barbers and Other Men,* Eddie Sanchez's *Unmerciful Good Fortune,* Roy Conboy's *When El Cucui Walks,* Elaine Romero's *The Fat-Free Chicana and the Snow Cap Queen,* and Alicia Mena's *Las nuevas tamaleras.*

In the chapters that follow, we offer textual readings and critical pairings of Latina plays that might, on the surface, appear to share no common denominator. In the labyrinthine world of Latina playwrights and solo performers, women protagonists literally stage their lives and their bodies. As many Latina playwrights and solo performers have affirmed, their playwriting grew, in the first instance, out of a desire, need, and urge to see themselves represented on the stage in roles other than virgin, whore, or maid.[21]

Consequently, a new poetics of Latina theater has emerged with its own dramatic structure and aesthetics as the playwrights have brought to the stage women's struggles to give birth to new hybrid identities and interstitial moments of cultural transition and transformation. What is specific to this theater is the use of Latina protagonists, women-centered action, and Latinas in general as the focus of the dramatic conflict. Given that Latinas must reclaim, reuse, and re-create their own history, the dramatic action is not based solely on the interaction of the characters, but also on an exploration of the self. If in male playwriting the object of desire is to solve an external conflict, in Latina playwriting the reverse seems to be true: the object is to solve an internal conflict. Because these plays revolve around self-definition, articulation of identity, and cultural affirmation, the action barely seems to move. In fact, a number of Latina plays have suffered from the same "stagnation" in the plot that the protagonists lament in their lives, as in Caridad Svich's *Gleaning* and Migdalia Cruz's *The Have-Little.*

Latina theater is a woman-dominated genre—that is to say that the majority of the characters are women—and Latina playwrights stage their work in a variety of both traditional and contemporary settings, juxtaposed with one

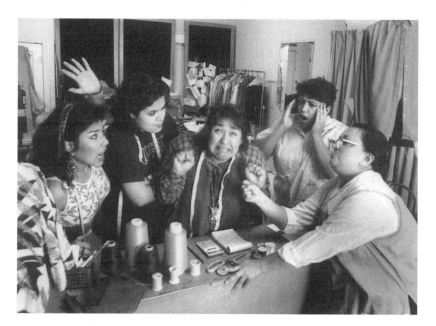

2. Josefina López's *Real Women Have Curves* at Guadalupe Cultural Arts Center, San Antonio, Texas (1990). *Left to right:* Lisa Suarez, Mariana Vazquez, Irma Escolar, Sonia Rodriguez, and Ruby Nelda Perez. Photograph by Al Rendon.

another across generation, class, educational level, ethnicity, and political point of view. As a result, mother-daughter relationships are emphasized, and at the closing of the plays the characters celebrate womanhood and these newly forged coalitions among themselves *(Real Women Have Curves, Novena Narrativas, Beautiful Señoritas).* The unison is accentuated by the absence of male characters, sometimes deliberately, giving credence to Teresa de Lauretis's (1984) observation that once men and their actions are decentered and the female characters are no longer distracted by them, these characters cease to be the object of male desire and can thus be the subjects of their own agency.[22]

By removing male characters from their plays, Latina playwrights have not dismantled patriarchy in one fell swoop. Rather, they have begun the action of deconstructing the institutions that privilege male power and restrict or constrain women's agency, potentiality, and independence. Among the most common institutions Latinas confront are the requisite Catholic school, abusive marriages, and the Catholic Church. Some playwrights prefer to specify their diatribe on the institutions that have trivialized, infantilized, and objectified women and women's experience—such as the beauty contest *(Beautiful Señoritas)*, the sweatshop *(Real Women Have Curves)*, or cosmetic surgery *(The Waiting Room)*. That diatribe extends to a refusal to condone or silence the ultimate exploitation and abuse of women in such criminal acts as rape, incest, child pornography, and serial killing (in the plays *Giving Up the Ghost, Salt,* and *Lucy Loves Me*).

Distanced from a male-centered world, the protagonists are now poised to reappropriate and take authority over their location regardless of previous definitions and behaviors dictated by that space. However, not all protagonists become empowered in the course of these plays. Failing to reconstruct an existing space of their own, they resort to experimenting with an alternative discourse and with new ways of being, seeing, and doing: dreams and phantasmagorical worlds populate this imaginary alternative space in *Roosters, Botánica, A Dream of Canaries, Cigarettes and Moby-Dick, Another Part of the House,* and other plays. Rather than viewing such spatial creations as idiosyncratic acts of "irrationality," escapism, and madness, we may interpret them as acts of intervention and survival. The protagonists expand their territory and ultimately locate themselves in these imaginary topographies as a way to save themselves, for these experimentations permit them to fantasize and create utopian "imagined communities" (Anderson 1991) of women. As a result, the playwright and her characters are free to envision a new transcultural definition of themselves in their newly reclaimed geographies.

Because Latina theater centers on the interconnectedness between the cultural construction of race, class, gender, ethnicity, and sexuality, it is practically impossible for Latinas' plays *not* to include their ideological agenda. Although that agenda may vary from playwright to playwright, almost all the plays tackle specific issues: immigration matters to Josefina López, Yolanda Rodríguez, and Milcha Sánchez-Scott (in *Real Women Have Curves, Emigración: An American Play,* and *Latina,* respectively); gentrification underpins Dolores Prida's *Savings* as well as Ofelia Fox and Rose Sánchez's *Of Barbers and Other Men;* environmental and health issues concern Cherríe Moraga in *Heroes and Saints;* the health-care system and its application to women concerns Lisa Loomer in *The Waiting Room;* Diana Saénz chronicles disappearances in Latin America in *A Dream of Canaries;* Maria Irene Fornes depicts repressive military regimes in *The Conduct of Life;* Midgalia Cruz concentrates on the victimization of women in *Lucy Loves Me* and *Salt;* and Cherríe Moraga and Marga Gomez confront homophobia in *Giving Up the Ghost* and *Marga Gomez Is Pretty, Witty, and Gay,* respectively. As AIDS

3. Poster for Milcha Sánchez-Scott's *Roosters* at Guadalupe Cultural Arts Center, San Antonio, Texas (1988). Used by permission of David Mercado Gonzalez, Guadalupe Cultural Arts Center.

proliferates in Latino communities, playwrights such as Ofelia Fox and Rose Sánchez use the theater didactically in *Siempre Intenté Decirte Algo (SIDA)* to raise consciousness, as do Janis Astor del Valle in *Fuchsia* and Migdalia Cruz in *So . . . ,* which are resonant with Moraga's earlier play *Heroes and Saints.*

Yet it would be simplistic as well as reductive to limit Latina theater merely to political and ideological agendas. What is at stake here is a new way of doing theater—that is, a poetics of Latina theater propelled and driven by its own structure, style, grammar, rhetoric, and aesthetics, and, ultimately, by the creation of a new genre.

A primary characteristic of the innovation of this new genre is its non-linear structure; it tends to be fragmented and nonchronological, allowing for the staging of short scenes and vignettes that are frequently autobiographical. Innovation reigns as Latinas experiment with staging sequential scenes instead of the traditional few scenes in a three-act play. Thus, it is not uncommon for Latina plays to stage up to twenty-five separate scenes in a single performance. As we show in chapter 3, many plays commonly follow the structural model of the bildungsroman, which chronicles the phases of a woman's life in the course of her education or concientización. These vignettes are principally dialogues of self-discovery, which at times appear testimonial and nondramatic. In this sense, little action takes place. Instead, the real drama goes on in the protagonists' consciousness and in their interactive dialogue with other women.

Although this theater endeavors to stage real life (as Migdalia Cruz has stated, "we have to be honest"[23]), it is not limited to a theater of realism. Rather, parody, sarcasm, cynicism, irony, and humor serve as filters for its expression. In consequence, laughter permits the audience to negotiate the underlying political message of the play without feeling threatened by the radical alternative politics being played out. Thus, feminism loses its fearful edge, lesbianism ceases to be so intimidating, and even La Migra (the short name for the U.S. Immigration and Naturalization Service) is confronted by a female collectivity. Ultimately, women's body is the site of laughter instead of shame.

Just as Latinas have a unique story to tell, they also have a new way to tell it. Like their counterparts in fiction, poetry, and essay writing, Latina playwrights and solo performers have invented a theater of hybrid genres. What began in the 1980s as teatropoesía has evolved into new types of theater, mixing poetry, monologues, and dramatic dialogue into one play or performance. The playwrights and solo performers themselves are conscious of their new genre by naming it originally and creatively: Denise Chávez has dubbed this new genre "novena narrativa"; Midgalia Cruz calls it "plovel" (a play and a novel); Ana Mitchell considers it "teatromentira"; and Cherríe Moraga might well call it something else related to myth, as one of her plays, *Heart of the Earth: A Popol Vuh Story,* reinvents and rewrites myth intersecting with history. But most innovative is Fornes, whose ambiguous and elusive dramaturgy undermines traditional theater to such an extent that failure to notice her new genre in fact does violence to her work.

In their search for new forms of expression, Latina playwrights and solo performers have reinvented the theater, a cultural expression that reflects the intersection of all their concerns—of their consciousness as women, Latinas, artists, and people of color. The creation of these new genres has allowed Latinas in teatro to stage in its totality a poetics where the politics of identity and representation intersect with the politics of location. The dialectic that they produce between form and content and between space and identity allows new generations to see themselves on stage, articulating their trans-cultural identities in novel, dramatic, and performative ways. As Latinas continue moving toward center stage, we can most assuredly affirm that now, at the beginning of the new millennium, the show that Dolores Prida presaged in 1989 "will go on, and you might as well get your tickets now" (1989:188).[24]

THREE

LATINA THEATER

STAGES OF LIFE

Part I: History

From the mid-1980s onward, the proliferation of Latina playwrights literally opened the door and set the stage for a new poetics of theater and solo performance, both in content and in dramatic structure, as we have just seen. Of the three main ethnic groups, Chicanas played the most predominant role in developing Latina theater from its inception. Together, Chicanas organized and founded their own theater groups, which promoted and fostered their specific political concerns and feminist agendas. Their ideological platform, then and now, centered on bringing to the theater strong leading roles for Latinas, debunking stereotypes, and promoting Latina playwrights, producers, directors, and actresses. Their work in the theater responded to urgent issues concerning their female experience and centered on articulating a trans-cultural identity formation. One of their major contributions was their questioning of the machismo and chauvinism inscribed in male-centered theatrical productions. In particular, many Chicanas disagreed with the representation and participation of women in Luis Valdez's Teatro Campesino. In their task of demythification, revisionism, and reconstruction, they worked collectively and individually to write themselves into history. Chicanas' creative combination of poetry and performance gave birth to their new way of doing theater in the form of teatropoesía.[1]

Teatropoesía, as Yvonne Yarbro-Bejarano has stated, was the "creative fusion of drama and poetic texts" (1983:79). Indeed, in its beginning, Latina theater—owing to the absence and almost nonexistence of women's plays—turned to poetry in an effort to stage a Latina experience within a theatrical discourse. Although these staged montages of poetic texts were powerful acting performances, the dramatic and feminist content of the writings reinforced the collective's theatrical practice. The commingling of poetry and performance embodied the theatrical representation of a Latina subjectivity-in-process, a hybridity just beginning to articulate itself in those years. Although that hybrid identity began as an experimental form of theater, it is now one of the major constitutive elements of Latina transcultural discourses, regardless of genre. In many of these cross-pollinated montages, the dramatic structure is characterized by short scenes, monologues, or poems in which women break silence, find a voice, and enunciate their subjectivity in relation to other women across generations. The 1981 teatropoesía production *Tongues of Fire,* for example, performed at Mills College in Oakland, has become an influential paradigm and a cornerstone of Chicana feminist theater. A dramatic adaptation of selected poems from the now classic *This Bridge Called My Back* (Moraga and Anzaldúa 1983)—an anthology of texts by "radical women of color," which denounces racism, sexism, and social oppression—gave primacy to the spoken word. The theatrical productions of Latina poetic works in the 1980s might have been called poetry readings or declamaciones, which are a legacy of poetic recitals that have from generation to generation of Latinas/os been a mainstay in preserving and transmitting key texts in schools and community events. These events in the 1980s served as precursors to the overwhelming popularity of Latina performance in the 1990s.[2]

In these poetic performances and in the ones that followed, Chicana solo performers and playwrights drew on their Mexican heritage and legacy in their search for women characters and role models. Almost inevitably, as Chicanas created a women's theater of their own in the mid-1980s, they discovered, recovered, and reclaimed as well as reinterpreted the iconic figures of Sor Juana Inés de la Cruz, La Malinche, the Virgin of Guadalupe, and Frida Kahlo.[3] The same act of cultural reappropriation takes place all across the spectrum in Latina playwriting in such plays as Migdalia Cruz's *Lolita* and Yolanda Rodríguez's *La Causa.*[4] Ultimately, the process of reclaiming has involved celebrating the unsung heroines of Latina daily life, such as the characters in Denise Chávez's *Novena narrativas,* the garment workers in Josefina López's *Real Women Have Curves,* the women strikers in Cherríe Moraga's *Watsonville,* and the historical Chicanas in Elaine Romero's *Walking Home.*[5]

Latinas' role in the theater was not limited, however, to the mythopoetic, but also extended to social action.[6] As Latinas demanded decision-making participation in the theater, they intervened for positive images and roles, child-care policies, network development, and support groups. In the early

years of Chicano theater, their voice and activism even led the official organization of Chicano theater, Teatro Nacional de Aztlán (TENAZ, 1971), to found
Women in Teatro (WIT) in 1978.[7]

A first attempt to study the evolution of Latina theater and solo performance is Alicia Arrizón's *Latina Performance: Traversing the Stage* (1999).
This pioneering book concentrates solely on Latinas in the theater, confirming
the genre as a legitimate site of research and study. Arrizón's interest lies in
describing the dynamics of a cultural politics and not necessarily in writing a
history. Her goal is to draw a tentative cartography of a Latina tradition and
legacy en el teatro, consciously contributing to the urgency of a scholarly
recovery of the archives of Latina performance. She begins this task with the
two founding mothers of Latina theater, Beatriz Escalona and Josefina Niggli,
both born in San Antonio, Texas. For Arrizón, each of them formed part of a
Mexican American aesthetics and identity, each with her particular way of
doing theater, that is, minority and women's theater. Escalona, using the
artistic name La Chata Noloesca, entertained Spanish-speaking audiences in
the 1930s and 1940s with humor, maintaining the tradition of carpas (tent
theater) and vaudeville (see chapter 5).

Also in the 1930s, Niggli, on the other hand, produced a theater from a
sophisticated and more academic vantage point (she received a graduate
degree in playwriting in 1935 from the University of North Carolina, Chapel
Hill) by addressing Anglo audiences with her crossover plays. The fact that she
wrote in English signals her as the first Latina playwright to participate directly
in and to contribute artistically to the Anglo imagined community by staging
plays that romanticized and emphasized Mexican folklore and a nationalist
sensibility. She says: "The United States needed the folk drama more than
Mexico. I wanted people to know the wonderful world south of the border
and that there was something besides Europe" (cited in Arrizón 1999:47)
Indeed, Niggli's conscientización was both a political intervention and a cultural affirmation that was highly unusual for her historical moment. If she is in
fact the only Latina playwright between that era and the Chicano Renaissance,
it would take another four decades for another Latina playwright to emerge
(Estela Portillo Trambley). Such a gaping lacuna indicates the vast need for the
kind of archeological work that Arrizón has initiated. Whether that recovery
project exists in the West or Southwest, it is clear that no matter where a
scholar locates herself or himself, there are stories of Latina performance and
playwriting everywhere, waiting to be found.[8]

When we move to the East Coast, however, women's participation in the theater manifests a history of irregularities and contradictions that, although still steeped in the political cohesion that we saw in Chicana theater, made their work seem more fragmentary. A practitioner since the 1970s, Magdalena Gómez, whose "performance poetry" was delivered in alternative venues, contributes her memories to this history of the early Nuyorican theatrical movement: "We came from the ranks of the poor, the marxist, people of color, the mentally alternative, straight, gay, transgendered, bisexual, young, old: lavaplato poets, dazzlingly unlike anything I'd read about in school" (Gómez 2000). These performances took place everywhere, from cafés in the village to various living rooms and lofts, but always with the intention of combining the theater and community of it all. The incipient Nuyorican poetry movement attracted many young poets such as Gómez and was instrumental in her meeting with the woman she considers to be her mentor, Sandra Maria Esteves. According to Gómez, a variety of theatrical venues opened up for Latinas/os in the 1970s, including playwriting workshops at the Henry Street Settlement House, the Puerto Rican Traveling Theatre, and Joseph Papp's Shakespeare Festival Hispanic Writer's Unit. Gómez's goal in these early theatrical spaces was to use "performance as a form of insurrection and healing." Even today, in one of her latest pieces, *You Don't Look It,* the transgressive nature of her art is designed to facilitate "the audience to share their own stories with each other about their own identity experiences," so that they leave "more connected to each other; that to me is the most important function of theater as I live it" (Gómez 2000).

Gómez's testimony reveals the fact that there is also an oral history of theater by Latinas/os in the New York area, a history yet to be written. No matter how local or community based Latina/o plays have been in New York City, they must always still compete with the dominant and powerful commercial theater of Broadway and off-Broadway. In other words, Latina theater has had to construct itself in the margins and interstices of official, hegemonic, capitalist theater. Furthermore, in their struggle for recognition, Latinas have found themselves pitted against Latinos for the few playwriting spaces allotted to works by "people of color." This is not to say that Latinas could not do theater in the East, but to date most Latina participation has occurred in "ethnic" commercial theaters: International Arts Relations (INTAR), the Puerto Rican Traveling Theatre, Teatro Duo, and El Teatro Repertorio Español.[9] The "language policy" of each of these theaters (English only, Spanish only, or bilingual) has been yet another consideration that has defined each group; and the playwrights working for or with them have had to adapt their plays to the policy of the theater in question. When competing with English-only play-wrights for spaces in national theater productions, they have often been told that their few words of Spanish are "too bilingual" for a national audience. It is interesting to note that Repertorio Español's box office successes—Gloria González's *Café con leche,* Carmen Rivera's *La gringa,* and Josefina López's *Real Women Have Curves* (staged in New York as *Las mujeres de verdad tienen curvas*) were originally written in English and translated into Spanish for these productions.

Another aspect of doing Latina/o theater in the New York area has been the consideration of an already existent theatrical infrastructure that is the result of the ideological and economic paradigm of individualism, competi-tiveness, profit making, and entertainment as commodity that characterizes Broadway and off-Broadway. With the exception of theater groups such as Teatro Pregones in the South Bronx, the African Caribbean Poetry Theatre (1980), and the Nuyorican Poets' Café, movements or traditions comparable to Chicanas' "teatropoesía" were less visible in this area. Thus, Latino conven-tional and commercial theater did not offer alternative theatrical models, dramatic structures, and ways of doing theater such as street theater, popular political theater, agit-prop, or collective theater that became popular in the West. In spite of all this, a community-based alternative collective theater also developed in addition to Latino commercial theater (Pregones, El Puente), an alternative committed to addressing the issues, concerns, problems, and needs for social change in the Latino community.

As one of the most visible and active Latino theaters in the New York area, INTAR, founded in 1972, has served in the capacity of developing play-writing among Latinas/os. Its many activities since it initiated its annual Hispanic Playwrights-in-Residence Laboratory (1981–90) include its sponsor-ship of plays-in-progress, workshops, dramatic readings, productions, and net-works for Latina/o playwrights. In a similar manner, the South Coast Reper-tory Hispanic Playwrights Project in Costa Mesa, California, also sponsored a Playwrights-in-Residence program in 1986, as did the Puerto Rican Traveling Theatre as early as 1977. These writing workshops were the single most important factor in the training of a new generation of Latina playwrights, for many of them were mentored into the theater with these residency programs. Also notable was the Latino Playwrights Lab at the Joseph Papp Public Theatre (1993), led by Dolores Prida and George Emilio Sánchez, which devoted itself to the development of performance, character, and dialogue.

Although always present previously, Latinas played an increasingly important and active role as organizers, directors, actresses, and playwrights in Latino playhouses throughout the country during the 1980s and 1990s. Women's hard, consistent labor and perseverance contributed significantly to the founding, functioning, and survival of many Latino theaters and theater groups. Clearly, it is apparent that Latinas have served as the anchor for Latina and Latino theater in the U.S. One after another, women have manifested themselves as leaders in as well as practitioners of theater arts. In her informative and diligent study *A Report to the Ford Foundation: Hispanic Theatre in the United States and Puerto Rico* (1988), Joanne Pottlitzer mentions no fewer than twenty Latinas actively engaged in theater work.[10]

One of the most prominent figures of these Latinas is Miriam Colón, founder of the Puerto Rican Traveling Theatre (1967), who has been instrumental in its productions and is responsible for its financial survival.[11] As early as 1969, when Teatro Duo began, there was always a corps of women in its organization: Dolores Prida, Magali Alabau, Gloria Celaya, the late Ilka Payán. Likewise, Rosalba Rolón has been the heart and soul of Teatro Pregones; María Mar produces an innovative theater in the New York area that she calls "theatre of transformation"; Silvia Brito has been the founder of and artistic director at Teatro Thalia in Queens; Carla Pinza, a Puerto Rican actress, founded Latino Playwrights Lab at the Henry Street Settlement House in the late 1970s; Carmen Zapata made a name for herself in founding the Bilingual Theatre Foundation of the Arts (1973), with Margarita Galván and Estela Escarlata in Los Angeles; Laura Esparza was a founding member of the Latina women's theater group Las Comadres and was an active director based in Seattle; Amy Gonzalez was the first female director of a woman's play at Teatro Campesino and has been instrumental in bringing to the stage the works of women playwrights such as Cherríe Moraga, Josefina López, and LynNette Serrano-Bonaparte; and Susana Tubert has directed powerful and important theatrical pieces nationwide. In addition, Ana María Simo and Magali Alabau cofounded Medusa's Revenge, a lesbian-feminist performance group in New York City, which operated from 1976 to 1981. More recently, Janis Astor del Valle, a Bronx-born Borinqueña, cofounded Sisters on Stage (s.o.s.), a multicultural lesbian theater devoted to developing lesbian playwriting; and Diane Rodriguez is the co–artistic director of the Latino Theatre Initiative at the Mark Taper Forum in Los Angeles.

In terms of connections between all these women, Marta Moreno Vega's newsletter *¡AHA!: Hispanic Art News* (1985–97), a publication dedicated to the enhancement and advancement of Latino arts and to the promotion of Latino and Latin American culture in the New York area, acted as a kind of bulletin board for many of them, and playwright Dolores Prida served as its editor until 1991. In the Massachusetts area, Magdalena Gómez's solo performances and community-based productions bespeak the continual activism of Latina playwrights, as do the work of Brenda Cotto Escalera and Noelia Ortiz Cortés in Boston. In the West, Denise Chávez's Border Book Festival brings together many Latina/o artists in an annual event in the Las Cruces, New Mexico, area. Cherríe Moraga's work at the San Francisco–based Brava! For Women in the Arts Theatre also highlights the innovative cultural work Latina playwrights have been doing. Always the innovator, activist, and community organizer, Moraga endeavored to establish "DramaDIVAS," a theatrical group for gay and lesbian teenagers in the Bay Area and described as "a place for young people to come to a positive awareness and expression of their identity through the theatre arts."[12] Also composed of young women of diverse backgrounds and between the ages of seventeen and thirty-one is the San Antonio–based group the Women of Ill Repute: REFUTE! What began as plans for a single performance has evolved into a highly requested politicized show. As in teatropoesía, one of their concerns has been to find a way to fuse the poetic with the dramatic, a more developed form of the slam. In the group's written call for works, the prized characteristics of a work include "collaborative," "interactive," "theatrical," and most importantly, "challenging the ideas of a 'woman's reputation,'" especially regarding bias and stereotype. Finally, the overtly political agenda against rape propels both the dramatic action and the impulse of this group, whose proceeds go to a Rape Crisis Center (Guzman 2000). Also in Texas is the Cara Mía Theatre Company, which produces quality plays by women, especially Latinas, including works by Prida, Fornes, Sánchez-Scott, and Moraga. Their mission, in their own words, is "to broaden the understanding and appreciation of Latino culture through theater, literature, and educational programming" (brochure).

Beginning in the 1990s, Latina playwrights found another venue for their tremendous talent and energy. Schools of performance art throughout the country have honored them as "artists-in-residence," where they teach playwriting in undergraduate and graduate programs to a new and diverse generation: Dolores Prida (Dartmouth College, University of Michigan), Midgalia Cruz (Amherst College, NYU), Edit Villarreal (UCLA), Cherríe Moraga (Stanford), Caridad Svich (Yale), Amparo García Crow (University of Texas, Austin),

4. *Women of Ill Repute: REFUTE!* San Antonio, Texas (2000). *Top row, left to right:* Andy Garcia, Heather Mockeridge, Victoria Garcia-Zapata, Shannon McGarvey, Elain Peña, Celeste Guzman. *Middle row, left to right:* Lisa Cortez-Walden, Amalia Ortiz, Maria Ibarra, Frances Trevino. *Bottom row, left to right:* Jackquie Moody, Ana Deluna. Photograph by Celeste Guzman.

Laura Esparza (University of Washington), Yareli Arizmendi (California State University, San Marcos), Monica Palacios (UCLA), Elaine Romero (University of Arizona), and Susana Tubert (Stella Adler Conservatory).

No discussion of Latina teaching, mentoring, or playwriting is complete without a long aside for the Cuban-born playwright Maria Irene Fornes. Fornes has consistently supported young playwrights, who are indebted to her mentorship and vision, as demonstrated in their grateful acknowledgments.[13] The writers Milcha Sánchez-Scott, Migdalia Cruz, Josefina López, Caridad Svich, Ana María Simo, Edit Villarreal, Dolores Prida, and Cherríe Moraga have all worked closely with her in various capacities.[14]

Although Fornes is known today for her workshops, a long list of theater publications stands behind her, an unusual phenomenon in the Latina playwriting community. Normally, a wide margin separates Latina playwriting from publications and productions. With this paucity of Latina works in circulation, it is hardly surprising that only a few Latina plays received critical attention until the late 1990s. The sole exception is Fornes, whose plays continue to garner academic interest. To date, only a handful of Latinas (including Fornes) have had their plays anthologized in a single volume of their own work: the late Estela Portillo Trambley, Dolores Prida, Cherríe Moraga, Lynne Alvarez, and Carmelita Tropicana complete the list.[15] At this writing (2000), however, we are constantly being apprised of new anthologies of Latina playwrights now in press or preparation and new critical appraisals of these playwrights.[16]

Another factor that contributed to the current renaissance of Latina playwriting was the visibility and professionalism of Latina literature in the 1980s. As a result, a subtle shift began occurring as more works appeared in print, were circulated, and then produced. Although some of these works were anthologized as new American plays, only the pioneering collection *On New Ground: Contemporary Hispanic American Plays* (Osborn 1987) alerted the Anglo theater community and university drama departments of the diversity of Latina/o theater. For women, this collection signaled a presence in the playwriting community because the anthology contained at least three plays by Latinas (Fornes, Alvarez, Sánchez-Scott).[17] The biggest splash, nevertheless, was the 1992 anthology *Shattering the Myth* (edited by Linda Feyder), which included plays *only* by Latinas: Cherríe Moraga, Migdalia Cruz, Edit Villarreal, Caridad Svich, Josefina López, and Diana Sáenz. Of these six, only Cherríe Moraga had previously published a play (*Giving Up the Ghost,* 1986). *Shattering the Myth* was the first anthology on Latina theater to create a collectivity of Latina playwriting in much the same way that the earlier anthology *Cuentos: Stories by Latinas* (Gómez et al. 1983) did for fiction. It helped to consolidate a Latina dramatic corpus in its inclusion of plays by three Chicanas, one Puerto Rican, one Cuban American, and one Central American. Not surprisingly, a playwright herself, Denise Chávez was responsible for making the selection. In less than two years from the publication of *Shattering the Myth,* most of the playwrights included there had another play in print or were preparing anthologies for publication. Although such visibility made it appear that a canon of Latina theater had suddenly emerged, in fact a very respectable history was behind the formation and maintenance of that theater over the years. Our own anthology, *Puro Teatro: A Latina Anthology* (Sandoval-Sánchez and Saporta Sternbach 2000), participates in this history by publishing Latina theater, solo performance, and testimony in one volume. *Puro Teatro* attests to the hefty solidity of this lengthy historical process now materialized in print.

Inasmuch as it is possible to pinpoint a single moment in the emergence of contemporary Latina theater, that date would have to be 1972, the year that Estela Portillo Trambley published *The Day of the Swallows* in the collection *El Espejo* (followed by publication in the 1973 collection *We Are Chicanos*). In so doing, she initiated the process of the constitution of a Latina theater canon, which has finally gained consolidation with the publication of *Puro Teatro* nearly thirty years later. Both *Shattering the Myth* and *Puro Teatro* stand in great contrast to the 1979 theater issue of *Revista Chicano-Riqueña,* where the only play by a Latina was *Sun Images,* also by Portillo. For a long time, it appeared as if Portillo were the only Latina writing plays, as Fornes was distanced from the Latina community at large. Portillo's collection *Sor Juana and Other Plays* (1983) historicized Latina playwriting by being the first published volume of plays by a Latina. Yet, although the 1970s were characterized by lean and spare publication of works by Latinas, once we move into the 1980s and with increasing vigor and visibility into the 1990s, we can see a steady production of plays and solo performances by Latinas. From the mid-1980s onward, at least one play by a Latina has been published per year, and a host of solo performances have been witnessed, a trend that reached full circle at the end of the 1990s (which we trace in chapter 5).

Part II: Toward a Poetics of Latina Theater

For a genre—Latina theater—that has been historically undertheorized and is practically devoid of a critical apparatus, almost any approach to it would widen its analytical field. Of all the possible literary approaches applicable to Latina theater, the bildungsroman, as we develop below, may seem the most unlikely. Nevertheless, the paradigm of the coming-of-age novel replicates the stages of life—and especially one particular stage of life, early adulthood, so prevalent in many Latina plays. Precisely because Latina theater is often staged in a series of vignettes, each signaling a moment in the path of life, the bildungsroman model provides the structure with which to conjoin the performative with the narrative. Indeed, Latina theater conflates these two seemingly disparate genres by linking them at the juncture of a politics of identity and a politics of representation, thus redefining the limits of the bildungsroman itself.

Once again, the evolution of Latina writing becomes apparent as we witness its transition from poetry to narrative to theater. A brief review of the model of the bildungsroman is useful before we discuss its application to

Latina theater. Scholars concur that this literary form usually involves an initiation of the protagonist into adulthood, or is a "coming-of-age" novel. In its first definition (1913), Wilhelm Dilthey conceived it in the following terms: "A regulated development within the life of the individual is observed, each of its stages has its own intrinsic value and is at the same time the basis for a higher stage. The dissonances and conflicts of life appear as the necessary growth points through which the individual must pass on the way to maturity and harmony" (Dilthey 1913, cited in Swales 1978:3).[18] The immediate problem that a Latina studies scholar encounters is the obvious masculine, white specificity, and exclusivity of both the genre itself and of the criticism of it. Under these circumstances, the classic definition of the bildungsroman describes a male hero who operates within a clearly defined patriarchal world and discourse, which relegates all women and people of color to invisibility. Based on this hegemonic conception of the bildungsroman, Jerome Buckley's definition makes explicit the dominant plot of the genre: the inadequate education the "hero" receives in his father's home and his consequent quest for the "real world." In Buckley's analysis, after leaving home, the young hero goes to the city, where his development and true education occur (1974:17–18).

Feminist theory and criticism were the first to question the premises of such a phallogocentric genre. In the first instance, they deconstructed the actions of the male heroes and the ideology of the male writers who created them, exposing the gendered limitations and conventions of the genre, plot, and its politics of representation. Second, once the characteristics of the genre were applied to female protagonists, the model itself required a major paradigmatic shift not only in structure but also in characterization. This shift registered women's ideological and political awareness of their own lack of access to the power and privilege of men. From a woman's experience and a feminist consciousness, however, that privilege could be attained only if the woman protagonist had the necessary education and opportunity for social mobility. As women recognized their differences and as the category *woman* was de-essentialized, women of color dis-placed the bildungsroman of the industrialized world. As Bonnie Hoowver Braendlin has written, "In contemporary American literature . . . the bildungsroman is being resuscitated, revived not by males of the dominant culture but by societal outsiders, men and women of marginality groups. The *bildungsroman* of these disenfranchised Americans—women, blacks, Mexican-Americans, Native Americans, homosexuals—portrays the particular identity and adjustment problems of people whose sex or color renders them unacceptable to the dominant culture" (1983:75).[19]

The emergence of the feminist bildungsroman into an altered genre, with its particular women's perspective, however, was still limited to white, middle-class, educated women. Immediately, once women of color started writing their stories and experiences, not only did they transform the reading of the genre, but they also began to appropriate it. As ethnic coming-of-age stories reached publishers' shelves and university classrooms (works by Cisneros, Morrison, Alvarez, Walker), the tenets of the bildungsroman eventually also made their way to Latina theater. If the starting point for the male and/or white bildungsroman is after the protagonist leaves home, for Latina playwrights what action there is often takes place *at* home. Whereas in a white, male bildungsroman, privilege—or access to it—is assumed, for Latina protagonists, stuck in the marginal places and positions assigned to them not only by gender but also by race, ethnicity, and class, their fantasies and the real possibilities of getting out become the core of the work. For men, accessibility to geographical and social mobility is possible, but for Latina protagonists, leaving home is often not even an option. Thus, many of the plays by Latinas that we discuss center around the limitations of a politics of location in which women are stuck in no-exit situations.

Paradoxically, that "stuckness," often read negatively, anchors them in their own quotidianity. This quotidianity is concretized in the theater by the series of vignettes that characterize Latina playwriting. These vignettes often take place in the traditional spaces—private and public—assigned to Latinas and are populated mainly by women. Such spaces as the kitchen, the botánica, the factoría (*Real Women Have Curves,* Josefina López), the bedroom (*Lucy Loves Me,* Migdalia Cruz), and the bathroom (*Living Dolls,* Elaine Romero) permit the protagonists to interact within and to transact—and, as we argue, to transculturate their women's world of intergenerational families, women's bodies, identity affirmation, and, ultimately, community. Specifically, these works register a moment of cultural transition that stages a new politics of representation in which hybrid transcultural identities are always being questioned, being constructed, and evolving in relation to location. By appropriating these often domestic spaces—once limiting, marginalizing, and confining—Latina playwrights empower their characters, for a transformation of consciousness now takes place in these woman-specific spaces. The insistence on daily life and experience permits the playwright to draw from women's personal belongings and so-called subgenres. Hence, the scenes are staged like testimonials, diaries, or photo albums. The installation of an altar to La Virgen de Guadalupe or to another saint in the dramatic space reproduces the familiarity of such scenes at home. This process of reappropriation of space also implies a recognition and recovery of culturally specific icons, traditions, and value systems. In addition to the presence of these Virgenes, we also find food items and recipes, spiritism and medicinal cures, and an acknowledgment of the wisdom of the abuelas and tías (aunts). Indeed, this cultural reclamation—a transcultural act in the making—testifies to a recognition and legitimization of knowledge passed on from generation to generation, replicated from actors to audience. In these terms, with Latina appropriation of the bildungsroman, the entire genre is transculturated. This transcultural genre occurs when a politics of identity is fully staged and when Latina protagonists articulate and redefine their identities not only within a feminist consciousness, but also within the parameters of transculturation.

Although a formal education is the structural and ideological element of the bildungsroman, for people of color, who may not be middle class and who might have slipped through the cracks in the educational system, that educational journey leading to upward mobility, privilege, and power is fraught with complexities, struggles, and displacements. In Latina plays, the protagonist's process of educating herself entails juggling her informal education with a formal one (Of Barbers and Other Men, My Visits with MGM, Botánica, Real Women Have Curves, The Have-Little, The Fat-Free Chicana). Her effort to educate and raise the consciousness of members of her family, friends, men, and even the audience is one of the most important elements that produces the dramatic tension, a conflict both determined and resolved by the processes of transculturation as it displays "toma y daca" dynamics.

Whereas in some plays the mere acquisition of an education and its consequences for the protagonist, her family, and the community are the most important aspects of both the protagonist's and the playwright's work, in others educating oneself is tantamount to educating the community. In fact, the entire performance manifests itself as an educational transcultural act. Hence, the play's didactic function mobilizes and activates audiences and protagonists alike: feminism leads to the questioning of cultural constructions of gender and to knowledge of her female and patriarchal constructions of sexuality; a class consciousness allows for the possibility of a solidarity between educated and uneducated women; a racial consciousness problematizes issues of mestizaje, nationality, and ethnicity; sexual awareness breaks taboos for lesbians and heterosexuals as it exposes homophobia in Latino/a communities. Finally, an acknowledgment that transcultural, hybrid identities are valid and full of potentiality leads to an affirmation and celebration of the protagonists' achievements and experiences as Latina women. In each of these cases, the main protagonist, by her words and deeds, exemplifies to a younger generation the satisfaction, reward, and ultimately the need to re-invent themselves as Latinas. The educational process is completed by the fact that women dare to speak out and reimagine themselves. In this process of education, transculturation, and performance, the play itself has taught women how to speak and how to *remember* how to speak. In this sense, a new empowerment also arises from the enactment of transcultural ethnic memory. As a result, the theater itself becomes a rite of passage from one identity to another, from one stage of life to another, from one sexuality to another, from one single location to multiple sites of intersection.[20]

Because so many Latina plays center their action on staging the many phases of woman's lives, our chapter subtitle, "Stages of Life," not only derives from a theoretical and structural model inherited from the bildungsroman, but also reflects the ontological substance of the plays themselves. In this sense, we can see why many protagonists in these plays enact on the theater stage the process of their passage from childhood to womanhood. In the first wave of Latina playwriting, a typical Latina play would, for example, represent a woman at various stages of her life: the stage directions would indicate that she is to start the play in her childhood, reach adolescence and puberty in the second act, and end the play in maturity (*The Have-Little, Simply Maria, Sarita, Beautiful Señoritas,* etc.). Therefore, the structure of the bildungs-roman described above is the scaffolding for the staging of women's experi-ences and phases of life from childhood to adulthood. Even when certain roles are stereotypical or problematic, Latina playwrights deploy them as a point of departure in their contestation of social and cultural constructions of Latina gender. For example, if women are the traditional bearers, transmitters, and preservers of culture, in Latina plays such as *My Visits with MGM, Botánica,* and *Las nuevas tamaleras* those roles are reconfigured and negotiated in ap-prenticeships typical of the bildungsroman. In this process, those roles that are considered negative, stereotypical, and demeaning are reappropriated and re-imagined with a new appreciation made possible by the protagonists' initia-tion into a transcultural state of mind and into a political agenda that Gloria Anzaldúa has called the "new mestiza consciousness" (1987:79).[21] This new consciousness, as in Anzaldúa's case, almost always is the result of the commingling, juggling, and hybridity of a formal education with a nonformal one at home. Often in the protagonist's quest for education in the public sphere, she brings new knowledge back to the home to share with her family or community. In this way, the learning process extends from the individual to the collective via the female protagonist, within the context of transculturation.

Whereas some Latina playwrights focus almost exclusively on feminist issues, others have begun writing about race, class, ethnicity, sexual preference, and a variety of political issues facing the community at large. Learning about the simultaneity and intersection of oppressions, a Latina playwright manifests her outrage beyond gender-specific concerns. As Yvonne Yarbro-Bejarano has observed, "In her defiant self-definition, the Chicana writer commits herself to the denunciation of injustice, the injustice of social and economic oppression and well as the unjust imposition of sexual stereotypes" (1983:88).

If in the first instance of Latina playwriting, what we shall call *Phase One,* Latinas concentrated on deconstructing sexual and cultural stereotypes from within the dominant Anglo culture, eventually they could no longer ignore Latina representation in plays by Latinos, a necessary response that would inaugurate a second phase essential to identity formation. During that first phase, the "beautiful señorita" exoticized by Anglo culture triggered the satire in the eponymous play by Dolores Prida. In 1977, *Beautiful Señoritas* embodied the discourse on Latina identity at that historical moment and limited itself to deconstructing those one-dimensional constructions of femininity. In what we call *Phase Two,* the obedient, passive "virgen" and "madre sufrida" roles that Latino playwrights had perpetuated and audiences venerated were the next target of attack. In *Novena narrativas* (1986), Denise Chávez explores and makes possible self-representation and multiple identities that manifest the heterogeneity of Chicana identity and the protagonists' self-affirmation. Having been classified into roles that were said to be unidimensional, passive, and submissive, Chávez's protagonists are human, Latina, and, above all, mujeres. The spectator cannot forget the pachuca artist, the homeless lesbian, or the religious fanatic.

In the 1990s, as Latina theater evolved into what we call *Phase Three,* these acts of contestation transformed the focus of Latina playwriting from issues solely of representation to issues of identity formation, giving diversity and transculturation a firm footing. Chicana playwright Josefina López was thus able to build on characters created by her predecessors of a previous generation: her new protagonists are either educated or searching for the education that will free them from the stagnant roles to which they have been assigned by class, race, and gender. Without that education, they lack the means to find new alternatives to empower them with ways of seeing and being. In López's *Real Women Have Curves* and *Simply Maria,* the young protagonists have no need to preach about or apologize for their feminism: on the contrary, it is almost taken for granted, and they are able to convince the older women of its urgency and applicability. Given that each play centers on a single character and her process of acquiring an education, López is able to move the audience's consciousness from merely the politics of representation to the politics of identity. As these writers were freed from the restraints of limited representative models and constant deconstruction of stereotypes, a politics of difference truly cohered for them in this decade, bringing to the stage a variety of perspectives that began with Moraga's *Giving Up the Ghost* (1984, 1986) and took further shape with her later works *Heroes and Saints* and *The Hungry Woman: A Mexican Medea.*[22] In all these plays that scandalized traditional audiences, Moraga opened the door to a new Latina theater by incorporating the shock of sexuality, debunking Catholicism, breaking sexual taboos, and staging the scars of incest and rape. Not only do her protagonists graphically acknowledge their women's bodies, they speak through them in order to represent lesbianism and difference.

In short, through these three phases of Latina theater and theatrical evolution, we may now affirm a double bildungsroman: not only do many plays employ the structure and conventions of the genre, but the entire ensemble of plays—which when put together is the corpus of works we may identify as Latina playwriting—*also* resembles a bildungsroman, as if each play were a different, processual component of the whole. Thus, Dolores Prida created a young girl in *Beautiful Señoritas* in 1977, but Migdalia Cruz, one of Prida's successors, showed an adolescent in *The Have-Little* in 1992. Once this girl becomes a Latina woman, she is no longer pigeon-holed into the one representational slot available in 1977. By 1992, the complication of identity is acknowledged on stage, making room for diverse sexual orientations, ethnic and racial differences, varying homelands, and singular performative styles that show the complexity of the Latina imaginary on stage. Within this politics of difference and affinity, a new type of male character is beginning to emerge, including gay men.[23] Gay or straight, these new male characters are not threatened by the strong women and female sexual autonomy in these plays.

Thus, in the wealth of diversity that is Latina womanhood, the whole world becomes her stage.

At the end of the twentieth century, it is clear that these three phases of Latina playwriting and performance have served as a necessary genesis and embryonic seedbed for the efflorescence of solo performance that will undoubtedly define the first decade of the new century.

FOUR

THEATER MATTERS

FOUNDATIONAL FEMINIST PRACTICES

Up until the 1980s, the existing paradigm of U.S. Latino theater was almost exclusively male. With very few exceptions, women's roles were marginal, secondary, and tangential to the established genre. But as the decade progressed, Latina playwriting gained momentum, and male theatrical supremacy began to lose its currency as the sole defining factor. With the turning of the new decade, as the number of Latina publications in all genres soared and a national readership began to define itself, Latina playwrights and solo performers also found an audience.[1] In retrospect, we can now see that at a point in history when male Latino theater had seemingly come to an impasse, Latinas, on the other hand, were revitalizing and reinvigorating the stage by marking new directions and staging new subjectivities. Just when it seemed that Latino theater—that vital, important, socially conscious, and politically oriented genre of the 1960s and 1970s—had become an anachronism, women quite literally appeared on the scene, displacing, replacing, and upstaging male playwriting. Latina playwriting offered an alternative vision of the world, a fresh new view of society, and new ways of doing theater.

In spite of the fact that theater is not written to be read, but rather produced, from the early 1990s onward Latina plays were published in either collections of plays by ethnicity, their own individual publications, or anthologies that grouped them with other playwrights. Because theater is a cultural domain where values, beliefs, ideologies, and identities are put to the test, it is not surprising that it has served as a forum where Latinas stage, play out, dis-play, and act out alternative models of and for social action and imaginary social constructions of reality.

Before we can understand or chart precisely how Latinas moved from backstage to their current prolific theatrical productivity, we must examine, interrogate, and problematize their historical participation in the theater. How does one dramatic work connect to another? Why did it take so long for the playwrights to become visible? What obstacles did they encounter? Did they have contact with one other? Is there an intertextuality among their works? Even if we establish a genealogy, that dialogic interrelationship itself answers some questions while generating others: Why the absence of Latina theater in collections of Latino literature? Why the invisibility of Latina theater in collections of feminist plays and critical anthologies? Why have Chicana playwrights received the most critical attention? Has the existence of a Chicana feminist movement and theoretical discourse contributed to the recognition of Latina performances and playwriting? Finally, when we take into consideration the fact that every Latina writer faces the triple jeopardy of being a woman, a Latina, and a writer, does the Latina playwright face a quadruple jeopardy for writing in a genre as marginalized as the theater?

To begin with, no writer, Latina or otherwise, emerges from a literary vacuum. The plays we consider in this chapter, all of which we classify as the foundational works and historic theatrical moments of Latina playwriting, demonstrate their interconnectedness on many levels. Regardless of the playwright's intentions or even of the extent of her knowledge of others working in a similar vein, we argue that a dialogue exists among these works. This dialogue has rarely been perceived, much less examined critically, but that neglect does not diminish the fact that when grouped as a whole, these plays have a coherence and cohesion that has initiated a historic moment we call a *foundational discursive site.*[2]

Consequently, we insist that Latina theater was not born of spontaneous combustion, but rather is a process in the politics of representation and identity formation, articulated in part by feminist consciousness and in part by Latina playwrights' reaction to the Latino gendered national and ethnic consciousness developing at this time. As we unravel and recover Latina plays and performances in order to reveal the roots of their theatrical practices, we center on a woman's tradition constituted by definite themes, dramatic structures, characterization, and conventions. Furthermore, as we place Latina theater works in dialogue with one another, it becomes clear that their alternative tradition has inaugurated a process of representation and identity formation whose discursive practices not only question cultural stereotypes and social constructions of gender, but also demonstrate their intertextuality and ideological agenda. In their refusal to continue to play the secondary roles assigned to them in early Latino theater, Latinas have redefined and challenged theatrical spaces and have engaged in a genre with its own poetics. As we analyze the dynamics of this new genre, we observe how works that center on sexual abuse, oppression, sexual repression, and compulsory hetero-sexuality, among other ills, dramatize the psychic patriarchy that traps women into static positions.

Superficially, it may appear that the foundational plays emerged as isolated events: Portillo's *The Day of the Swallows* (published 1972), Fornes's *Fefu and Her Friends* (produced 1977), Prida's *Beautiful Señoritas* (produced 1977), Sánchez-Scott and Blahnik's *Latina* (produced 1980), Moraga's *Giving Up the Ghost* (produced 1984), and Chávez's *Novena narrativas* (produced 1986). Nevertheless, their deep structure reveals how they resonate and intersect with one another. Given the absence of an established history of Latina theater, a dialogic reading of these texts—connected to each other and viewed as a whole—illustrates how indeed a politics and an aesthetic coherence unite them. Our critical reading demonstrates just how many commonalities these works have, despite their varying historical moments and scenarios. If the surface structure in Latina playwriting adheres to a chronological develop-ment of plot, the deep structure, in contrast, reveals the ideological apparatus around which the play functions. In every case, that ideology foments, fosters, and affirms women's consciousness as a subjectivity-in-process. If we position these works synchronically rather than view them as isolated examples of Latina playwriting, a theatrical canon in its own right emerges. Each of these six playwrights, when read on her own, represents a singular discursive mo-ment of Latina playwriting. However, when read together, an exciting develop-ment materializes as a new foundational discursive site.

Perhaps it is ironic that the 1980s, a long decade of ultraconservatism in the U.S., served as a kind of incubation period during which performances and productions by Latinas flourished. Although the pivotal figure of the decade is Cherríe Moraga with her play *Giving Up the Ghost* (1986), even its taboo-breaking, pithy core requires us to trace its matrilineal genealogy to at least one previous play by a Chicana. *Giving Up the Ghost* triggered a reaction that immediately opened Latina theatrical space to women's, feminist, and sexual concerns.[3] But even Moraga's open lesbianism in this play had its antecedent in Estela Portillo Trambley's lesbian character in *The Day of the Swallows,* published more than a decade earlier in 1972.[4]

When *Giving Up the Ghost* burst onto the theatrical scene, it was hailed as the first dramatic production by a Chicana in which lesbian sexuality was finally represented on stage. Many were the critics, both within Chicano/a studies and in women's studies, who proclaimed the formation of a new dramatic subjectivity-in-process—namely, the Chicana lesbian. These critical readings seemed to adjudicate to the play the first stirrings of Latina playwriting. At first glance, it appears that Moraga initiated the art of representing Latina desire, Latina lesbianism, and Latina feminism simultaneously on stage. These critical works acclaiming Moraga launched her into a position of visibility and prestige as her play was analyzed from a variety of perspectives, all of which placed it at the forefront of an emerging Chicana literature, but especially a Chicana theater (Alarcón 1988; Rosenberg 1993; Yarbro-Bejarano 1986a, 1986b).

And how could this play fail to attract attention and critical acclaim? At a time when white feminism was being challenged for its Eurocentricity, homophobia, and politics of representation, a play emerged that filled in the void of a national feminist agenda in the performing arts: it established a Chicana theater that was defined by a politics of sexuality and ethnicity that in turn disclosed multiple, transcultural identities. *Giving Up the Ghost* develops the plural selfhoods of a Chicana whose identity revolves around a younger self (Corky), an older self (Marisa), and a sexually ambiguous lover, Amalia. In the course of the play, which is performed as a series of long monologues by each character, we witness the flashback of a rape scene. In the retelling of this event in her young life, Corky also questions the taboos and stereotypes placed on her within her own culture. Her struggle is to break away from compulsory heterosexuality and to defy gendering in dress codes and in social and sexual behavior. In effecting this break, her lesbian desire emerges both as a contestation to prescribed gender and cultural roles, and as a force in its own right. It is a powerful, provocative performance from which audiences cannot leave unaffected. Even on the written page, its power is palpable to the reader. For both spectator and reader, the play succeeds in dismantling dominant heterosexual stereotypes and patriarchal imprisonment. As a result, "giving up the ghost" becomes a coded construct whose meaning is to (1) recall the past, (2) examine its contents, and (3) reappropriate only that part of it that serves to edify a new identity. Upon examination, the "ghosts" signify a closeted lesbian existence, the painful memory of which has brought nothing but shame and unhappiness. In being able to give up that ghost, the character is well on her way to constructing her new identity, a proud lesbian existence that fuses her cultural and ethnic identity with her sexual identity.

Although *Giving Up the Ghost* is the milestone marker of the emergence and existence of a Latina/Chicana theater, most critics are content to discuss the play as an isolated event, which corroborates their detailed critical interpretations. These important close readings have aided students and readers in their analysis of a difficult and confrontational play. Nevertheless, they treat Moraga's play ahistorically, seeming to suggest that it germinated spontaneously. This is not the case. In Moraga's own admission, Estela Portillo Trambley's play *The Day of the Swallows* (1972), had a profound impact on her and featured largely in her consciousness as a Chicana writer. She observes:

> I've always loved *Swallows,* although it is a 'classic' lesbian work in the worst sense of a 1950s view where all lesbian protagonists are punished for their disobedience to the male hegemony. They all end up dead or howling at the moon on all fours in a crazed frenzy, as does Josefa whose suicide is described as a sensuous reunion with the body of the lake. . . . Still the value of *Swallows* remains in its daring and complex depiction of a lesbian who is actively desirous, whose desire is equal to the urges of a man, but who rightly fears for her life to face it. (Moraga 1993:161–62)

Moraga's remarks clearly recognize the significance of Portillo's audacity in portraying a lesbian character. Furthermore, her appreciation of Portillo establishes a historical context that permits us to read the two plays against each other. Consequently, *The Day of the Swallows* cannot be seen as an anomaly or a fleeting paradigm in the history of Latina theater. It is, rather, nothing short of the inaugural moment of Latina playwriting. This first symbolic signature of a Latina playwright significantly occurred even before the term *Latina* was in circulation. Likewise, it was the first work by a Chicana to be published within a canon that was predominantly male. That this initial example demonstrates not only how women have no sexual need of men, but also that they may castrate them indicates what a scandal it caused.

By center-staging a lesbian relationship, Portillo problematized the issue of compulsory heterosexuality and squarely placed it right at the forefront of public consciousness. Although her later theater is more conventional, she might have unwittingly cut her ties with the Chicano community, which is not the case with Moraga. 1971 was still too early for a lesbian play to succeed with Chicano/a audiences. The play was scandalous not only because it offended any homophobic instincts that might have been present, but also because any mention of sexuality at all, hetero- or homosexual, was taboo. When in 1984 Moraga staged *Giving Up the Ghost,* the circumstances had radically altered. First of all, she spent those intervening years at work on feminist collectives that would place her at the center of what was then called a third world or women of color lesbian movement. In this role, she quickly gained national prominence and became a spokeswoman for a new politics of sexuality and identity. In this regard, she already had a hefty community composed of feminists, women of color, lesbians and gays behind her when her play was finally produced. At that point, there was no question of being ostracized. Unlike Portillo, she created her community before she wrote the play.

Although *The Day of the Swallows* is a problematic text, it would be a mistake to dismiss it flatly as homophobic. The fact that Moraga is attracted to the play and its central protagonist indicates how compelling the character doña Josefa is. Although the plot may be summarized in a few sentences, the interrelationships between characters is far more complex and disturbing. Doña Josefa, who is a devout Catholic, has a secret lesbian relationship with her young protégée, Alysea, who in turn is in love with a man. At the moment the play opens, doña Josefa is cleaning up the blood of the child whose tongue she has removed in order to silence him. His crime, in her world of ethics, was to witness her and Alysea kiss. Doña Josefa's drunken uncle Tomás enters the scene intermittently as blackmailer and voice of truth. At the end of the play, after confessing her sexuality and secret love affairs to the priest, doña Josefa drowns herself.

This tragic event, embedded within a play whose symbolism is redolent of Lorca's tragedies, points to the extent to which Portillo relied on a European canon as part of her formation. She readily admits: "I read philosophy, history, psychology: Bergson, Jung, Jaspers, Neitzsche, Huxley, the Bible, Toynbee, Aisley. I read Buddha, Lao-tzu, Kahlil Gibran, Pierre Tielhard de Chardin," and "In college because I was an English major, I had a sober and delightful exposure to the English and American classics. T. S. Eliot, Pound, Sartre, Get, Balzac, the Russian writers" (Bruce-Novoa 1980:168). It was not until much later that she discovered Mexican writers Octavio Paz, Alfonso Reyes, and others. Although she does not mention Lorca as an influence, critic Janice Dewey makes a convincing argument for the parallel between *The Day of the Swallows* and Lorca's *La casa de Bernarda Alba* (Dewey 1989:41). Like Bernarda, doña Josefa worries incessantly about her reputation in the community, the famous "el que dirán" (what will be said about one in public). Similarly, passion, desire, secrecy, and sexuality are the axes around which both plays revolve. In the repressed societies of Lorca's Spain and Portillo's border community, women's passion, desire, and sexuality constitute a presence whose power is overwhelming, but which cannot be named, much less spoken. Inevitably, that passion plays itself out in the only way the protago-nists of both plays can assert themselves: through their final act of death.[5]

If we take a step backward to analyze that passion, we can find other parallels between the two works. In Lorca's text, it is the playwright's covert homosexuality that cannot be named and that is displaced as the passion of the daughters in the house. In Portillo's work, however, it is the protagonist herself who is a closeted lesbian and whose passion for women must be silenced, kept secret, and never named. Following through on Lorca's model, which is a well-known tragedy, there is only one possible outcome: self-sacrifice and predetermined death.

As we work our way back from the tragic, "shocking and mystifying" (Dewey 1989:39) ending of Portillo's play, it is obvious that we are no longer in Lorca's Spain. There, the homosexuality of the playwright was indeed the "love that dare not speak its name." At the opening of Portillo's play, however, the reader/spectator is alerted to an event that must be silenced. Although homosexuality is also a taboo here, there is a marginal space in which the reader and spectator are free to imagine the true homosexual underpinnings that motivate the plot. As the action progresses, doña Josefa's disclosure of her lesbianism does not constitute such a shock because the playwright has pro-vided intermittent markers and clues that are meant to guide readers and spectators in decoding Josefa's sexuality. In the play, there is a group of characters who either know, witness, or suspect such proclivities. That they are blackmailed, maimed, or silenced evidences the rampant homophobia that pervades the community of the play.

Rampant homophobia also sparks Moraga's play *Giving Up the Ghost,* but in the fourteen-year gap between the publication of the two works, enormous social changes occurred. For a contemporary queer audience, like the one that attends Moraga's plays, there is an identification process with the lesbian character. Unlike Josefa, these characters bear no shame in their coming-out stories. On the contrary, Moraga imbues them with a sense of pride and jubilation at being their own speaking subjects. Because doña Josefa manifests an embryonic pride in her lesbianism, she does not succumb to the silence that the reader and audience almost come to expect. Yet mixed with her declaration is a sense of guilt and shame. That her coming out occurs during a confession with the priest allows for multiple interpretations. Because the Catholic Church is not renowned for its understanding of homosexuality, it might appear that Josefa is caving in to patriarchal authority by asking forgive-ness for "sinning." Yet her audacity to confess her love for another woman also results in her liberation. Read in this manner, her final act, which has been interpreted as homophobic and desperate, can also be viewed as liberating and jubilant: she is finally in control of her own person, she decides her own fate, nobody makes decisions about her body except her.

When considering Josefa's suicide, several factors must underscore our analysis. Her death is circumscribed by the genre of tragedy itself. But her life, too, is predetermined by a slim set of parameters open to women in her pueblo. Of course, one of these possibilities is marriage. Josefa rejects any mention of marriage, though we are told that she is "still" a very attractive woman. For women in her circumstances who choose not to get married, their options are limited to the convent, prostitution, madness, or death. To her credit, Josefa does not choose madness. The audience and reader are fully aware of the fact that she is a woman with all her mental faculties intact. To a certain extent, she chooses the convent, but again on her own terms. She is considered a kind of high priestess of the village and praised for her kindness and goodness. In this role, she could be viewed as the "beata" figure, also resonant of Lorca. As we have seen, she chooses death, but, like the other options, it too is a complex negotiation that points to all the ambiguities of the text and of Portillo's own moment in history as she composed it. In the first instance, homophobic audiences might celebrate the death of a lesbian as a just and deserved punishment for her transgression of social, sexual norms. But in the second and more important instance, her death may be viewed as liberating, like the death of Kate Chopin's protagonist in *The Awakening* or of Alfonsina Storni or Virginia Woolf, all by drowning. These real-life women as well as fictional figures find a communion with nature in the soothing water— and none of these deaths has been seen as a punishment. In all these cases, it was clearly a separate agenda that led the women to these final, fatal acts.

Our critical reading strategy places Moraga's and Portillo's works alongside each other in order to demonstrate that Moraga's text is anchored in her reading of Portillo and that Portillo's text initiated a discursive cultural moment in a much greater way than had previously been acknowledged. In this sense, Portillo not only inaugurated Latina playwriting, but her text must be seen as the harbinger of a transitional moment, exactly the kind of work that Catherine Belsey has theorized as an interrogative text. For Belsey, such a text "disrupts the unity of the reader by discouraging identification with a unified subject of the enunciation. The position of the 'author' inscribed in the text, if it can be located at all, is seen as questioning or as literally contradictory.

Thus . . . the interrogative text . . . literally invite[s] the reader to produce answers to the questions it implicitly or explicitly raises" (1992:91).

As a play penned by the first contemporary Latina to write a play and as the first woman's play to portray the first lesbian protagonist to come out, Portillo's work cannot be dismissed, even if the circumstances surrounding its genesis are somewhat ambiguous. Readers may feel ambivalent about Josefa's character: on the one hand, she is a lesbian who determines her own destiny, yet on the other she represents a classic static and one-dimensional lesbian stereotype. Consequently, her limitations are marked within the parameters of the play; she is never able to break away from the stereotype. Regardless of these factors, what is clear is that despite Portillo's own sexuality, the play marks historically a foundational discursive site in Chicana/Latina playwriting and identity formation. In other words, it is anchored. Whereas Teatro Campesino spent these same years doing agit-prop theater and theater of social protest, Portillo's play was serving as a precursor to the plays about sexual identity and about the formation of multiple and hybrid ethnicities, which would not evolve for another decade. Finally, it is interesting to note that in its singularity, *The Day of the Swallows* is also marked by its lack of production. As a play that openly dealt with Chicana lesbianism, it became as much of a taboo as the subject had been for doña Josefa. That it is now out of print is perhaps the clearest indication of its continuing marginalization.

It would not be until 1977 that two more pivotal foundational texts for Latina theater would appear. Maria Irene Fornes's *Fefu and Her Friends* and Dolores Prida's *Beautiful Señoritas,* both produced that year, not only represent the most eminent genesis of Latina theater but also assist us in tracing its coherence and evolution. With the possibility of historic distance and with the queer movement firmly placed, another set of coordinates emerges from which to examine these crucial plays by two women whose lesbianism was not open for public consumption in 1977. Given their insertion into both Latina playwriting and queerness, we can see how rereading their plays provides us with a lesbian continuum, despite the fact that lesbianism is not the ostensible agenda of their plays. Rather, both use their feminism to advance their political platform. Their plays, as well as the plays by Portillo and Moraga, account for a more inclusive politics of sexuality, one that demonstrates queerness as a historic discursive site of Latina theater. (In chapter 5, we theorize how queerness is also a foundational discursive site of solo performance.) If these four plays represent that discursivity as emergent, when we reach solo performance, lesbian discourse becomes a legitimate and valid means of expression for a politics of identity and difference.

Collectivities of Women

Although at first glance differences between Fornes and Prida seem to be greater than their similarities—they both write for drastically different audiences—a closer examination of their plays divulges the first manifestations of the synchronic model that we describe. In essence, each of these 1977 plays deals with a collectivity of female protagonists, thus mirroring on stage what is occurring everywhere behind the scenes. Women are involved in all aspects of theater production, but many of their individual signatures are lost. These two playwrights, both Cuban immigrants who later call themselves Cuban Americans, vary from the anonymity that characterized the norm in that they sign their plays individually. Both plays are deeply informed by feminism and the women's movement, either explicitly or implicitly, as well as by the playwrights' covert lesbian experience.

Fefu and Her Friends and *Beautiful Señoritas* also share another consequential and purposeful trait: both stage female protagonists who defy their role as passive recipients or spectacles of patriarchal domination and representation. Despite their differences, the two plays share the feminist agenda of their creators. Each playwright is concerned with writing scripts for women wherein their agency develops and thrives. Prida accomplishes this task with a fast-paced, sardonic, parodic style, which is the result of her deconstruction of stereotypes, especially those of Latina womanhood. That the objects of her parody are Latino and Anglo males places her play at a critical vantage point that exposes the constantly shifting transcultural subjectivities of her characters. Like Prida's, Fornes's play situates her female protagonists at the center of the action, with little or no male intervention.

The overarching characteristic of these plays is their structure: a series of vignettes—which will become the trademark of Latina theater in the coming decade—that move the dramatic action forward and locate the protagonists in their historical, ethnic, geographical, class, and sexual contexts. Prida's technique cannot escape the legendary choices present in *The Day of the Swallow* and *Giving Up the Ghost:* nun, wife, prostitute, or madwoman. Here, what concerns her especially is the commodification of women, which she parodies in her depiction of the beauty contest on stage. Thus, each vignette presents a woman who has "evolved" one step further in the path of life known as womanhood. The protagonist's story begins at her birth as a girl-child and follows her through the stages of her life until she reaches adulthood as a woman. The final result is a liberated new Latina generation that has the tools to confront both patriarchy and ethnic discrimination. It is no coincidence that the location of this multilayered performance is the beauty contest because it is the institutionalized site where colonialism, commodification, and racialized and racist ideals of beauty intersect.

Fornes's dramaturgy is modeled on Brechtian and experimental theater, so *Fefu and Her Friends* relies on an audience familiar with avant-garde theatrical techniques. Classified as minimalist, Fornes's work has, in all probability, its greatest impact when actually performed on stage. The clearest example of the difference between reading the play and seeing the production is in her stage directions in Part 2, which indicate: "These scenes are performed simultaneously. When the scenes are completed, the audience moves to the next space and the scenes are performed again. This is repeated four times until each group has seen all four scenes. Then the audience is led back to the main auditorium" (4). That ironic distancing fragments the actions as well as the characters' behavior and alienation, and contrasts radically with Prida's work. Whereas Fornes makes the spectator an active participant of the theatrical space, Prida didactically utilizes the stage and her plays in her desire to propose a model of Latina/o identity that her audience, mainly Latino, can take home and put to the test. Such a "rehearsal" is not possible with Fornes, whose audiences are well versed in the radical chic performances of sophisticated urban theater. Although class markers exist in her work, the ethnic and racial markers that characterized Latina/o theater up until this point (the late 1970s) are absent. Whiteness seems to escape representation and is assumed without question in *Fefu;* it is unmarked and therefore invisible, so that early audiences could leave the theater without ever questioning issues of race and ethnicity. Significantly, it was not until later, when Fornes herself began to work with Latino theater groups, that the beginnings of an ethnic identity crept in her work, as depicted, for example, in *Sarita* (1982).

Undoubtedly, with *Fefu and Her Friends,* Fornes initiated a thematic paradigm that was to become characteristic of almost an entire decade of Latina playwriting (1977–86). Specifically, she stages a collectivity of women, Fefu and her friends, who decenter male protagonists and characters. Using the "dis-ease" (Kent 1996b:121) of male/female relations as the unspoken agenda that underscores her work, Fornes also hints at the possibility of a sexuality beyond compulsory heterosexuality in her suggestion of a possible lesbian relationship between Cecelia and Paula. Sexuality also figures into the equation in that one of the characters has been sexually molested, a subject that later resonates in Moraga's work. From the innovative staging of four simultaneous scenes at its beginning to its shocking ending, when Fefu deliberately shoots her friend Julia, *Fefu and Her Friends* has generated a vast amount of speculation as to its meaning. The reader, who is clearly at a disadvantage compared to a spectator, may have trouble visualizing the type of fragmentation that characterizes the play. Furthermore, there is virtually no plot and very little action. What little cohesion there is centers on the meeting of eight college-educated women who gather at Fefu's country home to plan a fund-raising event.

The play's deep feminist underpinnings suggest the extent to which patriarchy has invaded the characters' lives. The fragmentation of the action and the lack of any kind of linearity parallel Fornes's message about women's position in a patriarchal system and underlies the deep structure of the play. Her technique results in a de-essentialization of women that serves as a counterpoint to their usual position in patriarchy. Although they have internalized their oppression and the misogyny from which it derives, they nevertheless attempt to resolve the contradictions in their lives (Kent 1996b:120). In this sense, each character brings to the play one other instance of a woman's "dis-ease in society" (Kent 1996b:121). Each one of them embodies in her female flesh one more outrage against women—from molestation by secret police to spousal abuse to actual paralysis. Their confrontation of these ills forms the corpus of the play: one is bound to a wheelchair, another drinks too heavily, another is plagued by hallucinations.

In its suggestion of the social ills women face, *Fefu and Her Friends* lays the groundwork for full development of such issues in the 1980s by the playwrights that Fornes herself will mentor. By focusing solely on feminist issues, Fornes gives the impression that ethnicity, race, and class are secondary in her theater. Nevertheless, the Latina playwrights that have emerged from her workshops have learned to take on their own individual projects; the cornerstone of Fornes's teaching is individuality. In this context, Fornes's play does not represent an isolated example of a Latina writing theater, but rather forms part of a continuum that is constantly manifesting itself through the theater and its practitioners. Her own way of doing theater and her feminist practices have served as the seedbed for a new generation of Latinas who simultaneously incorporate her philosophy while learning her greatest lesson: that they cannot imitate *her*. Thus, she has transformed the art of doing theater in that she has given them the tools to explore their own theater practices. In this regard, her contribution has been invaluable.

Given that this new generation of Latinas is producing plays about trans-cultural subjectivities-in-process, it is of vital importance that they not lose sight of their audiences, who are found in either community-based or regional theaters. These playwrights have no desire to marginalize or alienate those very communities or audiences on whom they rely. Thus, they negotiate and accommodate a Fornesian philosophy to a community-based way of doing theater, whose entire essence is the complexity of the transcultural subject. That the most produced playwrights to come out of Fornes's workshops (Josefina López, Caridad Svich, and Migdalia Cruz) are those who use her messages but imbue them with their own stories attests to the necessity of a theater that is hybrid in its nature.

Although Fornes remains the indisputable mentor and role model of many Latina playwrights, her personal politics have shown as much contradic-tion as her characters display. For example, she says that although "[there is] a rich Spanish tradition of classic theatre . . . there hasn't been a strong modern Hispanic theatre—by that I mean since the turn of the century. . . . the Hispanic-American doesn't have a model yet" (García-Johnson 1993c, 163). Many playwrights and theater practitioners, from Teatro Campesino to the teatro de protesta on the East Coast (1960s), would take issue with such a remark. It is clear that Fornes speaks from a positionality of class privilege, whiteness, and Eurocentric dramatic models. That she relinquished these positions to some degree through her work as director, mentor, and role model manifests both her own evolving subjectivity and her solidarity with a younger generation. New generations of Latino/a playwrights continually acknowledge the fact that she respects their autonomy and inspires them to find their own voices. For her, then, it is "very important to try to work with Hispanic playwrights at a level where they are just beginning to write, so that they do not dismiss possibilities of ways of writing that would be very original to them but ways they would not see models for in the active American or English or German theatre" (Garcia-Johnson 1993c:163).

If we consider how symbolic, fragmented, and postmodern *Fefu* is and how it is noteworthy for its lack of ethnic markers, our assertion that it is a foundational piece of Latina playwriting may seem questionable. The women in the cast could easily be "everywoman." Nothing defines them or their creator as Latinas. Yet, once placed within the context of the genre of Latina theater, *Fefu and Her Friends* can clearly be linked with both Portillo and

Moraga's work. The play itself recognizes and decries the situation of women under patriarchy, even when the playwright can offer few solutions to their entrapment. Like Portillo, Fornes presents a character whose final desperate, destructive act may be ascribed to madness. Also similar to Portillo's play, the expression of sexualities is both muted and articulated, both hetero- and homosexual. In its own embryonic moment, Fornes's play anticipated the way Moraga's characters audaciously accuse their sexual abusers. The entire play, then, underscores the playwright's outrage at the paralysis and even doom that seem to confront women in patriarchy. If the action of the play seems to stand still, it is intentional. There is no moving forward when women are trapped physically, sexually, and psychologically within the confines of the male-dominated world. Thus, the final shocking action, when Fefu shoots Julia, the "paralyzed" woman in the wheelchair, is tantamount to declaring that Fornes's theater has taken a social and political position, an exhortation to rebel.

As previously noted, *Fefu and Her Friends* clearly connects with Dolores Prida's *Beautiful Señoritas.* Undoubtedly, the late 1970s was a pivotal moment for women's issues and in the gestation of Latina theater. A feminist consciousness made visible around the country also left its mark on the theatrical productions of these daughters of Cuba. Like *Fefu, Beautiful Señoritas* exposes the same "dis-ease" with psychic patriarchy. Similarly, both plays rely on a company of women that symbolizes a collective feminist consciousness. Nevertheless, each play exercises its own particular agenda. If in *Fefu* that agenda is informed by a politics of feminism, in Prida's play it is constituted by a politics of feminism *and* by a Latina identity.

Beautiful Señoritas follows the development of a girl from the moment of her problematic birth—her father wants and expects a son—to the moment when she becomes "La Señorita de Mañana" at the play's end. As she grows, a parade of stereotypes marches before her eyes as acceptable and expected role models of Latina womanhood. Without Prida's feminist intervention, those stereotypes might pass unscrutinized, to the point that they may perpetuate themselves. As the young woman witnesses various patriarchal role models, the audience experiences the educative process through Prida's use of parody, irony, and humor. The play offers a solution to break the silence on women's issues and to dismantle the taboos that had previously been in effect, thus creating a space where dialogue about sexuality, gender, and the body can take place. There is no institution that escapes unscathed from this gaze: the Catholic Church, marriage, and the beauty contest all become the con-

5. Video photograph of Bibi Ramahatulla in Dolores Prida's *Beautiful Señoritas,* a student production at Mount Holyoke College, Massachusetts (1984). Video by Patricia Gonzalez.

tested ground on which the play develops as it decenters the misogyny inherent in both Latino and Anglo cultures.[6]

The great contribution of *Beautiful Señoritas* to Latina theater is that it was the first to develop a speaking subject with a conscious politics of multiple identities. This new politics of representation constructed its scaffolding around the coordinates of gender, ethnicity, race, sexuality, and class. In this cornucopia of identities, which are also stereotypes that are enacted to be questioned, lay the foundation for a transcultural subjectivity-in-process that was to become the hallmark of a Latina theater of the 1980s. For the first time, we could see a play in which no one single ethnicity prevailed over another. Prida's new identity politics proclaimed a Latina self—whether the provenance be Cuba, Puerto Rico, Mexico, or the U.S., but whose *home* is in the U.S. By placing a new Latinita on the stage, Prida ushered in a way for women to exercise their own agency, even under oppressive conditions. And Prida's radical project certainly owes some of its success to her method, whereby side-splitting humor, new lyrics to popular songs, and outrageous parody camouflage her deeply feminist agenda.

It is at this point that Prida's work anticipates Moraga's creation of a Latina subjectivity-in-process in *Giving Up the Ghost.* Unlike Prida, Moraga does not explain or justify her protagonist's sexuality, but she is connected to Prida by their common historical moment, when feminism, plurality, and the heterogeneity of women's experience intersect, especially for women of color. This budding U.S. Latina feminist consciousness in Prida's work hailed a new moment, substantially altered from the one we saw in *Fefu and Her Friends,* for it is marked by the multiple juncture of gender, sexuality, class, ethnicity, and race. Whereas Prida's feminist politics continued to refer, however tangentially, to Latin America, Moraga articulates what she calls a "Third World Woman" within the U.S. Moraga's project complicates Prida and Fornes's agenda by shifting emphasis to a new politics of sexuality. It is precisely at this symbolic moment that Cherríe Moraga consolidates a U.S. Latina lesbian identity in her multiple role as essayist, poet, editor, translator, and, of course, playwright. As she anchors the concept of home solely to the U.S., Moraga establishes a place for U.S. Latina identity in general to flourish. Once home is no longer a floating signifier and Latina identity is firmly rooted in the U.S., Latina theater is uniquely poised to move to its next stage of development.

"Una latina completamente latina"

The first representative work of this next period is Chicana playwright Denise Chávez's one-woman show *Novena narrativas* (produced 1986), a work that stages the experience of Chicanas articulating their identities as U.S. Latinas. Based originally on a collaboration among five women, Chávez's powerful solo performance of the piece she later called *Women in the State of Grace* immediately drew in audiences. Chávez's skill in this performance lies in the fact that Chicanas could finally see their stories performed on stage by characters recognizable in the community. From the abuelita to the bag lady to the pachuca artist to the factory worker, Chávez's "familia de mujeres" (100) reminds spectators of people they know in their families, communities, and workplaces. The fact that Chávez re-creates this gamut of women with her flair for veritable dialogue allows spectators not only to identify, but also to empathize with them. By erecting an altar as a pretext for busyness while performing the characters, the "narrator" evokes feelings of comfort and warmth in her audience (*Novena narrativas* 85). With the Virgin of Guadalupe as a centerpiece, the performance functions as a ritual that theatergoers immediately recognize, cherish, and claim. Such feelings help to establish a general sentiment of community among women, a legitimization of identities. Despite the fact that this work is not the first Chicana play, its importance lies in that its characters are so readily identifiable as bona fide members of the community and of la familia, and thus its function is both sacred and secular in its inclusiveness.

In contrast to Corky and Marisa in *Giving Up the Ghost,* whose politics are always confrontational, these nine women imbue their audiences with feelings of love. Of all of these characters, though, it is the Latina lesbian who represents another innovative moment in Latina playwriting. Once we trace representation of the lesbian from *Swallows* to *Fefu,* from *Beautiful Señoritas* to *Giving Up the Ghost and Novenas Narrativas,* the stereotype, formerly trapped in immobility, now transforms and deconstructs. It is the theatrical formation of a subjectivity whose rejection, alienation, loneliness, and homelessness supersede the audience's possible homophobia. Yet this character claims no need for anyone's pity. Unlike Corky, Corinne is usually willing to accommodate to the circumstances. For example, when she asks a viejita (little old lady) to dance and is rejected for being "media weird," she immediately turns to a male dance partner so as not to evoke more feelings of alienation. Corky, on the other hand, constantly provokes audiences, causing more "disidentification" than does Corinne. Corinne's unabashed devotion to the Virgen and her "ofrenda" to the altar show her, too, to be a member of the community even in all her marginality.

Establishing the foundation of a Latina discursive site in the theater corrals a synchronic group of discrete plays into one unit; what was previously seen as isolated moments of theatrical representation can now be examined as a whole. Although the works discussed in this chapter are well known within a theater-going, theater-reading Latina community, another play virtually ignored by critics is indispensable to our discussion. Its author, Milcha Sánchez-Scott, is well-known for her successful play *Roosters,* which was filmed for PBS in 1989, but her earlier collaboration *Latina* (with Jeremy Blahnik 1980) was not published until 1989 and has yet to be treated critically. Given its early production date, its instant success, Sánchez-Scott's subsequent celebrity, the issues of identity that it raises, and our methodology of synchronic dialogism, no discussion of Latina playwriting in the 1980s should ignore it. Both its name and its early date indicate a budding consciousness that would continually emerge throughout the decade. But what is crucial here is that Sánchez-Scott creates a paradigm of a Latina immigrant reality that transcends the Chicana, Cubana, or Puertorriqueña ethnicities. By drawing women of different ethnicities and nationalities together under the title *Latina* regardless of their immigration status, Sánchez-Scott gives validation to a term whose currency had yet to be circulated. When we consider that 1980 was also the year that the U.S. government began to favor the term *Hispanic,* Sánchez-Scott's use of *Latina* becomes a counterhegemonic act of self-definition, contestation, and resistance.

Like *Beautiful Señoritas, Fefu and Her Friends,* and *Novena Narrativas, Latina* presents a collectivity of women. Similar to "Señorita de Mañana" of *Beautiful Señoritas,* this play also relies heavily on a model for the future, embodied in the character of the "new girl." If Prida centers on gender exploitation, here the action revolves around the dehumanizing labor conditions faced by undocumented workers, who in the play are principally domestics. In this sense, the play anticipates Josefina López's *Real Women Have Curves* (1992) in that the main characters struggle to define themselves in the face of adversity from the Immigration and Naturalization Service (INS) as well as within their personal dramas.

Most specifically, what this play offers its spectators and readers is the playwright's realization that only Latinas can name themselves, that their subjectivities as Latinas are constantly evolving as they confront the realities of the harsh life dished out to them. In some sense, the play accomplishes some of the same political work of *Beautiful Señoritas* in that it brings together a diversity of Latina ethnicities and backgrounds, but this time without the comic backdrop. Nevertheless, it is not *Latina* that has given Sánchez-Scott her reputation. Rather, she is best known for *Roosters,* a work hailed as the more recognizable "magic realism." *Latina,* on the other hand, accuses the system of cruelty and unfairness, and in that regard must be read as an openly political play. Perhaps its most political message is the final transformation of the most assimilated character when she finds empowerment and courage by her process of self-naming at the end of the play: "Ahora, sí, eres una latina completamente latina" (140). Given that *Latina* contains all the elements of an incipient Latina theater, it is important to place it in its rightful context beside the works of Portillo, Moraga, Prida, Fornes, and Chávez.

A Foundational Discursive Site

Each of these six plays, when read as a singular cultural production, represents a discrete moment in Latina playwriting. However, when read in dialogue with each other, the whole becomes greater than the sum of its parts. Now such disparate stylistic elements such as the monologue, the ambiguous ending, the interrogative text, the hybrid genre, the performativity of the play, and the collectivity of women protagonists become the hallmarks of this new canon and become particular to it. Thematically, their interconnections are even more suggestive: nobody can speak about rape without referring to *Giving Up the Ghost.* Nor can anyone now refer to *Giving Up the Ghost* without knowing Portillo. The same applies to plays that ideologically promote a women's agenda, such as *Fefu and Her Friends* and *Beautiful Señoritas.* The celebration of groups of women who become speaking subjects compels us to read *Beautiful Señoritas* alongside *Novena narrativas.* In matters of Latina ethnic affirmation, we cannot separate *Beautiful Señoritas* from *Giving Up the Ghost* and *Latina.* When it comes to staging marginalized characters, Maria Irene Fornes and Denise Chávez seem to have much in common. We are not suggesting that any of these playwrights directly influenced one another, although in some cases they certainly had contact. Our project regards those intertextualities that are landmarks of the historic moment that gave rise to these plays.

This is to say that there *is* a historic moment of ethnic Latina consciousness that has taken place on a national level and that each of these plays documents. Although it may appear that one play takes up where the other leaves off, it is more accurate to conclude that a level of consciousness is in constant motion toward defining itself, and each movement functions within the parameters of this particular Latina foundational discursive site in the making. Important, too, are the political movements that lay the foundation for women's theater: the Civil Rights movement, the Chicano movement, the women's movement, the women of color movement, the third world liberation movement, and the gay and lesbian movement. Far from isolating Latinas, as is sometimes affirmed, all these discursive sites cluster and intersect as they empower women at a moment when male writing and dominance is greatly diminished.

If the 1960s and 1970s are characterized in Latino theater as a time of marginalization and silence for women, the 1980s and 1990s in contrast bring us their stories in all their complexity and strength. Furthermore, as Latinas chronicle these moments of cultural transition and social, historical, and political change, we find in their plays the inaugural traces of transculturation. Repeatedly the message is clear: each play documents, registers, suggests, and celebrates a new transcultural subjectivity informed by new politics of representation and location, where identity's multiple coordinates are race, class, ethnicity, gender, sexuality, and education. What is curiously "missing" from this list is a politics of "nationality," based on country of origin. Women's solidarity and affinity supersede the divisions based on nationality that had previously defined Latino male theater (Chicano, Puerto Rican, Cuban). As a result, this corpus of theatrical works can rightfully claim itself as *Latina theater.* In the chapters that follow, we analyze specific examples of Latina theater as manifested in solo performance and in two specific clusters of plays centered around certain thematic issues (kitchen, home) that register the Latina transcultural experience in the theater.

FIVE

THE PERFORMANCE OF THEIR LIVES

A HYBRID GENRE FOR TRANSCULTURAL IDENTITIES

Spectacularly visible and prolific during the 1990s, Latina solo performance constitutes a genre in its own right. A concrete derivation of Latina playwriting, solo performance in its many manifestations—dare we say it?—has become the most highly original, irreverent, and innovative theatrical art form Latinas are producing today. All of a sudden, everyone is doing it, and everyone is writing about it. Within the realm of Latina theater, solo performance stages to the fullest Latinas' subjectivities-in-process in relation to given historical social formations and discursive locations. This is to say that the bicultural and mostly bilingual condition of U.S. Latinas has determined and will thoroughly determine those staged identities within the processes of transculturation that we have described up to this point. In this chapter, we aim to show just how Latina performance by its very nature may be read as a transcultural act as well as a cultural practice and political intervention. Latinas' increasing participation in solo performance demonstrates how those cultural practices and political interventions embed the articulation of transcultural subjectivities.

Any attempt to define solo performance—Latina or otherwise—may be slippery and elusive not only to the artists themselves, but also to theorists of performance. Even when theorists of performance disagree about a consensual definition of the term, all seem to concur that its very essence is writing and performing the body (Auslander 1994; Chin 1991; Phelan 1993). Since the 1970s, feminist performance has staged women's bodies in their subjectivity as sexual beings; however, earlier, the unspoken assumption was that those bodies were heterosexual and primarily white (Forte 1987:379). Elin Diamond, whose work on performance has gained much theoretical currency in these years, defines it "a doing and a thing done" (1996:1). Performance always manifests itself as a "doing" by its actuality in the here and now. However, at the moment that a performance is executed, it becomes a past action, "a thing done," which registers its ephemerality in space and time. In this space and time, the body—as a cultural artifact—functions as a site of that performance-in-the-making and as the "thing done," a reminder of what took place, as well as an indicator of future performances. Therefore, although the performance itself is ephemeral, it permits the audience a reminder of the past through the body that serves as a conduit to the future. Although the body is always present, each time it performs, it does so uniquely, making each particular performance an unrepeatable act. If the material body is the evidence of the executed action or performance, no two performances can ever be the same. In that the body is the evidence, it also becomes the text of the performance. In other words, speaking the text necessarily signifies speaking (with/through) the body.

But bodies are not isolated artifacts floating through culture. They are historically positioned in given gendered conjunctures that have everything to do with how they act and react in their "situatedness." Although performance lapses into nonexistence by disappearing at exactly the moment the spectator wishes to grasp it, as a text what remains is a system of signs or "semiotization" that cannot be divorced from the text's historical circumstances and rootedness.

In order to apply theories of performance specifically to Latinas, it is necessary to understand that transculturation itself is a performative act, always in process. In other words, transculturation is enacted in and through performance. Like all performative acts, transculturation is syncretic, improvisational, and transformational by the fact it "takes what is at hand and makes something else out of it" (Apple 1995:123). Most importantly, the goal in both performance and transculturation is always to signal a process and not the finished or conclusive product or act. In that way, both can have the urgency of social action and communication in their resistance and intervention. In this sense, Diana Taylor's observation that "transculturation is not a theatrical phenomenon but a social one" (1991c:60–61) evidences the fact that "performing transculturation" is indeed an act of subversion, resistance, and counterhegemony; ultimately, performing transculturation is an act of survival. For marginal subjects, this performance opens a space and creates a positionality for the construction of new interstitial, border, hybrid identities. In a transcultural performance, which is determined by the collisions, clashes, fusions, and confrontations of two or more cultures, there is no room for unified, monolithic, homogeneous identities. Such transcultural performances, rather, are defined by the fragmentation, simultaneity, and discontinuity that reject fixation and labeling.

The heterogeneity, partiality, fragmentation, and multiplicity that give transculturation its theoretical apparatus are precisely those characteristics that also define performance and that are evidence of the fluidity of the transcultural protean subject herself or himself. It is in performance where not only the contradictions of transculturation become evident, but also its very essence and nature. Thus, the transcultural subject is not the chaotic, bipolar character stereotyped in the media, but rather a creative, new subjectivity constantly reimagining itself. In Latina theater and solo performances, the third interstitial space—that culture in-between—becomes a site of resistance inscribed in the body of the performer and the performative space where the theater also functions as a border, a space not here or there, but rather a neither/nor location.

Considering that the strength of transculturation is precisely the fact that it defies all fixation, undoubtedly the overarching quality of a transcultural performance is its unpredictable outcome. In this way, we elaborate on Diamond's thesis of the "doing and the thing done." That is, all performance points toward the future, which includes the audience's horizon of expectations. It is not only a present past ("a thing done") and a future past (will have done), but also a future perfect (will have been done). Thus, Diamond's definition is a good starting point for a much more complex procedure than she puts forth because the action is not only in the past, but also in the future perfect. All audiences anticipate an outcome. This forward-looking definition of performative transculturation, in this context, allows us to be optimistic and hopeful about the new transnational, transcultural identities that will define the twenty-first century.

We may now turn our attention to what is specific about Latina solo performance and how it came to occupy this position of prominence.[1] For Carmelita Tropicana, performance art "is not film, theater, music, but it can have these elements. . . . Performance art . . . changes your perception of things. Objects are not the same as they once were."[2] Guillermo Gómez-Peña has written: "my art is undescribable therefore I'm a performance artist" (in Levy 1992:127). Both practitioners echo theorists of performance who also insist that the genre itself "defies precise or easy definition" (Goldberg 1988:9).[3] Despite this elusiveness, certain traits are evident. We understand Latina solo performance to be a postmodern representation in a hybrid medium that encompasses drama, comedy, multimedia, parody, and cultural critique. These monologues tend to use autobiographical materials with comedic or dramatic sketches that the writer/artist performs herself as one-woman shows. They range from intimate and confessional portraits to enactments or improvisations of a variety of diverse characters whose consciousness is informed by the wide spectrum of political, social, sexual-orientation, and gender issues that confront Latinas.

At times, a monologue can become an entire one-woman play with its own dramatic structure, including plot, characters, and scenes that move the action forward, as in Marga Gomez's *Memory Tricks* and Wilma Bonet's *Good Grief, Lolita!* On other occasions, the tendency is to perform a collage of personal experiences in which the artist/performer/protagonist transforms the often damaging experiences of marginalization into an act of self-affirmation that allows the audience to participate by laughing and identifying with her, as in the performance pieces of Yareli Arizmendi *(Nostalgia Maldita: 1–900–Mexico)*, Monica Palacios *(Greetings from a Queer Señorita)*, and Carmelita Tropicana *(Milk of Amnesia)*. Indeed, contemporary performance pieces involve and invoke audience participation, as in works by Cuco Fusco and her collaborators. In the 1992 installation *The Couple in the Cage,* Fusco and Guillermo Gómez-Peña staged themselves as native indigenous peoples on display at the world's plazas and museums. In addition to acting in the piece, Fusco was responsible for its documentation in video form, a part of which includes audience reaction.[4]

Just as Latina plays did not suddenly emerge from a theatrical vacuum, but rather derive from a long history of Latinas participating in the theater, so too may we reclaim Latina performance roots with the initial "performances" of Nuyorican poetry, Denise Chávez's pioneering one-woman shows of the early 1980s, and the collective performance *Tongues of Fire* of the same era. Whether "declamación," "poetry performance," "poetry recitals," or the artistic rendition of local corridos (a Mexican music genre), all of these forms served as the foundation for what we now know as solo performance.[5] When we locate Latina/o performance in its historical context, we must recognize that Teatro Campesino's *Actos* of the 1960s and 1970s were in fact "happenings," which today would encompass what is known as performance. In *Canícula,* Norma Cantú describes declamación as a kind of performative act of reciting poems in Spanish at school and family reunions. These declamaciones also included the bilingual and bicultural recitation of song lyrics from both Anglo and Mexican traditions (1995:62–63). Moreover, as Yolanda Broyles-

González has argued, the Teatro Campesino can trace a lineage to "Mexican popular performance tradition, both secular and religious" (1994:4). Within this popular tradition, we may locate such disparate forms of entertainment as carpas (tent shows), tandas de variedad (vaudeville), musical reviews, and corridos.[6]

Like the Teatro Campesino, the carpa criticized and satirized the dominant system of power, often through the use of humor. To wit, the comedic sketches of the carpa privileged the comedian to such a degree that his act already registered an incipient form of what we know today as performance, where the actor takes precedence over the text (Taylor and Villegas 1994:11). Using a combination of parody, improvisation, jokes, and satire, this artist also drew on his deep Hispanic roots, on popular forms, and on oral traditions in places where there was a lack of print culture and literacy. As we chart the genealogy of Latina/o performance, we may consider such diverse forms of entertainment as zarzuela, sainete, teatro bufo, revistas musicales, and, most importantly, the sketches of the late Mario Moreno (Cantinflas).

However important Cantinflas's films were in Mexico or to Mexican or Chicana/o populations in the U.S., there was yet another strand of Latina/o performance that Marga Gomez has memorialized in her tribute to her father and his acting career in New York, *A Line around the Block*. In recognizing and recovering the "Latin" entertainment world of the 1940s and 1950s at the end of her show, Gomez states that were her father alive today, he would be a performance artist.[7] Given this insight, it is perhaps not too bold to assert that Latina/o performance of the 1990s is indeed part of the historicocultural map of Latina/o entertainment, both rural and urban, professional and amateur, middle and working class. In other words, performance is not a new phenomenon to Latinas/os; it is a cultural legacy.

Although it is beyond the scope of this study to recover all the "Latin" stars of the pre-1960s period and the impact they had on the entertainment world of both coasts and the Southwest, it is also impossible not to recognize these precursors to Latina/o performance art today. In particular, Beatriz "La Chata" Noloesca (Escalona) (1903–79), who was born in San Antonio, enjoyed great popularity as a vaudeville performer from the 1920s onward, first in the Southwest and later in other parts of the country where she performed until the 1960s.[8] Given today's definition of a feminist performance artist as someone who is the "representer of herself" (Goodman 1993:182), who writes and performs her own material and creates her own characters, La Chata, in her role as her own agent and entrepreneur, was certainly a performer, evidenced by the creation of her own company, Atracciones Noalesca, Variedades Mexicanas (late 1930s). In contrast to stars such as Celia Tejeda, who was a singer, dancer, and actress (Ybarra-Frausto 1983:49), La Chata moved beyond the role of mere mimicry to a subjectivity of her own. During this time, the role of the pelado—"a penniless, urban roustabout" who gave "pyrotechnical displays of verbal wit," "a feisty underdog" (Ybarra-Frausto 1983:51)[9]—became increasingly attractive to and for the Chicano male population. What is original in La Chata's performances is that she refined the existing roles of the peladita and created a female paradigm at a time when the only roles for women were either as the star of the show or as a member of the chorus, both of which were written by men. La Chata's visionary perspective encompassed the uniting and consolidating of all three major Latino populations and sought to reach them in her show by instructing her troupe to give up their Spanglish for a more standardized form of Spanish (Kanellos 1990:94–95). Instead of perceiving Latin theater as a single ethnicity, she played to Puerto Rican audiences in New York and was instrumental in bringing other Chicana/o artists to that area.

In our own era, the new national interest in performance is not limited to Latinas alone, but rather is a phenomenon that has gained increasing cultural currency since the 1960s. In the 1990s, as ethnic groups acknowledged their differences and voiced their presence demographically, performance became a privileged medium in which to enact those differences. Certainly we may attribute the representational flourishing of people of color to a growing ethnic consciousness in the cultural imaginary. Likewise, economic variables, sexual preference, and political awareness are all factors that contribute to the highly visible popularity of performance, for the alternative styles and spaces available in performance are especially attractive to lesbians and gays as well as to other nonmainstream performers. In that performance incorporates storytelling to a select audience, both its style and content allow for a politics of identity to emerge. For lesbian and gay performers, the performance may take the form of a coming-out story, which accents the community-building process that is often part and parcel of the performative experience. Audiences filling these performance spaces are multiethnic, multiracial, and multisexual, so the sense of solidarity and coalition that fills the performative space has become a regular constitutive element of performance. From that "imaginary" space, an imagined Latina/o community consolidates,[10] this one not based on print culture or nationalism, but rather on orality, performance, and cultural identity, registering at the same time a counter response to global hegemony through their bodies' situatedness in specific local sites.

Perhaps this is the explanation for the fact that college campuses in the 1990s became a prime site for the staging of performance. Because more students of color are enrolled in higher education, the agenda of and commitment to diversity have greatly contributed to the community building, political platforms, and ideological purposes embedded in the artistic mission of solo performance. Therefore, despite the so-called culture wars, the growing population of Latina/o students on college campuses has been moderately successful in seeing their stories performed and Latinas/os represented by the historical experience and autobiographical sketches inherent in these performances. The very nature of solo performance dovetails with the circumstances that college campuses are able to provide: a low-budget, shortish piece of work with minimal stage set is at once accessible both culturally and economically.

Second, the economic factor plays a role in venues far from academia as well. Both for college campuses and for commercial theater, it is more viable to contract a single performer than to finance an entire troupe. Paradoxically, this low budget facilitates the entrance of performance artists or one-person shows into the mainstream—i.e., Broadway, off-Broadway, and television, as the examples of Lily Tomlin, Whoopi Goldberg, and Eric Bogosian have shown. Among Latinos, John Leguizamo and Marga Gomez's forays into television evidence producers' willingness sometimes to "address and deliver" a multicultural menu to their viewers. Nevertheless, mainstreaming is not without its cultural costs. Although the possibility for commercialization remains limitless—television, video, and film—ethnic marketing may also result in the actual commodification of Latino and Latina culture.[11] At the end of the millennium, the seemingly overnight success of Latino performers in the music world—Selena, Ricky Martin, Jennifer López, Marc Anthony—also indicates the existence of a new generation who celebrates their Latinidad, their bordered, hybrid, and, from our point of view, transcultural and transnational identities. Latinidad has never before been performed, received, or delivered with such pizzazz.

A third factor in the prominence of performance is the existence of an already flourishing Latina literature since the 1980s. With new publications by Latina writers (every month of 1994, for example), we are witnessing a virtual efflorescence of Latina writing in every genre. The very nature of this literature, transcultural to its core, makes the transition from poetry or narrative to performance a much more seamless venture. Such is the case of Denise Chávez's novel *Face of an Angel,* misunderstood by mainstream critics who failed to recognize or accept its hybridity as a constitutive element of Latina writing. Indeed, performativity is a manifestation of Latina mixing of genres where the narrative is theatricalized, and it consequently flourishes as Chávez "performs" given chapters in a public reading of her work. The same applies to the performance adaptations of Cristina García's *Dreaming in Cuban and Other Works: Rhythm, Rum, Café con Leche, and Nuestros Abuelos*[12] and of Judith Ortiz Cofer's *Silent Dancing: Memoirs of a Puerto Rican Childhood* by Teatro Pregones as *The Wedding March.*[13] If performance "fills the gap between entertainment and theatre" (Goldberg 1988:195–96), in the case of Chávez, García, and Ortiz Cofer, that performance, in all its transculturation, fills the gap between narrative and theater.[14]

The greatest visible presence in Latina solo performance belongs to Latina lesbians because once we enter the domain of Latina lesbian performance art, we cross the threshold of cultural and social constructions of sexuality, gender, class, race, and ethnicity. In the 1980s, we witnessed the first Latina coming-out stories in print, but artists such as Marga Gomez, Monica Palacios, Carmelita Tropicana, and Tatiana de la Tierra truly broke the theatrical silence by enacting Latina autobiographical coming-out stories on stage in the 1990s. In these pieces, the artists de-essentialize the stereotypical "butch-femme" relationship by approaching lesbian sexuality from a variety of differing positionalities and with a variety of differing audiences in mind. Each one addresses the topic from her own aesthetic and politics: in so doing, she simultaneously negotiates her relationship with her audience by engaging them in an exchange wherein gender and sexuality are rearticulated (Dolan 1988:81).

For Marga Gomez, whose work has received mainstream recognition, that positionality allows a comfort factor for both lesbian and heterosexual audiences given that lesbian sexuality is mediated by a large degree through comedy, as in *Marga Gomez Is Pretty, Witty, and Gay* and in Irma's character in *A Line around the Block.* On the other hand, Monica Palacios's creation of her Pilgrim lover, Manifest Destiny, in *Pilgrim Woman* situates her sexuality at the intersection of the implicit power relations between race, ethnicity, class, and colonialism. In this way, the performance functions beyond the role of mere entertainment as it confronts the audience with a cultural critique. In the case of Carmelita Tropicana, heavily informed by theories of lesbian performance, gender construction, and butch-femme aesthetics,[15] her performance problematizes the relationship between performer and audience by bouncing the lesbian gaze back onto the spectator. By reversing gender roles, cross-dressing, and deconstructing the "beautiful señorita" stereotype, she disarticulates dominant gender constructions and horizons of expectations of compulsory heterosexuality, thereby inviting the audience, who is already positioned in a web of reciprocity, to participate in a new lesbian subjectivity wherein desire and the spectatorial gaze validate lesbian experience and Latina identity.

In the following sections, we discuss solo performance pieces by three of the most visible Latina lesbian performers. In each case, their acts register just how transcultural dynamics mold and transcribe identity formation. We shall see how transculturation is determined and shaped through specific ethnic, political, national, and generational conditions visible in each performer's act within the context of sexual orientation and gendered relations. More than homogeneity of experiences, what we find here is a plurality of Latina lesbian identities always in the making and on the move, revealing how transcultura-tion per se refuses any fixity or stability.

Carmelita Tropicana

Alina Troyano's (a.k.a., Carmelita Tropicana) widely reviewed performance *Milk of Amnesia* (1995) serves as an ideal paradigm from which to discuss our concept of transcultural performativity. Inscribed within the evocative title of the piece, at work is the construction of a transcultural experience negotiated through a series of socio-ideological coordinates particular to the performer—such as lesbian identity, Caribbean masculinity, "exilic memory" (Muñoz 1995b:76), and the bilocation of home. As the performer attempts to recall her Cuban past, she almost immediately disavows the usual markers of Cu-banidad in traditional ethnic, racial, and nationalist terms; thus, not only is the milk of her title a metaphor of her assimilation, but in the piece the performer semioticizes it with a cultural charge that redefines it symbolically and discur-sively. Milk becomes a discursive construct and, as such, loses all its referen-tiality *in each location,* both in the U.S. and in Cuba, in the past and in the present, here and there, temporally and spatially. Carmelita's return to Cuba, dangerous and illegal, mirrors the balsero odyssey (the dangerous crossing in a raft from Cuba to Florida) in reverse form. Through this journey, Carme-lita shows us how the process of transculturation does not take place only in Latin America, as Fernando Ortíz imagined, but also in the U.S. This new layer of transculturation occurs at the crossroads of a globalized economy, a transnational subject, and a Latina sexual identity—all spatial signifiers beyond Ortíz's imagining.

The serious and parodic levels of signification in the title both encapsulate Carmelita's Cuban American hybrid identity and lay the foundation for the construction of a transcultural memory. To recover that past is to activate ethnic memory, a memory that, once recalled, projects itself into a future performance of being, of selfhood. In this manner, her performance is not only a "doing and a thing done," but also a "thing imagined," a "thing to be done," a thing projected forward, which truly is the solo performance *Milk of Amnesia* itself. In this title, milk is both literal and figurative: it refers to the various milks of her childhood and how each constitutes a particular sensory or locational association. Carmelita's memory of those associations is truly transcultural in that her recollection is fragmented, sporadic, and incomplete. Thus, milk is not a universal signifier, for it is historically determined by exile and thus contains different meanings in different geocultural and temporal contexts. In the piece, the natural/national milk that each child suckles at her or his mother's breast later can be read symbolically as the cultural milk of the mother country, which Carmelita lost after exile. If in Cuba she was nourished/nursed on condensed milk, desired for its sweetness and richness, once she migrated to the U.S., that native milk was substituted, displaced, and supplanted by the grade-A, pasteurized, homogenized milk served to American schoolchildren. "I learned to drink milk; it was my resolve to embrace America as I chewed on my peanut and jelly sandwich and gulped down my milk. This new milk that had replaced the sweet condensed milk of Cuba. My amnesia had begun" (*Milk of Amnesia,* 95). All of her resistance to the experience of exile was channeled into her distaste for American milk, assimilation per se. From the present moment of the performance itself, she engages the viewers in her binary opposition of places so that they are rapt with attention about her dilemma. How she will resolve it, always in relationship to the horizon of expectations of the audience, will eventually be the subject of reconciliation and ultimately transculturation.

On the metaphorical level, by evoking milk of magnesia, the dreaded childhood laxative used to purge the system, Carmelita addresses her real issue: the locked up, constipated, exilic memory that begs for release. In order to effect that release, manifested as a so-called crisis of identity,[16] the performance becomes both ritualistic and processual in its attempt to recover her lost memory. Second, the milk's whiteness serves as a point of departure for Carmelita's meditation on race and ethnicity, both in Cuba and in the U.S. On

6. Advertisement for Carmelita Tropicana's *Milk of Amnesia* at P.S. 122, New York City (1994), directed by Ela Troyano. Photograph by Paula Court. Poster design by Kukuli Velarde. Used by permission of Carmelita Tropicana.

a third level, most importantly, the referent, milk, within an Anglo cultural context stands for a product that has been homogenized and pasteurized. For an informed audience, this homo milk allows us to see a fourth level: Carmelita's lesbian identity and subjectivity, which would have been and still is denied and closeted in Cuba. Thus, if the first gulp of exilic milk is difficult for the child Carmelita to swallow, she allows the milk in its revised role in her adulthood to take on a new meaning that recovers her past and contributes to the articulation of her sexualized transcultural identity. It is this integration and fusion and capacity to select gender behavior—this constant negotiation, this constant questioning, this refusal to be either/or, or even half and half, always in excess and not enough—that throughly determine the dynamic construction of transculturation.

As the performance opens, Carmelita's voice-over narrates the painful process of exile and loss that she experienced as a child. When she appears on stage, cross-dressed as "Pingalito Betancourt," a Cuban bus driver before the revolution, her impersonation undermines a national symbol of Cuban masculinity that is entrenched in the adherence to compulsory heterosexuality and that gains its strength from the principles of "pureza de sangre" (purity of blood). In her parody of the Cuban male, Carmelita pokes fun at Pingalito's image, body language, and outfit. Sporting a guayabera, smoking a cigar, and scratching his genitalia, Pingalito is brought to the stage in a self-aggrandizing posturing as the expert on facts about Cuba to stimulate Carmelita's memory: "When I heard of Carmelita's tragic accident, I rushed right over. . . . the doctors have their methodologies for curing amnesia and I have mine" (95). As Carmelita becomes Pingalito, she transgresses the national patriarchal model of masculinity, a model that reveals the transformative power of transnational feminism, embedded in Carmelita's performance. This entire characterization registers a priori the extent to which Carmelita appropriates, subverts, and literally reconfigures Cuban manhood in baptizing her character "Pingalito"—literally, small prick.

This male-impersonation act, mediated with queer campiness and humor, imbues the show with satire and parody. Ironically, Pingalito is blind not only to Carmelita's lesbianism, but also to his own machismo and to Carmelita's bicultural experience. When he offers to show Carmelita the "facts about Cuba," his cultural mapping and reading of the island fail to consider her exile, her exilic memory, her sexuality, as well as Cuba's racism. Essentially, he is frozen in time, whereas she has moved forward. His perspective does not account for the fact that she has acquired new ways of seeing, new tools that aid her in deconstructing and demythifying the national imaginary of race and whiteness that she ascribes to Cubans of this era when he declares: "Three-fourths of all Cubans are white of Spanish descent." In this quip, the transculturated subject erupts; Carmelita is prepared to revise history as Pingalito/Carmelita adds, "a lot of these three-fourths have a very dark suntan all year round" (96). In her transvestism, transculturation, and transnationalism, Carmelita both interrupts and disrupts Pingalito's speech with a double-voiced discourse, not allowing the Pingalito character to go unchecked. Her intervention here demonstrates the difficulty of drawing the line between two separate characters, each with a distinct voice, sexuality, and point of view. Such a heteroglossic display registers once again the plurality and unquestionable simultaneity of a transcultural subjectivity.

The same applies to Pingalito's allusion to José Martí, whom he calls the "George Washington" and "Emily Dickinson of Cuba" (97). Who exactly is speaking here—Carmelita, Pingalito, or even Alina, whose voice-over narrates the show? Do they overlap, intersect, or transverse each other's geocultural discursive spaces? Even before Pingalito declaims "Ode to the Cuban Man," Carmelita Tropicana has androgynized the national hero, founding father, and "Apostol" by equating him with these two North American models. In this hilarious feminist mockery of Cuban men and in her many ideological permutations and discursive positionings, the performer has infiltrated and subverted machismo; no longer do unmediated machismo and its twin, nationalism, arrive at the audience without comment: "The Cuban man is persistent, stubborn / Like the mosquito, always buzzing around / Why you think yellow fever was so popular. . . . / To his mami, he's still the favorite / And at 80, she still calls him el Baby" (97). Carmelita's persistent feminist intervention thus serves to dynamite Pingalito's exaggerated masculinity and to de-authorize him as a rightful representative of the nation.

In a similar fashion, the signifier "fruit" materializes a multiplicity of meanings whose ironic deconstruction and androgynous labeling demonstrate yet again the performer's transcultural subjectivity. In a high school essay, a young Carmelita compared the North American apple to the Caribbean mango. "Americans were apples: healthy, neat, easy to eat, not too sweet, not too juicy. Cubans were mangoes: juicy, real sweet, but messy" (98). If her adolescent self enunciated her identity through the writing process relying on binary oppositions, now, in adulthood, that process leads her to the articulation of a performance that enacts a transcultural identity in these two particular fruits, whose representation is no coincidence. As an adolescent, feeling the pressure to assimilate, she "stood in front of a mirror and thought I should be more like an apple." Nevertheless, the mango persists in intruding and interrupting her assimilation process, just as Carmelita interrupts Pingalito: "A shadow appeared and whispered: 'Mango stains never come off' " (98). Here, mango not only represents a tropical fruit, but also encapsulates Carmelita's ethnic and national identity. Furthermore, its political connotations allude to the multinational corporations that export Central American and Caribbean fruit to northern industrialized nations. That mango, in contrast to the crisp "all-Americanness" of apples, functions as well in a metonymical relationship to female sexuality as juicy, sweet, and messy. In this regard, it resembles the guayaba, whose messiness and sweetness is often a metaphor for lesbian sexuality in the Caribbean: "Hacer el amor con una mujer es como comerse una guayaba" ("making love with a woman is like eating a guava").

If the mango and apple were binary oppositions in Carmelita's youth, when it comes time for Alina to choose a stage persona, she opts for a hybrid—namely, Carmelita Tropicana. Explaining the name as well as her differentiation between the performer and the writer, she says: "she who was baptized in the fountain of America's most popular orange juice, in the name of Havana's legendary night club, the Tropicana, she could [stand in front of an audience and tell jokes]. . . . she was a fruit and wasn't afraid to admit it" (98–99). As we unpack the significance of this new name, we must distinguish between Alina Troyano, a Cuban exile, raised in New York, and Carmelita Tropicana, an imaginary construct and performer (Román 1995a). The existence of this character permits Alina Troyano to conflate her past and her present, her Cuban self and her Anglo American education, and, as she puts it, her "mango Macintosh" (100). The first part of the name alludes, of course, to Carmen Miranda's campy performances in the 1940s, and *Tropicana* is a signifier that contains two signifieds: *(a)* the famous Havana nightclub, and *(b)* the name brand of the most popular orange juice in the U.S. As a whole, her stage name relies on audience recognition at the same time that it evokes the fusion of the Spanish language and English-speaking reality. The result is the hilarious and outrageous confluence of cultural and sexual imagery, stereotype and self-enunciation, linguistic memory and transgression.

Consequently, Carmelita and Pingalito constitute the two sides of Alina Troyano's gendered and sexualized Cuban identity. At work here is not only Troyano's queer agenda that confronts heterosexuality and homophobia, but also her feminist agenda that deconstructs stereotypical images of femininity and masculinity both in Anglo and Cuban cultures. As a Latina, Troyano uses

Carmelita as the arena where she will rehearse, perform, and eventually contest dominant Anglo representations of Latinas. In so doing, Carmelita not only asserts her agency, but also reveals the components of a subjectivity-in-process. Rather than allowing herself to be "tropicalized" by the system, she instead "tropicalizes" (Aparicio and Chávez-Silverman 1997:1) her self in order to empower her shifting positionality through the implementation of a politics of difference.

Both with Pingalito's reminder that she is Cuban as well as with her own urgent need to recover her past in order to construct her Latinidad in the U.S., Carmelita determines: "Maybe there is only one way to find out. To go back to the place I was born in. My homeland, the place that suckled me as a newborn babe. In the distance, I hear the clink, clink, clink of a metal spoon against glass. It is my mami stirring condensed milk with water. The milk beckons me. I feel a song coming on" (100). As she intones one of Carmen Miranda's famous songs, "Weekend in Havana," she situates herself within the dominant cultural representations of Latin America during the time of the Good Neighbor Policy, while parodying both Hollywood and Cubanidad.

But this business of negotiating a transnational identity is no easy task, as the traveling Carmelita discovers. She expresses her frustration by recognizing that life during this "special period" might not be "fácil" (easy). Once located at the Miami airport, an epicenter of Cubanidad in the U.S.—for the most part a reactionary Cubanidad—as well as the gates of America and the crossroads of the Americas, Carmelita's position is open to all kinds of alternative choices and possibilities. It is here that she discovers herself to be "underdressed" because she has come without her "hat," in itself a performance. For her fellow travelers, the hat is a way to provide relatives in Cuba with scarce and often luxury items, but for Carmelita the hat is another manifestation of her evolving hybrid self. The hat is a requirement and a kind of passport to return to the island because it signifies solidarity with the Cuban people and especially Cuban women (McLane 1994). Carmelita's hat serves as her survival kit and mediation on this journey to a place where she admits, "I don't know where I'm going" (100). The hat simultaneously is a baroque and postmodern inventory of life in Cuba under the embargo. If serious travelers to Cuba utilize the hat to take medication, paper goods, and other "luxury" items to an embargoed Cuba, Carmelita's agency in the act of constructing and wearing the hat turns a black-market transaction into a political identification with her people, whose life is not fácil. Thus, as she takes the hat to Cuba, she hopes that its currency on the exchange market will give her what she needs *from*

Cuba: a sense of bilocation and biculturalism, and the negotiated identity that comes from both of these places.

Yet Carmelita goes a step further: her entire trip to Cuba is imbued with her sexuality, even in ostensible nonsexual acts, such as wearing the hat. When she lands, she declares: "I tell my driver Francisco that I want to see, touch, feel, hear, taste Cuba. All my orifices are open" (102). Carmelita chooses to mark her hat by sexuality and gender, differentiating her version of it from that of her fellow travelers, who tend to adorn it with costume jewelry: she hangs tampons from it. This undercover trafficking with sexual overtones inscribes its wearer's sexual orientation and feminism. Not only is a hat a female garment, but many men seem to feel that wearing one in these circumstances represents an act of betrayal (McLane 1994:43) to the Cuban community in the U.S. Bringing goods to Cuba, even to one's own family, undermines their efforts at toppling Fidel. Finally, this hat represents the total deconstruction and reinvention of Carmen Miranda's tutti-frutti headpiece. If Miranda burlesquely and grotesquely stereotyped Latin America femininity and so Latin America, Carmelita appropriates that stereotype. In this reversal, she condemns the embargo, the exploitation of Latin America, and patriarchal authority in U.S. Latino homes, and squarely places herself on the side of the Cuban people. As she ceremoniously offers the hat, she assumes the rite of passage we have come to know from other border crossers. And as she enters the liminal space of Cuba and engages with the real, the necessity of the hat is less important now that the rite of passage proceeds and continues—that is to say, as the performance itself moves into the unknown territory of a distanced exilic homeland.

Carmelita documents her trip through Cuba with slides and stories that, despite their fragmentation and dispersion, make possible the reclamation of her ethnic memory. In search of that past, the history of Cuba itself, she visits a cemetery and impersonates an arriero, a horse from imperial Spain. This genealogy or ensemble of cultural archives lays the foundation by which she can reenter what was left behind: the house of her childhood, the home she lost, the imagined homeland. By revisiting her past, Carmelita distinguishes herself from the mass exodus of Cubans who failed to support the revolution. In order to establish her solidaridad, she explains that she is "not one of those Cubans that's planning to come back and take over their houses" (106) because her family "only rented" (106). In this, she distances herself from the exodus of the Cuban bourgeoisie, "who never would have said they rented"

(106). Carmelita reveals herself to be a product of history as she learns that her former home is now a construction company. In this regard, such a metaphorical articulation reveals that it is Carmelita *herself* who is the construction company: her project—a Latina transcultural and transnational identity in the U.S.

However much she is able to locate herself interstitially, nothing prepares her for the shock of the economic hardship of contemporary Cuba. The phrase "no es fácil" that reverberates among Havana's citizens becomes a link and symbol by which Carmelita rediscovers her memory and asserts her agency. The drastic food shortage that she continually encounters, coupled with the resolve of the people to maintain their sense of humor through the most dire circumstances, crystallizes in the slaughter of a pig. We must here underscore the pig's symbolic, historic, and material importance. The pig's story parallels her own story of displacement (U.S./Cuba, rural/urban) and replacement (mother's milk/bottled milk). The cultural paradigm of hunger—food for Cubans and culture for Carmelita—functions in the same way for both. Through a series of superimposed images, the pig narrates its highly evocative and suggestive first-person story, functioning in the piece as a sacrificial animal through which Carmelita and the Cubans recover their respective hungers: food for them and return of collective memory for her. If this "special period" in Cuban history "no es fácil" in terms of hunger, the pig also reminds Carmelita of other conditions that are not easy. "No es fácil" to be a Cuban American in Cuba, and "no es fácil" to be a lesbian in Cuba, nor is it "fácil" to survive the embargo.

"No es fácil," then, allows Carmelita to appropriate one phrase for another circumstance. As Carmelita politicizes her reentry into Cuba, she comments: "I remember. We're all connected, not through AT&T, E-mail, internet, or the information super-highway, but through memory, history, herstory, horsestory" (108). Reaching this provisional conclusion, we not only understand that memory is gendered, but it is also sexualized. At this point, Carmelita must sift her way through many strands of memory: Cuban memory, exilic memory, lesbian memory, childhood memory, home memory, official memory, silenced memory, and gender memory. The piece reminds us that memories exist in relation to given spaces and sensory experience, and that each memory has its own history (or "herstory") and location, which parallels the heterogeneity and plurality of identity that is at the core of the piece and that is emblematic of a transculturated memory.

Carmelita travels to Cuba to recover her ethnic memory and not necessarily to come out of the closet. Yet her lesbian identity, in place after many years in New York, will no more put up with being silenced than the narration of the horse story that she tells. Her sexuality, her Cubanidad, her New Yorker self in all their dislocations and fragmentations are part of her identity as she recites: "I REMEMBER / QUE SOY DE ALLÁ / QUE SOY DE AQUÍ / UN PIE EN NEW YORK (A FOOT IN NEW YORK) / UN PIE EN LA HABANA (A FOOT IN HAVANA)" (108–9). In spite of the fact that her displacements determine her identity in all it dispersion and incompleteness, she insists that she is not "ESPLIT / I AM FLUID AND INTERCONNECTED" (109).

It is a signature moment for all Latina writers when they construct themselves in all their creative transcultural potentiality. Here, that moment occurs near the end of the piece when Carmelita comments: "I thought by coming to Cuba I would have answers. Instead I have more questions. . . . Am I looking at Cuba from an American perspective? No es fácil. It's not easy to have clear vision. In seven days I can only get sound bytes. Cuba is a land of contradictions" (109). Locating herself at the Performance Space in New York City, P.S. 122, Carmelita puts into practice a feminist definition of the politics of identity in its intersection with geography. This subjectivity-in-process, disclosed at the end, conflates her sense of space and identity in her journey. When she realizes that home is having one foot in each place, that home is memory, and that home means embracing both her Cuban self and her American one, her amnesia disappears. It is then that she can drink both kinds of milk: "The sweet condensed milk of Cuba and the pasteurized, homo kind from America" (110). At this point, the performance comes full circle as she moves from the politics of representation to the politics of identity formation to a politics of affinity and coalition building that reveal her deep connections with two geographies. She says: "EVERYBODY FOR THE SAME THING / BETWEEN THE PAGES OF COLONIALISM, / CAPITALISTS, HOMOSEXUALS, ATHEISTS, SPIRITUAL-ISTS / MORALISTS / EVERYBODY FOR THE SAME THING" (110–11). This transnational political stance, although representing utopia, also allows Carmelita to become the architect of her own home, regardless of where she is located geographically and in direct relation to where she is located politically and sexually. Finally, then, we can see how the entire piece *Milk of Amnesia* serves as the culmination of the work that she began in *Memories of the Revolution,* which narrates the trials and tribulations of exile, her emergent lesbian identity, and her parting from Cuba.

Monica Palacios

Another lesbian performer, Monica Palacios, uses her sexualized lesbian body as the location at which her politics and performance conflate. At first glance, her performance piece *Greetings from a Queer Señorita* (first produced in 1995) may not appear to encompass the dynamics of a transcultural subjectivity that we have discussed above. It is crucial to differentiate here Carmelita's migratory experience and the experience of Chicanas/os, many of whom have always lived in the U.S. If in other plays and performances, the recent transcultural memory of migration was in constant evolution and progress, in many Chicano/a works, a different kind of transculturation takes place, an embedded one with many layers, a transculturation to the second power. Latino culture has become so visible because of demographic shifts, signifying the perpetual reconfigurations of Latino populations in their new or inherited communities. In this sense, *Greetings from a Queer Señorita* is informed and shaped by that Latino constituency, one that resides in the U.S. and already speaks English. Therefore, transculturation dwells not only in the surface structure of the piece, but also in its deep structure.

As the title indicates, the performer begins by deconstructing normative heterosexual stereotypes in the act of self-naming as a "queer señorita." In this designation, Palacios anchors her identity within differing cultural discursive landscapes. First, by calling herself "queer," she signals to spectators a political affinity that unites the Chicana lesbian with an Anglo queer community. At the same time, she queers the ultimate representation of Latina women as virgins by use of the noun *señorita,* which connotes the Marianista dichotomous tradition of women as virgins or whores. In this second move, she commits another act of deconstruction: a dismantling of the trope of the "beautiful señorita" as promoted by the dominant mainstream culture. If that image is most prevalent in the Hollywood representation of Latinas, what Palacios does is not only to debunk that representation, but more subversively to appropriate it on her own terms. It is here that transculturation registers in all its complexity: as in the case of Carmelita Tropicana, the irony of the performer overrides the blatant stereotypical representations. Palacios goes a step further within her performances: she translates "queer señorita" into "LATIN LESBO COMIC," her next piece. In this act of prestidigitation, Palacios reveals her political agenda in that she refuses to perform to a homophobic audience, representative of the dominant culture: "I stopped going to these

7. Poster for Monica Palacios's *Greetings from a Queer Señorita* at New World Theater, Amherst, Massachusetts (1997). Poster design by Yvonne Mendez. Used by permission of Roberta Uno, New World Theater.

clubs and those stupid auditions! I couldn't put my LATIN LEZBO COMIC self into those Hollywood molds" (*Greetings*, 1995 unpublished version, 10). If she sees those molds as examples of compulsory heterosexuality, what each of her shows does is to provide a place in which to perform and evaluate a shifting, sexualized ethnic identity.

Given that Palacios constructs her Latina identity within a queer consciousness, it is impossible to consider her act of transculturation without its sexual dimension. So predominant is that queer component, however, that it is easy to overlook the ethnic aspects of her transculturation. Yet Palacios provides her audiences with two discrete moments of transculturation: first, as she recalls the memory of sexual attraction, and second, as she reclaims a Latina entertainment legacy.

In the first explicit act of transculturation, Palacios sets the stage in the culturally specific location of the Mission District of San Francisco at her favorite and celebrated Taquería la Cumbre. It is in this marked ethnic and racialized space that sexuality turns into a Chicana culinary delight as Palacios drools over a potential lover's pleasure in eating a carne asada taco. Although her first attraction to this restaurant is its "dietary delight," she quickly uses the scenario as a way to invoke family, heritage, cultura, the Spanish language and sexuality. Although she knows it as a place in which to enact her "pura Mexicana" self, an added pleasure occurs as she watches "Miss Sabrosita" eating "con pasión" with "full Chicana lips" (16, 17). Palacios's voyeurism displaces the male gaze and refocuses the audience's attention and the sexual object into ethnicity. Sexuality reaches its peak with the ideologem "jalapeño," the emblem par excellence of Mexican culture. Watching this "hungry" (16) woman allows Palacios to usurp the place of the macho and his ultimate virile act of eating a jalapeño and exclaiming, "¡Ay, puro mexicano!" Just as Palacios appropriates Hollywood images in her title, here she takes possession of male representation as the ultimate cultural expression of mexicanidad. In doing so, she dynamites male flaunting of machismo by outdoing its posturing herself and redirecting it back on her audience. This consummation, coupled with hunger of memory and culture, reaches its climax in the sexual metaphor of eating. Each "¡ay!" produced during the act of eating implies one more sexual advance and another cultural bite: "Watching the carne asada grease / trickle from her mouth / Down her chin / Down her neck / Almost down her cleavage, / Her cleavage— / Almost. / Ay!" (17). Although there is no physical (i.e., sexual) contact per se, it is clear that Palacios has negotiated sexuality and ethnicity within their specific transcultural manifestations ("I need to watch her eat / CARNE ASADA TACOS / from afar" [18]). In this sense, transculturation can take place in the forms of ethnic memory, sexual desire within the context of that memory, and the pleasure of intersecting food and mexicanidad with lesbian sex.

Ethnic and sensory memory intersect with sexuality once again as Palacios reminisces about her childhood and family. Specifically, she refers to family get-togethers where again the conflation of home, family, music, ethnicity, and Spanish occupy and shape the performer's transcultural identity. For the adolescent Monica, the evocation of those recollections, seen now from her adult perspective, enables her to reprocess the compulsory heterosexuality of her youth. At those musical gatherings, what appeared to be a simple friendship of two women, comadres and singing partners, under the lens of Palacio's adult lesbian gaze now reappears in all its complexity and queerness. As she revisits the moment when the two singers intone the infamous "Cu, cu ru cu cu, paloma," complete with exaggerated facial gestures, trilling Rs, and histrionic performance, Palacios distances herself enough to reexamine the women's relationship: "Just *comadres,* I don't think so" (5). What a queer contextualization does is allow the song to acquire an erotic and sensual dimension as it progresses. That eroticism is expressed through "pasión" and "ruby red lipstick" in a transgressive and symbolic kiss between the two women. Because open lesbianism is of course still taboo, their performance is enacted within heterosexual (and frequently homophobic) norms. Nevertheless, from Palacios's lesbian vantage point, the desire and passion of these two singers for one another cannot go undetected: "And their lips would be really close together—quivering like this. . . . Full of passion and ruby red lipstick. Filling the air with music, culture, make-up, woman sweat, woman breath and beer!" (5). In the kiss that cannot be performed on stage, the present-absence and absent-presence, the two singers reach a climactic moment as they come together while crooning "Palomaaaaaaaaaaaaaaaaa!" in an orgasmic swell that will set the stage for the carne asada taco and its orgasmic pleasure later in the piece.

Once again, as in Taquería la Cumbre, Palacios isolates the experience from the outside world; thus, in the taquería, she sees only the potential lover, and in the family living room she has eyes only for these potential lesbian performers. In this manner, Palacios shows how they are the embodiment of culture, a hybrid body, a sexualized body, a conflation of sexuality and cultura. It is within this interstitial space, as we have argued before, where a transcultural subjectivity flourishes. In a constant flux of memory and desire (cultural memory and sexual desire *or* sexual memory and cultural desire), the stage has provided her with a place to perform her alternate queer identity.

An additional factor that mediates the expression of that tabooed sexuality is Palacios's use of humor. Just as she appropriates male behavior in some scenes of the piece, in one of her more memorable characters she evokes her desired "surfer chola," an export from male beach culture. The eponymous poem is full of irony, humor, and parody, and allows once again for a lesbian subjectivity in which the lesbian body reaches all its jouissance, this time in the form of pan dulce, an empanada of love. As Palacios's character lures the surfer chola to her bed with a homemade Mexican meal, this activity allows the performer to imbue cultura with sex and to imbue sex with cultura—all within a politics of lesbian activism of the 1990s, including safe sex practices. As the character describes the sexual encounter, the audience hears about the third orgasm in the piece, when surfer chola questions just how the salsa was made, exclaiming that her "*empanada* [is] on fire" (21). Although such a declaration contradicts the safe sex promised in the previous line, it allows the character, through humor, to negotiate sexuality through culinary metaphors. The continual repetition of this identity formation—its negotiation and conflation of cultural, ethnic, and sexual domains—reveals the transcultural paradigm once again. It is notable that this particular Latina identity, although making use of Spanish, is not a bilingual one. Nevertheless, as the character invokes words in Spanish, these words are specifically and culturally marked in locations or settings that evoke cultura. Especially visible is the way the character sings songs in Spanish, fantasizes about Mexican meals, also in Spanish, and interacts at family reunions, using Spanish when needed. In this sense, transculturation is registered within the deep structure of the piece—that is, through particular discourses, including humor, by means of which Palacios positions herself as a contrapuntal Chicana lesbian when it comes to food and sex.

Thus, we can see that Monica Palacios's political project, replete with activism, is both a legacy and springboard to the future of Chicana feminism and performance. This politics is celebrated at the end of the piece with a reaffirmation and self-confidence of the queer activist who has "reached / DEEP IN THE CROTCH OF MY QUEER *LATINA* PSYCHE" (28). Finally, the pièce de resistance where all taboos are broken occurs as she closes the show with her transgressive "Vagina Medley," in which the nouns of popular songs are removed and replaced by the word *vagina:* e.g., "I left my vagina in San Francisco," and "I'm gonna wash that vagina right out of my hair," and "La Vagina, La Vagina, ya no puede caminar" (30). Palacios's constant transgression of cultural and linguistic borders, a desacralization of pop culture, may very well alienate some of her more traditional straight audiences. When we add this to her refusal to perform to homophobic audiences, she thereby limits her crossover potential. Nevertheless, she has certainly found a place to articulate a sexualized lesbian identity that builds community at the same time that it delights queer audiences.

Marga Gomez

Whereas Carmelita Tropicana and Monica Palacios perform their transcultural subjectivities to audiences in the know, highly politically charged and subversive, Marga Gomez stages her acts in a less-radical milieu—more comfortable "mainstream" locations that have, until now, been closed to the previous two performers. Although Gomez's audiences are mainly lesbian, gay, and feminist spectators, they are also predominantly white, which signifies both that the Latino component must be adjusted and accommodated, and that Gomez's material is more likely to cross over.[17]

Gomez's gradual rise to fame and popularity began with her performance piece *Memory Tricks* (1990), which centers on her relationship with her mother. It was followed by *Marga Gomez Is Pretty, Witty, and Gay* (1990), a meditation on an evolving Latina lesbian subjectivity. In her next show, *A Line around the Block* (1994), a tribute to her performer father, the spectator witnesses the complementary and overlapping cross-sections of all the previous identities performed in each work—daughter, lesbian, Latina performer. Although each performance constitutes a text in its own right, when read together as companion pieces, the trilogy presents differing stages of Marga Gomez's historical subjectivity, her lesbian/feminist praxis, and her theatrical career.[18] Each solo performance on its own offers fragments of the processual construction of a heterogeneous identity at differing stages of her life. Her subject positionalities as an ensemble reveal the plurality, multiplicity, and fragmentation of a Latina identity formation through space and time. In other words, the three "autobiographical" pieces together provide a complementarity that none of them is able to accomplish on its own. As Gomez recovers her familial relationships and gradually articulates her lesbianism through each performance, she simultaneously configures herself at a transcultural intersection of both Latina and lesbian subject positions and discursive practices.

Her Latina lesbian-feminist consciousness provides her with mechanisms to reevaluate, deconstruct, and subvert gender-sex roles promoted and incul-

8. Poster for Marga Gomez's *Marga Gomez Is Pretty, Witty, and Gay* and *Memory Tricks* at New World Theater, Amherst, Massachusetts (1992). Poster design by Yvonne Mendez. Used by permission of Roberta Uno, New World Theater.

cated in both Latino and Anglo patriarchal cultures, where heteronormativity and woman-as-spectacle predominate. Through her multiple and strategic positionings, we witness her negotiation and accommodation within the process of transculturation, where sexuality shapes her identity as an "adult female homosexual."

In *Memory Tricks,* Marga, the character, rejects her mother's carefully controlled construction of femininity and in fact parodies the Latina gender-specific behavior to which her mother is so prone. On the other hand, in *A Line around the Block,* instead of rejecting her father and his ways, she creates a tribute to him. Through a series of sketches that are at once both respectful and lovingly parodic, Gomez recovers, documents, and traces the beleaguered history of her father's career as a performer, comedian, and impresario in New York Latin show business of the early 1960s. Yet it is his daughter, through her reconstruction of the Latin theater circuits, who accomplishes Willie's lifelong dream: she attracts a Latino constituency both on stage and on television. The recovery of this legacy is an act of transculturation itself; through it, Latino performance is placed in particular historical junctures at the same time that it provides Gomez, the performer, with an inheritance that will foment her future career. In this sense, although her transcultural theatrical and ethnic memory selects, mediates, and re-collects both her parent's careers, it is her father in particular who embodies the art of performance for Gomez. While impersonating her father, Marga/Gomez exalts those qualities in him that make him a survivor in her eyes: his bravado, his strength, his optimism, his improvisational skills, his cultural performance—in short, his perseverance as a dreamer and a performer. In contrast to the critical distance that she establishes with her mother, here Marga fills the gap between reality and parody by her desire to become her father.

Marga's identification with her father is reiterated during the piece as she recounts several defining moments in their relationship that are crucial for her future career as a Latina performer. Indeed, these cultural moments and memories register so deeply in Gomez's consciousness that they can be understood only within the parameters of transculturation. In the first instance, Marga reconstructs a summer spent with her father in his New York home after her mother has remarried and moved the family to Long Island. These summer visits to her father's house become a kind of apprenticeship or even her own Latino summer stock as she prepares for her career.[19] Marga hones her craft on stage and offstage by mere interaction with her father, for whom life is "puro teatro." If, for example, on an excursion to the beach

9. Poster for Marga Gomez's *A Line around the Block* at New World Theater, Amherst, Massachusetts (1994). Poster design by Yvonne Mendez. Used by permission of Roberta Uno, New World Theater.

Marga has no bathing suit, Willy produces the costume from the show's finale for her to wear there. This burlesque costume, the vestigial tropicalized attire of the Latina bombshell, signals Willy's inability to distinguish performance from reality, to separate exile from homeland, and to comprehend cultural gender roles, not to mention teenage daughters. Nevertheless, the costume does make some sense if we consider it as a prop for grooming Gomez in her future role as cross-dresser/performer.

Back at the house, Willy furthers Marga's apprenticeship by having her assist him in his home-recording studio. There, not only does she acquire the necessary skills for a second phase in her schooling as a successful performer, but she is also exposed to a variety of role models in the Latino entertainment world. In his love for theater, Willy never misses an occasion to place his daughter in the spotlight at the club or at home. As he passes the torch to a new generation of Latino performance, he establishes a tradition and bonds with his daughter.

In this way, Gomez's inheritance is twofold: in the first place, all this "home" rehearsing actually provided her with the education that she would translate into a career; in the second place, and crucial to the first, in her father's world, Gomez was immersed in a Spanish-speaking environment and cultural domain, all the while insisting that her Spanish was nonexistent. Even the smallest and most mundane acts provided the future performer, Gomez, with transculturated material and ways of seeing as she richly performs such characters as the bodega owner, La Gagita, or the closeted lesbian performer, Irma Pagán. In contrast, her mother's lessons represented a type of finishing school that she can "perform" and incorporate into the comedic acts she learned from her father. Thus, her mother's erasure of their Puerto Ricanness and her father's Cuban school of performance supplied Gomez with rich cultural imprints to flesh out her own act.

But the world of the father went beyond performance and ethnicity. Rather, it also set the stage for a young girl to express her sexuality. Her father's star, Irma Pagán, a closeted lesbian performer, awakened a sexual desire and eroticism that Gomez—the stand-up comic—is now able to recognize and acknowledge as her own lesbianism, as we saw in Monica Palacios. If in *Marga Gomez Is Pretty, Witty, and Gay* that desire is exemplified when Marga makes love to a lesbiana's chewing gum in order to be close to the person, in *A Line around the Block* it needs no metonymical displacement. Her simultaneous attraction to and infatuation with Irma signals the affirmation of her lesbian subjectivity when she has the opportunity to interact with

Irma backstage. This opportunity also affirms her desire to express her sexuality in a culturally "authentic" way with a Latina sexual encounter. Knowing Irma's sexuality, Marga's father intervenes with a patriarchal intrusive act. Refusing to name his own objection to Irma's sexuality and to acknowledge his daughter's sexual preference, he opts for the taboos of his Cuban ethnicity and politics: he tells Marga that Irma is a "communist." Not missing a beat, Marga immediately responds that she, too, is one. This witty response parallels what José Muñoz calls "choteo" (1995a), which we understand as a way of responding to sexuality through jokes. Although the humor is sexist, sexuality is always mediated through humor, a lesson that Marga has learned in her apprenticeship with her father. By aligning herself politically—read, sexually—with Irma, she expresses her difference from her father and speaks between the lines of her yet to be named lesbianism. In this manner, she is able to articulate her incipient lesbian identity and her commonality with other Latina lesbian performers.

At this point, it is significant to identify the fact that both Irma Pagán and Marga Gomez play to specific audiences. Irma addressed a Latin heterosexual audience in New York of the 1960s, and Gomez plays to a contemporary Anglo lesbian, feminist, and gay audience. Irma could not flaunt her lesbianism given her historical, gendered situatedness. Gomez, on the contrary, juggles multiple levels of gender codification according to her ironic handling of Irma in combination with an out Marga. Once we place both performances—Irma's and Marga's—within the dynamics of cultural worlds, Latino and Anglo, there and here, then and now, multiple readings emerge. For a Latin heterosexual audience whose horizon of expectations is a femme fatale, Irma delivered a unidimensional performance; but for Marga in *A Line around the Block,* who knows how to discern reality from performance, there is a deeper structure. Unlike Irma's Latin heterosexual audience, Gomez— distanced through time—recognizes the irony of Irma's campy act: she can decode lesbian messages that heterosexual audiences could not even see. This is nothing short of transculturation at work. Irma's hyperbolic expression of femininity accentuates Gomez's awareness that gender is socially constructed as well as performed. Furthermore, being bicultural and moving back and forth in a "toma y daca" offers Gomez an array of gender performances not available to Irma. In her own show, as Marga cross-dresses into Irma's glamorous, alluring, seemingly heterosexual Latina nightclub performer, she becomes, in her own words, a "female impersonator." With this exaggerated act, she reveals the superficiality of Irma *passing* as a heterosexual woman, but Irma's lesbianism interrupts and disrupts her "heterosexual" performance for those with the vision to see it. Marga's advantage is her capability of putting on a transcultural and transgendered act that shows how even at this young age she is equipped with the necessary antennae to recognize "puro teatro" when she sees it. Gomez's show reveals how Latina lesbians performing to a public eye in the 1960s were forced to hide their true sexual identities. The fact that Gomez revives these scenes demonstrates the impact that closeting had on her and her present political responsibility not only to be out of the closet herself but to liberate Irma by outing her, too. In this manner, we see how transculturation is also a liberating, revisionist process, even when the discourse of homosexuality is taboo.

The culminating act of transculturation takes place when Gomez cross-dresses into her father, Captain Willy Chevalier. There is a great sense of pleasure and exaltation in imitating the gestures, costume, body language, and humor that marked the father's performative life. In short, she revels in the similarities with her father as she simultaneously seeks to take over where he left off—thus, the subtitle for *A Line around the Block* as a work-in-progress is *My Art Belongs to Daddy*.[20] Given that her father loses his vocal chords in his final years, Gomez's tribute is more than symbolic: she not only recovers her father's legacy; she ventriloquizes his comedy acts. By literally speaking for her father, she gives words to his acts and to him, all within a lesbian context. Such a dramatic recovery is never present in *Memory Tricks,* where the mother's voice is usually parodied as an absurdity. Yet, Willy's macho bravado is practically never viewed in the same manner, nor is it ever parodied as an excessive gender construction.

How can we decode transculturation in this final act of cross-dressing? The key is not in how Gomez plays the role of her father, per se, but rather in the way she impersonates and embodies her father. In this manner, costuming enables and makes visible the transgendered act that closes the show. If Marga's mother and Irma emblematize excessive femininity at one end of the gender spectrum in their choice of feminine clothing and its power, her father represents the other end in the stiff, starched, white dress uniform that symbolizes his masculinity. Unwilling to identify with either of these exaggerated, cultural, gendered markers, Gomez places herself somewhere in the middle of the spectrum by creating an outfit to accommodate her newly defined lesbian subjectivity. However, in this third space, this interstitial performance, she enacts her transcultural subjectivity by performing her Latina self in relation to a Latin American theatrical heritage. Her models consist, on the one hand, of Latin American women who exaggerate their femininity and, on the other, of Anglo lesbians who are free to cross-dress. Thus, not only does she return to the comfortable androgyny of her childhood to fashion a costume that is at once both feminine and masculine, she also creates a hybrid category for her art that derives from both her parents: her father's career as a comedian and her mother's as an exotic dancer yield in Gomez the "exotic comedian" (*A Line around the Block,* video). This final outfit, a tuxedo dress, which combines the elegance and flair of a tuxedo with the fitted torso of a tailored dress, includes a "jacket" long enough to serve as a miniskirt, so that no other garments—save the black stockings—are required. Ultimately, that tuxedo facilitates the ease with which she will later be able to cross-dress into her father's persona, Captain Willy Chevalier.

When she impersonates her father, it is not an act of mimicry, but rather one of transculturated memory; nor will she be content to rely solely on body language and tone of voice, as she did in impersonating her mother. Here, the costume is as essential to re-create that persona as are the other props and body language. Thus, costume and masquerade become progressively complex in her three works as Gomez transmogrifies into an androgyny that has been informed by both femininity and masculinity in their most extreme forms, as well as into a bicultural being who oscillates between ethnic and linguistic spheres. In order to establish this new transcultural lesbian perspective, she picks and chooses from many available models, but ultimately the subjectivity that she "fashions" for herself is unique and individual.

Gomez's return to her parents, then, is a necessary act of survival made possible by her transcultural sweep through her childhood and adolescence. When read as a trilogy, Gomez's three performances reflect each other, the fragments of each piece belonging to its own and yet the other's puzzle. In the constitution of transcultural identity, especially one that is multiply marked because of its ethnic and sexual constituents, her work exemplifies the postmodern condition.

Critics and reviewers have pointed out how Gomez's theatrical monologues deal with the complexity of identity formation. In our study, although we recognize the significance of such representations, we think it is also important to explore her contribution to the performing arts in all its dimensions. In a way, she has created a new genre that eludes any facile categorization because of its heterogeneity as well as because of her own hybridity.[21] She combines theatrical monologue, personal anecdotes, stand-up comedy, one-liners, impersonations, and solo performance as she glides in and out of the characters and dramatic situations she stages. As she imbues her art with this heterogeneity of theatrical traditions and genres, she also makes history for feminist theater, gay and lesbian theater, and Latina/o theater. We must understand that this new history is a transcultural and even transnational one.[22]

Transcultural Performance

All three performers—Carmelita Tropicana, Monica Palacios, and Marga Gomez participate in what Mary Louise Pratt calls an "autoethnographic text," which she defines as "a text in which people undertake to describe themselves in ways that engage with representations others have made of them. . . . [They] are representations that the so-defined others construct *in response to* or in dialogue with those texts" (1991:35, emphasis in original). For our purposes, Pratt's theoretical model unfolds as we analyze the features that constitute minority performance. First, there is the issue of the "subaltern" or marginal subject who constructs an identity in relation to the one assigned to her by the metropolitan or dominant culture. Second, these works are addressed to the dominant culture as well as to the subject's own community in the form of "print culture" (Pratt 1991:35). Finally, the fact that these performative texts constitute collaborations between the subjects themselves and their audiences, they may be said to materialize a space for negotiations and resistances in Pratt's celebrated "contact zone," the space of transculturation.

In this way, each Latina solo performance is not simply an autobiographical act, but a collective collaboration through which the self becomes a communal experience; in the fact that one person speaks for the whole, performance, as Pratt has described autoethnography, also resembles the Latin American testimonio tradition, this time without the educated intermediary as scribe. If testimonio emerged in the 1980s as the urgent way to denounce human rights abuses in the Americas, in the 1990s within the U.S., Latina solo performance also center-stages a single person's experience, one that is shared by her audience, who has experienced different kinds of oppression and marginalization (racial, ethnic, and sexual). In their "out"rageous, "out"spoken performances, Latinas create a hybrid genre that oscillates between theater and testimonio, between ethnography and autobiography, between confessional and stand-up comedy. As this new transcultural and transnational voice gains recognition, Latina solo performance leads the way into new modes of expression, representation, and performativity in the cultural imaginary of "América."

SIX

FROM MOLCAJETE TO MICROWAVE

AGENCY & EMPOWERMENT IN CHICANA "DINNER" THEATER

Among the fragrance of crushed garlic and chopped cilantro, in an altar room of every Latino home—the kitchen—mother and daughter share a special moment.
—Dolores Prida, "Janis Astor del Valle"

In the North American context, multiculturalism has catalyzed an array of political responses, each with its favorite metaphors, many of them culinary: "melting pot," "ethnic stew," "tossed salad," "bouillabaisse," "stir-fry," "gumbo."
—Ella Shohat & Robert Stam, *Unthinking Eurocentrism*

Our refried beans are 100% free of animal products.
—Sign at La Veracruzana Restaurant, Northampton, Mass.

Historically, anthropologists had until recently cornered the market, so to speak, on writing about foodways as structural systems that centered on the link between ethnic, social integration, and community. For them, the ritual preparation of meals and the ethnocultural interaction of dietary traditions with identity and food practices determined the specificity of social groups and their cultures. More recently, historians and social scientists have also observed the significance of food in relation to national, cultural, and regional identity, paying close attention to the sociopolitical significance of cookbooks, menus, and the often gender-specific stories embedded in them.

A pioneering voice in developing a semiotics of food, Mary Douglas has identified a cultural theorization of food as a code pointing to the "pattern of social relationships being expressed," including "degrees of hierarchy, inclusion and exclusion, boundaries and transactions across boundaries" (1972:61). On another tangent, feminists, although concentrating on women's "subgenres" of literature—works such as diaries, autobiographies, and letters—opened the door for cultural criticism that recognizes the feminist potential in cooking, recipes, and the kitchen as a gendered space with its own politics. We shall see in the Chicana plays that we discuss below how recipes, "oral cookbooks," and menus operate in relation to identity formation wherein ethnicity is a process, not a product. In the gendered space of the kitchen, where generations of Chicanas interact, each in her own discursive positionality and practices, notions of cooking depend on performative acts.

If performance is a "doing and a thing done," as we discussed in the previous chapter, then the cooking of food is a prime example of how this conceptualization works in practice. The "doing" reveals itself as the actual making of food, while the "thing done" results in the production of a prepared meal. In the "doing of the performance" (i.e., the cooking of the food), each dish's uniqueness at the time of the doing demonstrates that no two dishes can be the same each time, just as no two performances can ever repeat themselves exactly. Under these circumstances, recipes, menus, and cookbooks are always in the making and point toward a future making, which will vary each time they are "made" or "done."

All performative acts contain a combination of elements that when put together produce a certain result. At the same time, there is simultaneously an alteration of these very elements each time the act is performed, which registers its newness, uniqueness, and variation. Historically determined and culturally manifested, these acts crystallize into new cultural artifacts each time they are "enacted" in a specific ethnic and national(ist) context. For this reason, it is possible to demonstrate this truism by placing cooking and culinary acts within the theory of transculturation. Like performance, transculturation is never duplicated; rather, it is always open to new cultural possibilities and alternatives, which depend entirely on the historical location of transcultural subjects, as well as on their given positionality when cultures clash.

Once again, we turn to Fernando Ortíz, whose notion of ajiaco provides us with a metaphoric understanding of transculturation in Latin America. Ajiaco is a kind of stew autochthonous to Cuba. In his theorization, Ortíz's definition of the term *ajiaco* resists the Anglo-American melting-pot metaphor in that it depicts the cultural and ethnic culinary complexity of the region. Ortíz thus undermines both the loss of identity and the expected accultura-tion that the melting pot demands. With his counterhegemonic intervention of ajiaco, he demonstrates the specificity of race, ethnicity, and nationalism in terms of a pioneering postcolonial disruption way ahead of his time. For him, Cuba emblematizes the ideal location to study mestizaje/transculturación, for in Cuba a multiplicity of mestizajes took place: "mestizaje de cocinas, mes-tizaje de razas, mestizaje de culturas" ("mestizaje of foods, mestizaje of races, mestizaje of cultures;" 1940:22). This "caldo denso de civilización" ("dense broth of civilization") cannot be better visualized than through Cuban ajiaco (22). Ortíz's concept of heterogeneity and fusion rely more heavily on process than on final product. For a culture that is constantly inventing itself, his idea of "amestizamiento creador" ("creative mestizaje" [22]) underscores the dy-namism, the creativity, and ultimately the performative aspect of identity as a crossroads ("encrucijada de las Américas" [23]).

Ortíz's model provides us with a way to articulate a new understanding of Chicana intervention in the politics of cultural identity. Because both plays and solo performances in this study display processes of identity formation, the stage is a particularly suited venue to enact the clash of cultures and the drama that such encounters produce. In the "contact zone" of the kitchen on stage, culinary traditions are transmitted, rituals are performed, and recipes are altered, while the protagonists experiment with oral cookbooks, revive ethnic memory, and gain agency through the process of transculturation. Although gastronomic traditions are maintained, these culinary practitioners simultaneously accommodate themselves to the immediate circumstances and conditions of a new transculturated generation conscious of its place in history.

It is precisely this generation of U.S. Latina playwrights, specifically Chi-cana playwrights, in whom we encounter the conversion of the stage into a kitchen. The dominant paradigm in these plays is the staging of a protagonist in the moment of crisis preceding cultural transformation. Thus, the kitchen, a legitimate space of social relations and dramatic action, becomes a public domain where agency is developed and identity is established, and, most importantly, where hybrid subjectivities result from new historical positionali-ties, where a new combination of ingredients conflates.[1]

What could be so important about a recipe that it needs all this theatrical and critical attention? Deceptively, recipes adhere to quite strict linguistic codes that can be analyzed in much the same manner as other narrative texts. Colleen Cotter, for example, discusses these components, which consist of (1) seeing the recipe as a narrative or a story, (2) discussing the recipe's semantic and syntactic features, and (3) examining the way in which "language constructs community, establishes personal identity, and tells us who belongs and who is the outsider" (1997:52). As cultural narratives, recipes, like no other social signifier, encapsulate cultural traditions, modifications, practices, and belief systems. Cotter adds that recipes, as such, are a "form of cultural cohesion . . . a text that is 'locally situated' as a community practice" (53). In this manner, both the author and addressee " 'co-construct' an artifact of their community" (69), visible here in the plays and solo performances we examine (Diane Rodriguez's *The Path to Divadom,* Alicia Mena's *Las nuevas tamaleras,* Ruby Nelda Perez's performance of Rodrigo Duarte Clark's *Doña Rosita's Jalapeño Kitchen,* and Elaine Romero's *The Fat-Free Chicana and the Snow Cap Queen*).[2] In these works, entire families gather around tables and kitchens to discuss the veracity, texture, taste, and nutritional value of the ingredients and the menu.[3] In addition to their mouth-watering function as appetite teasers, the menus and recipes in all these works signal a moment of cultural transition in their role as catalysts. The new tamale makers and the fat-free Chicana protagonists allude to an emerging identity formation among second- and third-generation Chicanas, who exalt the position of the cook and celebrate the transition from the home and the kitchen to the public arena of the restaurant and the stage.

The play *The Fat-Free Chicana* concretizes the confluence of private and public space, the generational conflicts, the new ingredients, and the consciousness-raising model of and for a hybrid identity. Once the kitchen metamorphoses into the restaurant, as in two of these works (*The Fat-Free Chicana* and *Doña Rosita's*), its former privacy becomes a communal experience that the protagonists "co-construct," for it shows how kitchen and theater function dialectically. Like other ethnic groups, Chicanas/os mitigate the violence of migration, occupation, and domestic colonialism through the recollection and preparation of native foods, particularly at moments of celebration and festivity. These "food memories" (Shigley 1997:120) not only activate the past through "heritage foods," but also provide a meaning to the present. Individuals and the community as a whole can revive and preserve their legacy and survive colonialism, neocolonialism and the evils of assimilation through a recuperation of their foodways because in "recipes lie memories of food and history" (Shigley 1997:121), of home and family, providing a way to "reterritorialize" a usurped social space.

Specifically, the recipe on the Chicana stage operates as more than a mere how-to. Its significance is manifold. First, an older generation of women transmits knowledge and wisdom to younger, college-educated Chicanas, who must be trained in the art of cooking. Second, younger Chicanas take pride in the recipe, but they always alter at least one ingredient from the original. For example, they remove the lard from the recipe, causing an intergenerational dispute regarding past and present, oral tradition and cook-book, nonformal and formal education, Spanish and English, lard and fat-free foods. Third, if assimilation signifies discontinuity and amnesia, memory, under these circumstances, must be activated and mobilized by returning to its residual home in the recipes of the abuelitas, tías, and mothers.[4] That menu, a site of a new transcultural memory, and its "instructions"—the recipe itself—are a repository of cultural and familial memory that is activated through cooking. Fourth, each culinary performance directs audiences in the "how-to" of cultural performance: cooking food unfolds into a metaphorical cooking of identity. Sharing the recipe with the audience triggers the double conversion from a domestic activity, which had previously confined and isolated women, to a springboard that manifests a public and politicized self. The end result is not only the dish itself, but also community building and solidarity across gender, generation, class, and levels of education.

As the recipe is transmitted from one woman to another, from one generation to another, and from stage to audience, the Latin root of the word recipe—which is recipere,[5] to receive—becomes significant. Sharing recipes, cooking, and participating in the bustle that accompanies these acts, all imply or suggest a way for one group of people, namely women of a certain generation, to engrave their memory on another group of people, namely women of a certain other generation, who will ensure the recipe's survival in the community; or, in Anne Goldman's words, these acts are "an affirmation of cultural difference" (1992:173), which provides the cook with the necessary agency to assert sufficient authority to speak (179). In that generational engagement, the cook becomes acquainted not only with the recipe, the ingredients, and the menu, but more importantly with what Susan Leonardi describes as the "embedded discourse" (1989:340): all manner of information peripheral to the actual recipe, such as advice and sharing, community building and female bonding, storytelling, and, most important, gossiping—all of which are the necessary ingredients of a good recipe. Finally, the situatedness of recipes comprises succinctly what Tey Diana Rebolledo calls their "rooted-ness and place" (1987:102), precisely the discursive space where a politics of cooking and the politics of location intersect in the formation of identity.

Ethnic Memory and Foodways

If food is culture, as it is in these works, each and every ingredient mentioned registers as a symbolic, cultural marker of ethnic affirmation. Given the visi-bility, tangibility, and materiality of food—its prominence as a cultural sig-nifier—it serves migrating populations as a means of preserving an ethnic identity whose values and traditions are either trivialized, commercialized, or exoticized by the dominant culture. These populations may see migration as a double-edged sword: on the one hand, preservation of ethnic foodways pro-vides them with a kind of authenticity. On the other, that very affirmation also runs the risk of becoming stereotyped if it is appropriated and hence frozen by the dominant culture, as in the case of Taco Bell. Jeffrey Pilcher argues in his *Que vivan los tamales* that the notion of authenticity can stereotype an appropriated culture. For the Mexican migrant population itself, the issue of appropriation is a recovery, a reclamation, and even a recycling of culture versus the commodification of Mexican food in the Anglo mainstream. In the constant innovation that forges transculturation, identity functions as a me-dium for nurturing and nourishing that culture whose reach goes far beyond the physical body.

Thus, everyday acts—such as making tamales—that were once common occurrences in the culture of origin and taken for granted now achieve the status of cultural icon and are indispensable for maintaining ethnic memory and identity. Furthermore, that icon has the potentiality not only of becoming an item of nostalgia, but also of achieving folkloric status with a veil of sa-credness: for example, Puerto Ricans long for their Christmas pasteles, and Cubans cherish their arroz moro and habichuelas negras. In the case of Chicanas/os, whose long residence in the Southwest does not always imply migration, there has always been a deep connection to Mexican food rituals. Undoubtedly, in addition to their celebratory role, these rituals may also serve as a contestation to the double-edged sword of assimilation and Anglo pirating.

The importance of food as a preserver and carrier of culture acquires even a greater status in situations where other cultural markers, such as language, may have been lost. Although newer generations are schooled in "English only," the home often is the only place where culture is preserved through food rituals. In such cases, the food remains constant as that cultural umbilical cord to national and ethnic identity. It is in this way that food underscores cultural identity, especially when connected to ceremonial occasions, festivities, and rituals. Whereas certain types of food are considered a part of such major holidays as Christmas, Easter, Cinco de Mayo, and El Día de los Muertos, other kinds of foods are themselves the cause of the celebration or a special event. Of all of these celebrations, it is the tamalada that takes precedence in Chicana/o culture; and of all ingredients, lard and chile are the key culinary artifacts that hold the most revered place.

In the Chicana works we analyze, a new generation of playwrights is not content merely to copy the recipes of their abuelitas; rather, their vision is to transculturate those recipes, literally giving and taking. The process of reproducing (cooking) a tamal, a burrito, or an enchilada is metonymic to the configuration of the playwrights' identity as new mestizas. Cooking tamales, in these plays, is tantamount to finding their identity as Chicanas. In these staged tamaladas, we learn not only how to make tamales, but even how to "make familia from scratch" (Moraga 1986b:58), creating a community of women in the kitchen. It is a process that cannot be prepackaged or "store bought" because just like those prepackaged tortillas, it will never taste right or will come "out of the microwave" like a frisbee (Elaine Romero, *The Fat-Free Chicana and the Snow Cap Queen,* 129). Furthermore, the ingredients are not simply a staged prop (Rodriguez's *The Path to Divadom*); once placed within given discursive constructions, these props are the metonymic tools that edify those ever-evolving transcultural subjectivities.

Even when the original Spanish language is lost through the rigors of assimilation, the oral tradition that passes on information from one generation to another survives. In these works, the oral tradition, from which the recipes derive, manifests itself discursively in such a variety of forms as proverbs, gossip (chisme), and humor (chiste). Each recipe contains not only ingredients, but an "embedded" narrative that retells its history. When Spanish is used, it refers to that ethnocultural history. In this way, each work provides its audience with a panoply of proverbs, always in Spanish. These refranes, dichos, or proverbios (proverbs, sayings), serve as a part of a condensed cultural belief system, embodying wisdom and humor, and like the medieval exempla, they highlight sociocultural world values based on oral tradition. Such cultural formulae exalt women's knowledge, and when taken into the province of the kitchen, they not only are part of the recipe, but actually validate it. Just like the recipe itself, proverbs preserve and condense culture into a few key phrases. Their capacity for consolidation facilitates the didactic function of the proverb, which resonates in the ingredients functioning as cultural artifacts. By collapsing the recipe and the proverb, each one takes on the characteristics of the other in their symbiosis. If the proverb has a moral, so too the recipe. If the recipe contains ingredients, so too the proverb. It is almost as if the proverb immediately puts into practice the inventory of the ingredients. In this sense, both proverb and recipe retain their cultural significance and serve as a model for/of social action and identity formation as well as of ways of doing cultura. Just as the proverb needs the embedded discourse to give it meaning, the recipe also needs an embedded discourse to gain *its* meaning.

In each of the works we discuss, that embedded discourse takes the form of chattiness and humor: chisme and chiste, which provide, accommodate, and validate the context in which the phrase was spoken. For this reason, broken hearts are cured with the dicho: "Con pan las penas duelen menos, con mole son sabrosas" ("With bread sorrow is less painful, with mole they are delicious"; Duarte Clark, *Doña Rosita's Jalapeño Kitchen,* 19). Food's curative and restorative function is made apparent in such refranes as: "Con lo que sana Susana, cae enferma Juana" ("What cures Susana may make Juana sick"; *The Fat-Free Chicana,* 98), and "a cada uno su gusto lo engorde" ("may each one's taste fatten him" or "you are what you eat"; Romero, *The Fat-Free Chicana,* 114). Thus, we see that the proverb itself, both by its linguistic articulation in Spanish and its reference to food, serves as the repository of cultural memory insofar as neither language, nor food, nor tradition have fallen into oblivion. Therefore, when we ask the question "What is the moral of the proverb?" we can see that its function is to guarantee the preservation of culinary traditions, the Spanish language, and ways of seeing, doing, and performing cultura, all of which are essential for the construction of the protagonists' and the audience's bilingual and bicultural identities.

The importance of the proverb relies on its ability to register the signifiers that refer both to food and to chisme. If in the original proverb there are allusions to panza (belly) and engorde (fatten) in the plays, those words will refer to specific gossipy remarks about certain characters as a "gordiflona" (big fat lady), "nalgona" (big fat ass), and "panzona" (big- bellied lady). As to their relationships with men, these protagonists satirize patriarchal domination of women, evidenced in such proverbs as "ni padre que me ladre" ("no father to bark at me") and "contento como un pig en el lodo" ("as pleased as a pig in mud"; Duarte Clark, *Doña Rosita's Jalapeño Kitchen,* 4). That Rosita has altered the original proverbs "perro que ladra, no muerde" ("a barking dog does not bite") and "contento como un cerdo [swine] en el lodo" indicates disrespect for and trivialization of patriarchal authority. Her bestialization of the father in "padre" and in "contento como un pig en el lodo" jokingly mocks men as well as poking fun at the refrán. Just as Rosita is prone to add her own ingredients to the new tamales, so too her own bilingual lexicon substitutes for the traditional. Now what appears to be a simple chiste is yet another example of the way in which chisme creates a subjectivity-in-process constructed through language and, in so doing, creates transcultura. By claiming their rightful place within a framed linguistic code, the chisme, these women assert a self-affirmation and self-determination within a women's particular transcultural discursive mode.

If the chisme functions as the embedded discourse of the recipe, the embedded discourse of the chisme itself is the chiste. Within the chisme there is the capacity for myriad transgression. The freedom to make jokes such as "Cesar Chávez would come back from the dead" and "you look like you saw the Virgen of Guadalupe having sex" (Romero, *The Fat-Free Chicana,* 105, 104) signals a moment of cultural history in which the playwright knows that she can simultaneously reaffirm the cultural and political values of the 1960s while also maintaining an ironic distance from that history. What seems to be a desacralization of the pillars of the Chicano movement and Catholicism attests to the success of those figures in entering the general consciousness and to the revision of history in a more human and humorous context. These protagonists are now poised to appropriate, transform, and take their physical space within cultura. And where do they begin? The kitchen, of course . . .

La Tamalada

For millions of Chicanas, whose daily chore is/was to slap out the family's tortillas, the kitchen would hardly be a transgressive or even a transformative space. Yet, in these scripts, the kitchen changes from a space of confinement to one of autonomy, self-empowerment, and community building. The kitchen is removed yet once again when it is converted into a restaurant as the private becomes public in two senses. First, one woman's kitchen is now her restaurant, open to customers in her new entrepreneurial role. Second, this woman-owned space allows the protagonist to interact with the audience as the kitchen/restaurant is transformed into the setting of a play. In several Latina theatrical works *(Botánica, The Fat-Free Chicana, Of Barbers and Other Men, Doña Rosita's Jalapeño Kitchen)*, when gentrification threatens this safe space of home and kitchen, the woman steps into a leadership role, protecting and defending it. Just as Dolores Prida has affirmed, the kitchen is an "altar" of safety and security, comfort and spirituality. In other words, this sacred reverential space concretizes and materializes a place of worship, a sanctuary. In *The Fat-Free Chicana and the Snow Cap Queen,* that sanctuary predates Anglo occupation and has its own culturally marked history. Although the building sustains and nurtures Chicana/o identity in its resistance to Anglo encroachment, its occupation by men and women reveals it as a gendered space. If in the beginning Chicano men built and owned this piece of Aztlán, for the last fifteen years women have owned and occupied it. Indeed, in all of these restaurants and kitchens, men are either absent or occupy only a figurehead role. That they cannot, will not, or are not permitted to interfere allows the women literally to usurp that previously male-identified space and exercise their control, power, and agency. By claiming that space, they also usurp the male code of honor and fame, as they translate it to the honor and fame of good cooking. Repeatedly, the protagonists flaunt their culinary skills and fame in the community. In the older generation, each cook claims her rightful spot: "mis tamales were famous . . . los mejores de toda la región, todo el mundo me lo decía" (Mena, *Las nuevas tamaleras,* 164); "Sometimes I think some people would rather eat my / enchiladas / than listen to my stories" (Duarte Clark, *Doña Rosita's Jalapeño Kitchen,* 14); "we have a reputation for having the best beans in town" (Romero, *The Fat-Free Chicana,* 98); "it's dangerous to change my recipes" (*The Fat-Free Chicana* 114).

A reputation for making excellent tamales is not merely a matter of boasting, as Brett Williams asserts in "Why Migrant Women Feed Their Husbands Tamales" (1984). Rather, a woman's fame, place in the community, marriageability, and authority within the household and the survival of her family depend on how she uses the strategies and weapons of the tamal to keep her family together. Thus, the tamales serve as a bartering tool to keep her husband in line, as Williams describes: "Tamales help her maintain that influence, and she uses them to express affection and obligate others, as well as to gather a network of tavern owners who watch out for her husband when she cannot be there" (1997:118). In traditional families, a refusal to cook tamales is grounds for divorce because it is understood that a proper wife does not defy her husband, especially in something so critical as tamales. However, in second- and third-generation Chicano/a families in the U.S., where women are not migrants, may be single mothers, are professionals, or simply do not have the time, the making of tamales must be adapted to their own positionality and transcultural lifestyle. The question of how these modern Chicanas will *adapt* the tamal—considering both its difficulty and its desirability—to their life as mestizas is at the core of many works.

First and foremost is the questioning of the use of lard. If in traditional settings the cook's fame depended on the sacred, irreplaceable, and incomparable manteca (lard), contemporary Chicana playwrights stage the generation gap in terms of lard usage. In every theatrical piece, the reference to lard is much more than mere coincidence, but rather is a trope that inscribes cultural transition. Rather than lard serving as merely "part of the recipe," it is the basis of the dramatic tension around each generational and dietary conflict. In this sense, lard is not only a matter of taste, but rather a cultural signifier across historical periods and generations. For the older generation, lard not only marks the family name, synonymous with the honor of the clan, but is the family's secret and unsubstitutable ingredient. Furthermore, the use of lard, too, is part of a long process of transculturation whose genealogy begins in the colonial moment, as Pilcher describes it. Historically, he tells us, Spanish colonists scorned the use of lard over their beloved olive oil. But economic necessity impelled them to turn to lard as the price of importing olive oil became astronomical. Indigenous populations, too, found lard distasteful, until they discovered that tamales made with lard were "fluffier and more delicate" (Pilcher 1998:36). If this transition was a transcultural moment, the one that we analyze in the plays is transculturation to the second power as the younger generation again revises the use of lard in traditional Mexican and transfrontera cooking.

For the older generation, nothing can provide the authenticity of lard's taste, flavor, and texture, a way of cooking that was not open to question, ever. As such, lard, and nothing else, can make cultura the way abuelita used to make it. Whereas this older generation often waxes nostalgic about a return to the origins of their cultura, a frozen moment in time, a younger generation struggles to retain cultura but at the same time to remain contemporary. For them, the dictum "you can never put too much manteca in a tamal" is not acceptable for reasons of heart health (Mena, *Las nuevas tamaleras,* 162). In the case of Romero's *The Fat-Free Chicana,* one sister wants to eliminate any trace of lard in her mother's restaurant, a sentiment she expresses sarcastically by rebaptizing the business "The Heart Attack Café" (100). Her younger sister, in contrast, when making the decision to return to *her* Chicana roots, requests "the greasiest taco [you can find]" (115). The residual and symbolic need for manteca reaches its climax and hyperbolic moment when the building that houses the restaurant begins to "sweat manteca," an action that can be interpreted in at least two possible ways. On the one hand, a personification of space occurs when the manteca substitutes for tears shed over Anglo occupation and deterritorialization. But at the same time, the manteca serves as a reminder that cooking—and especially with manteca—is an integral component of cultura.

Throughout these pieces, the succulent ingredients of the Mexican kitchen tantalize the spectators. The suggestion of the aroma and flavors of garlic *(The Path to Divadom, Las nuevas tamaleras),* cilantro, mole, salsa, and cebollita (onion) *(Doña Rosita's Jalapeño Kitchen)* evoke sensory memories of childhood in the protagonists' mothers' kitchens, where their feelings of safety and home conflate with the pleasure of eating a burrito, tasting a chile, and reaffirming their mexicanidad. Yet, although all these dishes call for an ethnic memory, none can match or meet the requirements as well as a steaming pot of tamales. The tamalada takes a place of sentinel importance as the protagonists cherish the making of the tamal as much as the eating of it. And no tamal worth its salt can be relished without its secret ingredient: manteca. Indeed, Diane Rodríguez's character in *The Path to Divadom* sets up her own little tamalada right on stage. Her transgression—replacing the manteca with shortening—evokes the allegation that such tamales are inedible; her uncle Sam finds them "secos" (38), a pronouncement that denotes her failure as a cook and perhaps even as a Chicana.

In order to understand the critical issues at play here, we must begin by tracing the history of tamales. In Pilcher's description of Mexica (pre-Columbian) ritual feasting, tamales formed a core part of the celebration: good ones elevated the reputation of the cook, and bad ones resulted in loss of stature. Revered in the community as the sacred food of the gods, tamales "provided the hallmark of festive banquets" (1998:11) for Mexicas to such a degree that overt and covert social battles were decided over the competition between rival nobles to sponsor the most lavish feast (14, 15). If, as in most cultures, the task of feeding is woman's domain, in Mexica ritual, women fed the men, but men fed the gods, all of which was considered essential to "maintaining the cosmic balance" (17). Respect and reverence for maize defined the social construction of reality for pre-Columbian peoples: if the tortilla was the daily bread, the tamal was its lavish manifestation. Revolving around the aura of its intense labor, the tamal and the consequent tamalada have retained their value precisely because the time-consuming effort that they require represents the halt of time characteristic of ritual or performance, and, indeed, the tamalada is both.[6]

In this way, Alicia Mena's *Las nuevas tamaleras* center-stages the act of cooking tamales by two generations of women. The older generation knows that "una buena tamalada" is much more than a mere cooking lesson; in fact, they understand completely its ritualistic performative function. The younger generation, raised in a prepackaged consumer culture, must learn that ritualistic aspect step by step in order to perceive and create cultura. In the play, the older ones, long dead, return from heaven to supervise this arduous task, but are invisible to the younger Chicanas. Whereas for the older cooks a tamalada is an occasion to gossip, to take up their rightful place in their culture, to reclaim that space and their legacy, it is only in the actual making of the tamales that the younger generation learns of its ritualistic value as a celebration and a performance. Furthermore, the act of making tamales facilitates the ways in which identity construction is informed by ethnic memory. The time-consuming labor of the tamal conferred status and fame on the viejitas, and the younger generation, although complaining that making tamales is "hard work" (168), undergoes the process of transculturation in this rite of passage. The play serves as a didactic medium whose main purpose is to highlight the sacredness of the event of the tamalada. By lighting candles for "spiritual guidance" ("Some spirit or something will come and help us" [152]), they communicate with the afterlife in the form of the viejitas and manifest their reverence for the Virgen de Guadalupe. This aura of sacredness confirms the general belief that tamales are the "food of the gods" (Rodríguez, *Divadom,* 39). By recognizing the tamal's ancestral roots, they not only recover their history, but also place the viejitas as the "high priestesses" (*Divadom* 40) of cultura.[7]

In this manner, the kitchen becomes a sanctuary whose ultimate deity is a woman. In contrast, the patriarchal world allegorized in heaven indicates the artificiality and sterility of Anglo culture, represented in *Las nuevas tamaleras* by the whiteness of heaven and by the modernity of the high-tech equipment used by the younger Chicanas. Even more crucial to the undertaking is the idea that making tamales is synonymous with making chisme. As the viejitas dream of returning to earth, they are silenced in heaven by St. Peter, renowned for his dislike of chisme. In order to regain their speaking voices, the

10. Alicia Mena's *Las nuevas tamaleras* at Guadalupe Cultural Arts Center, San Antonio, Texas (1993). *Left to right:* Maria Elena Garza Salcedo, Kim Hemley, Ruby Nelda Perez, and Sonia Rodriguez. Photograph by Al Rendon.

viejitas must enact a tamalada. Just as the younger women traverse a trans-cultural identity through the tamalada, the older women, too, also perform a rite of passage in regaining their voices and asserting their identities.

Similarly, in *Doña Rosita's Jalapeño Kitchen,* the crucial ingredient is chile, whose alliteration with *chisme* is apparent and intentional. In *her* allegorical dream, Rosita tries to conceptualize heaven's kitchen, "Do you think they have chile in heaven?" (11). In this performance piece, whiteness again symbolizes Anglo culture, whose conception of heaven is as white as it is. In her allegory of heaven, Rosita panics at the predominance of "white food and white people" and at a refrigerator full of "white milk, mayonnaise, tofu, cauliflower, all white foods" (15). Neither frijoles, fajitas, salsa, nor, of course, chiles are heaven's culinary ingredients. Thus, the denizens of heaven's kitchen must call upon Satan in hell's kitchen to procure these essential ingredients. In this move, Rosita leaves heaven not because she fails to meet its requirements, but rather out of her own volition. St. Peter, repre-sentative of the law of the father and of the patriarchal silencing of her voice, is substituted by her choice to live in a place where delicious, spicy food is the norm. Her transgression reverses the myth of the original sin as she, a woman, takes a scrumptious bite out of a chile. As she reclaims her space, she simultaneously rewrites her history, her authentic Mexican history embedded in her recipes and contrasted with the artificiality of Anglo food. Here, then, she resembles the protagonists of *Las nuevas tamaleras* as she, too, experiences a rite of passage from assimilation to resistance.

In all of these cultural productions, the rite of passage is never an isolated act. Rather, a story accompanies the transcultural process, a story that always relates to culture—that is, to woman's culture and ethnic identity. For example, in *Doña Rosita's,* the most important story of the performance is the embedded discourse of Rosita's courtship with Tomás, the love of her life. Instead of following her heart and marrying him, as he requests, Rosita instead allows her father's dictum of an arranged marriage to prevail. As Rosita retells this story, it is framed within the context of the restaurant and the recipe for flan, which she prepares during its narration. This recipe activates her memory about "the man of her dreams," lost because she didn't have "permission from my father, the priest and God" (25). The telling of the story and the art of cooking intermingle as they do in Laura Esquivel's *Como agua para chocolate.* Rather than see *Doña Rosita's Jalapeño Kitchen* as derivative of Esquivel, we witness here a cultural phenomenon of food and its value that transcends the political border with Mexico. What Cecelia Lawless has observed about Tita, the protagonist of Esquivel's novel, applies to Rosita: "[she] uses the kitchen *and* the recipe to expand the confines of the site and to set up her own discursive territoriality" (1997:228). Indeed, the patriarchal law evident in the holy trinity that denies women's agency is usurped by these cooks as the kitchen becomes a transformative space where women's bonding and reconfiguration occur. The chattiness of the recipes consolidates the mother/daughter relationship and thus serves to bring generations—including those in the audience—together.

While the recipe for flan helps Rosita revise and recover her story as a girl, *that* story enables her to make an adult decision about the future of her restaurant. In so doing, the character, as a speaking subject, elaborates a dialectical construction of her identity. The conflation of her life and culinary experiences enunciates her subjectivity, which is activated by the use of embedded discourses of recipes and stories. In this new "reciprocity," her recipes and stories are embedded in each other, giving shape and meaning to each other. Remembering how she caved in to pressures as a young girl, she resists harassment from priest, children, and neighbors, this time as the Anglo developers harangue her to sell the restaurant. Each story and recipe of this process take her one step back to her politicoethnic affirmation and one step closer to her decision. Thus, the piece straddles her indecision about whether to comply (sell out) or resist (exercise her agency). As Rosita finishes giving the recipe and once the flan is ready, the audience understands the power of the recipe, for it has the capability to awaken ethnic memories in Rosita. In that regard, instead of miring in nostalgia about what was lost, Rosita instead has utilized that past experience to mobilize and activate an agency that she is just coming to know in herself.

Chicana empowerment again manifests itself allegorically when one of her customers in a vision sees Rosita "bien macha," ready to take on the bulldozer (11). In this vision, Rosita is brandishing a frying pan that gets larger as the dream progresses and the encroachment becomes ever more threatening. Such a hyperbolic use of her weapon (sartén, a frying pan) indicates that she has put the refrán "la sartén por el mango" ("grab the frying-pan by the handle") into action. In the dream, Rosita has taken matters into her own hands, the customer literally claiming that Rosita has "un sartén in your hand" (11). Rosita's tactic of territorial defense awakens her political consciousness. Just as we saw in the previous usage and appropriation of proverbs by women, here, too, we witness a similar maneuver. The manipulation of the original proverb, "tomar la sartén por el mango" (to be in control of any situation), demonstrates a control of language, autonomy, and especially code-switching. Rosita's political construction of reality is always in relationship to cooking utensils, the kitchen itself, and the art of cooking. In the substitution of *mango* for *mano,* and *mano* for *hands,* we can see in the friend's vision how Rosita's linguistic, political, ethnic, cultural, and social identities are constructed in relation to food and culinary traditions.

These works articulate the preservation of culture, the empowerment of women, the transformation of the kitchen into a public space, and the constitution of identities, as well as the way in which recipes and gossip cohabit kitchen space. The relationship between identity and location, domestic and public arenas, the personal and the collective concretizes in these pieces at the moment that Chicanas take "la sartén por el mango," producing a reterritorialization of the space. The play that accomplishes and emblematizes this act of reterritorialization as a political feminist act in Aztlán's kitchen is Elaine Romero's *The Fat-Free Chicana and the Snow Cap Queen.*

In this full-length play, Amy, a Chicana college student majoring in dietetics, returns home to an undetermined place in the Southwest to help her family run their business, a restaurant. She knows they need her because of a visit from the good witch of the North, who alerts her to an impending crisis. In Amy's confrontation with her family's eating habits and cultural past, the audience witnesses the full display of the dynamics of identity formation. In her attempt to become a Chicana of the 1990s, Amy experiences a gamut of emotions, positions, and transformations: from scorn and rejection to crisis, negotiation, conscientización, and, finally, accommodation and pride. *This* rite of passage is not simply a matter of assimilating or of eschewing family values and cultural traditions, but rather the dramatic staging of the process of transculturation.

Like other protagonists and second- and third-generation characters in Latina/o theater, Amy must find her way back home while negotiating her formal and nonformal education.[8] Through apparitions of Doña Norte and the Snow Cap Queen, her cousin's graffiti art, her mother's heart attack, and her sister's impending anorexia, Amy learns to articulate her ethnic identity in relation to her place at home and in her community. Her assimilated way of seeing requires the constant and continual negotiation of cultural and family values and of ethnic memory inscribed in the recipes, cooking, and menu of her mother's restaurant. As the play progresses, and as Amy gains agency, the recovery of the past becomes her new transculturated memory, which is neither nostalgic nor unproblematic.

Around the coordinates of home, education, and cultural identity, Amy's dilemma develops into a crisis situation as she delves into the archives of cultural memory. As in the previous plays, the connecting tissue continues to be lard—hence, the title of the play (Snow Cap is the most famous brand of lard sold in the Southwest). The role of the Snow Cap Queen in the piece is of vital importance in that she also represents a plurality of identities: she is both the Good Witch of the Norte as well as the Snow Cap Queen; she claims to be from the Andes, but later confesses her Mexican roots; she is a shaman and a coyote trickster. Her act of intervention compels the characters, especially Amy, to take a political position. For example, in her role as Good Witch, she advises Amy to take courses in Chicano history. As the Snow Cap Queen, however, she encourages consumption of great quantities of lard. By first repudiating and then reclaiming her mexicanidad—that is, her own multiple identity—she serves as a catalyst to Amy's bicultural condition. But if lard serves as the connective tissue of the play, it also functions as the signifier that separates theory from practice. When lard is divorced from cultura, as it is in Amy's biology classes, she learns only about its negative effects on blood pressure and cholesterol. Thus, in her curriculum on dietetics, she has

11. Elaine Romero's *The Fat-Free Chicana* at El Centro Su Teatro, Denver, Colorado (1997). *Left to right:* Manuel R. Roybal Sr., Valerie A. Bustos, and Louis Lopez-Esquivel. Photo by Jose Mercado, courtesy of El Centro Su Teatro.

implicitly learned to erase her cultura. Her return home, on the other hand, occasions the need for attitude adjustment on her part after assimilation. In practice, her mother's restaurant, cooking, and recipes affirm, continue, and promote the cultural heritage and legacy of their forbears, in this sense constituting an educational program at home. Amy thus moves from the public educational domain of Anglos into the private realm of the home and its center, the kitchen. Not a simple binary opposition between private and public, this play represents a dialectical fusion wherein past and present, old and new values are juggled and reconfigured as transculturation defines the characterization of the protagonists and the dramatic action.

As a representative of an educated younger generation, Amy has put aside her lessons in the old ways of cooking. In this sense, education, although empowering, produces cultural dislocation and historical amnesia, as evidenced in the remark Silvia makes, echoing one of their cousin Rumaldo's: "Inside you there is somebody who will remember. Everything. And it's stronger than that other part of you that went up north to get an education and, instead, she was erased" (133). By assimilating a new symbolic Anglo law of the father, Amy distances herself from her Chicano community. As a result, she is continually searching for her way back home, in this case to the maternal center, emblematized in the restaurant. The kitchen and food (collectivized in the restaurant) become the cultural signifiers by which this younger generation can return "home." Thus, Amy rehearses here a transcultural performance of Anne Goldman's statement that "food and its preparation, within the context of personal narrative [serve] as metonyms for the reaffirmation and maintenance of traditional Hispano cultural practices as a whole" (1992:179).

If reentering home occasions a crisis of identity for Amy in the collision of formal education with family tradition, alienating and estranging her simultaneously from both home and community, in contraposition, her cousin Rumaldo, an artist and activist, supplies her with new lessons in cultural identity and citizenship in Aztlán. Despite his lack of a college education, he is informed about M.E.CH.A. (Movimiento Estudiantil Chicano de Aztlán) and its activities. In his painting, he unites the syncretism of the political and the artistic, the collective and the individual. Grounded in the mural art of the 1960s, he moves the dramatic action forward with his political graffiti art of the 1990s. Although not abandoning the principles and political platform of the muralists, Rumaldo's art is firmly rooted in the present: what was once collective is now individual. At stake is an artistic expression that inaugurates a new form of identity. That Romero chooses an artist as the character to wave the banner of this new transcultural identity, which is anchored in the politics of the 1960s and the Chicano movement, inscribes how space and gender are related. As a male artist, Rumaldo metaphorizes this new hybrid self in his murals, which represent the public domain, commonly understood as a male space.

Women's space, on the other hand, has traditionally been the home and specifically the kitchen. In a way, in these plays women take up the kitchen as artists of food, but do not remain marginalized and silenced in the private sphere. Instead, they put their signature on their recipes and, in so doing, reverse the public-private dichotomy at the same time as they genderize and decolonize the public space with their own experience and history. If that public space was the cultural domain of men during the Chicano movement, represented by a predomination of mural art by men, as we move toward the century's end, Romero and other playwrights become cultural workers whose solidarity with men shows us that issues of survival depend completely on the community building and the collaboration between both sexes.

Once the artists achieve a collectivity, the didactic function and intention of their art, be it creative or culinary, become more visible. In *The Fat-Free Chicana,* not only does one character learn from another and from an organization such as M.E.CH.A., but more importantly the play itself becomes the medium by which the general audience, in its identification with the characters, is also able to share the lesson Amy learns, which is the lesson of history, memory, and transculturation. Nowhere is this more apparent than in the symbolic function of the restaurant's sign, prepared by Rumaldo. In the beginning of the play, it simply read "Café Lindo," but by the end of the production the new sign celebrates the transcultural process by proclaiming the restaurant's menu to be "low fat" and "third generation." The process of self-naming is an indispensable component to identity formation and a way to "compete" with the encroaching Anglo culture, personified in the form of a threat of Denny's opening up across the street. Although these neighborhood restaurants are also microcapitalist endeavors, they are simultaneously cultural icons: their existence points to the preservation of cultura and the empowerment of identities. As a whole, the restaurant is the privileged space to continue producing culture. Unlike Denny's, it is not limited to the business of private property and profit, but rather is the business of the cultura. When the young protagonists of *The Fat-Free Chicana and the Snow Cap Queen* learn that their restaurant is housed in a historic building, they implicitly reclaim their ancestral, ethnic roots in Aztlán.

The preservation of the restaurant as culture entails a rite of passage wherein its transmission is ensured. Just as in *Las nuevas tamaleras,* the younger generation is initiated into cultura through cooking. This cultural performance is activated at the moment the younger generation is separated from the maternal center—i.e., home—through their formal educations. As for the older generation, their separation from Aztlán produces the need to transmit history, knowledge, and wisdom in the cooking lesson. When seen as a rite of passage, the dramatic action of the play serves as an apprenticeship not only for the younger generation, but also for the older one and, most significantly, for the audience: they are *all* initiants in the process of reintegration into cultura. In order for the younger generation to make the complete passage into their reterritorialized space, at some point in the work the older generation needs to be literally removed from the premises. In *The Fat-Free Chicana,* the mother's absence takes the form of an arrest and then a heart attack. During her sojourn away, the daughter experiments with new recipes while she fills her mother's role. Such a cataclysm, although traumatic, registers the transference of values and authority from the older generation to the younger one.

It is precisely liminality, the betwixt-and-between condition, that guarantees the future resolution of the dramatic action and its didactic ending. Younger women have learned that the art of cooking is a tool of empowerment fostering women's consciousness. Thus, all initiants must pass through the kitchen, the sacred space where the rite of passage is performed. Successful transmission of culture and tradition result in remarks such as "Te hiciste mujer!" ("You became a woman!" Mena, *Las nuevas tamaleras,* 166). Even cultura is defined as a woman in the matriarchal definition of these works (as in, for example, Rodríguez's *The Path to Divadom,* where "la cultura es una mujer" [43]). While the older generation nods their approval and gives their blessing, they, too, profit from this symbiotic exchange. The final phase results in the younger generation's reintegration into the reterritorialized Aztlán and in the older generation's re*installation.* Both repositionings complete the rite of passage.

This rite of passage functions dialectically with the constantly increasing tension of the dramatic action. Therefore, it is no coincidence that when Amy finally understands her place in her community, her mother declares, "I am glad to have you home, mi'ja" (144). In this resolution, each character, in addition to Amy, achieves an awareness of personal and social change: the grandfather resolves not to ride his lawnmower as much, but rather to get real exercise. Silvia stops starving herself and takes up her rightful place in the restaurant. Mami advertises and cooks a leaner menu inspired by the recent events in the family. Rumaldo feels enough confidence to attempt a college education himself. What Amy's presence has crystallized for these characters is a recognition of their condition of transculturation, however heterogeneous, contradictory, and transitory that condition may be.

Given that food is the most potent marker of ethnocultural affiliation and identity, its significance in all these plays is more than merely casual. For these reasons, each protagonist of each piece discusses and defends *her* ingredient that will transform the menu. In this sense, the private recipe becomes the public domain as it finds its way into the restaurant menu. In each of these cases, the menus accommodate a transcultural subject gaining agency in a bilingual, bicultural world. If in Rodríguez's *The Path to Divadom,* the protagonist tentatively substitutes lard with healthier ingredients, she still asks for family approval before doing so. As for *The Fat-Free Chicana,* instead of such tenuous approval, the younger generation proclaims their hybridity and bicultural condition with such signs as "Order from Our Original Style or Third-Generation Menu" or "Low-Fat Food Available Here" (142).

Each of these dramatic works has brought to bear the cultural agency of the lard package and how it shapes the transcultural process paramount to the piece. If in *The Path to Divadom* lard is absent, its significance has more to do with cousin Rachel's nalgona contours. In *Las nuevas tamaleras,* the moment of transculturation occurs during the process of modernity itself. In the old days, when the viejitas lived on the rancho, the manteca was obtained by slaughtering the animal, the masa ground in the molcajete. In the sleek modern kitchen of the new Chicanas, these traditions are lost to blenders and microwaves. Thus, when the viejitas mourn the loss of certain cultural components, they are equally lamenting the loss of cultura. Finally, in *The Fat-Free Chicana,* it is neither the size of the woman nor the kitchen gadget that motivates the new menu, but rather a new generation concerned with the health of its community. This is to say that college-educated Chicanas/os, in order to preserve their culture, must ensure that they eat properly, and therefore they adjust the menu accordingly as well as recover and preserve ethnic memory in all its fragmentation, ambiguity, and discontinuity.

The transformation of the menu in each generation may be different. Even within a generation, each individual modifies the recipe according to her cultural, economic, and social needs. Yet the artifact that visually registers all these cultural transitions is the final menu in each of these dramatic pieces. The menu's serving as a cultural guide is not simply a matter of juxtaposing an Anglo menu to a Mexican one, but rather of interspersing such comparisons throughout the piece: for example, Rosita's Oaxacan style enchiladas are juxtaposed with Denny's grilled cheese; homemade tortillas rival cheese and crackers; flan soothes in contrast to apple pie à la mode; and chiles outdo the blandness of tofu and mayonnaise. In *Doña Rosita's,* as in the other pieces, any change in the menu entails more than culinary know-how: each is a political act, as in Rosita's resistance to gentrification. Those transmutations keep the protagonists alive and inscribed in a historical process in which transformation is essential for survival. Thus, Rosita is better equipped to resist the threat from the developer or from Denny's because of the recipes in her kitchen. In each case, the knowledge of how to wrap tamales, roll tortillas, and bake enchiladas is the end product of a long line of maternal wisdom passed on from mothers, tías, and abuelas to newer generations via an oral tradition that surpasses the formal cookbook. Thus, one protagonist whose tamales are the envy of her compañeras proclaims: "I remember watching my mother . . . and my tias" (Mena, *Las nuevas tamaleras,* 170), thus confirming the visual educative effect of watching older women prepare what Sally Bishop Shigley calls "heritage" foods (1997:121). Just as cookbooks create a community of readers who share a national cuisine (Appadurai 1988:3), the "food memories" (Shigley 1997:120) that elide formal cookbooks also accomplish this task through the visual performance of an act of cooking.

As we have seen, the information that women pass in the kitchen is not limited to recipes or, shall we say, to recipes only for food. Just as the word *receta* tells us, the Spanish recognizes no difference between a culinary recipe and a pharmaceutical prescription because their function in healing is so intermingled. Throughout the pieces we have discussed, the restorative value of certain foods takes center stage, as Rosita's utterance makes clear: "the urge . . . from way down in my tripas [for chile]" (Duarte Clark, *Doña Rosita's Jalapeño Kitchen,* 15). When Amy's mother suffers from a heart attack, her two concerned daughters recite a long list of Mexican dishes to her until they find the one that will restore her to health. As Rosita narrates the tale of her lost love, she deliberately cooks a sugary flan to cure her own daughter's heart. In this sense, ethnic foods are both nutritious and nurturing, healing not just the body but also the social wounds of assimilation, fulfilling their prophecy as "recipe" and "prescription." In all of these cases, food has a restorative, therapeutical power as a remedio. The women who prescribe such remedies often double as curanderas (healers), who also happen to be cocineras (cooks). They know that what a person eats can change not only a mood, but even a temperament.

As the aforementioned dishes and ingredients tantalize and whet the audience's palate, so they naturally expect the recipes. However, we soon discover that there is no recipe in these works, rather only fragments of recipes. Thus, the recipe functions as pre-text on at least three levels. On the first, the text of the recipe itself, a material cultural artifact, is either the written page or the oral instruction on how to concoct a finished product with a predetermined set of ingredients. In this sense, it is a pre-text because it foregrounds and predates the dramatic, literary text. On a second level, the telling of the recipe occasions the need for more stories, anecdotes and gossip. In other words, the recipe is the pre-text for women to get together to tell each other juicy gossip, as in *Las nuevas tamaleras.* There, once the tamales, lacking in uniformity and made under great duress, are safely placed in their pot, the new tamaleras can engage in the fun part of the tamalada, the gossip. Finally, on a third level is the recipe's embedded discourse—its metaphorical and allegorical function—which becomes apparent in Rosita's parodical story of the chicken who tries to migrate from Mexico to the U.S.

The chicken is an undocumented worker "sin [without] papers" who personifies Mexican migrant workers in their efforts to cross la frontera. The inquisitorial practices of the Migra (INS) take center stage as the border patrol interrogates the chicken: "Como tu llamar? What's your real name, chick? You're not carrying any contraband down there are you? While I'm down here I might as well check your liver. You had a tb check-up last month? Can you name your last ten sex partners? Were they all roosters? We don't want marimacha chicken sneaking onto the menu, this is a family restaurant you know" (Duarte Clark, *Doña Rosita's,* 8). Clearly, the allegory displays a double narration: that of the chicken on its way to becoming cooked enchiladas and that of the trials and tribulations of undocumented workers (*pollo* is the slang for *wetback*). When La Migra puts the chicken's health and its sexuality into question, at work here is the fear of the Other, the fear of the abject, the fear of contamination from those who are not desirable "ingredients" or "members" of the "American menu" and the American national imagined community. Both menu and restaurant represent the U.S. metonymically as a nation that practices discrimination and racism against Mexican migrants. As the allegory develops, politics play a significant role in the inquisitorial trial: "Are you a member of the Communist party? The socialist party? The Che Guevara knitting club? What about your character? Do you believe in abortion? Do you know how to flush the toilet? How many unfertilized eggs have you had in the last year? Have you ever been to Cuba?" (8).

The list of questions discloses the ridicule and the absurd situation that the migrant chicken has to endure. Most important, the questioning reveals the female gender of the chicken, whose assumed sexuality, hygiene, and promiscuity makes of her an unwanted migrant to the U.S. The harassment continues as the Migra undervalues her by assuming that she will be a financial burden to the country and whose migration will perpetuate the dependence of the poor on government programs: "Do you renounce Food stamps? Welfare? Unemployment benefits?" (8). In parodying real and brutal migration stories as well as Migra abuses with its technologies of intimidation, Rosita engages herself in a political act of resistance and contestation. Her allegory positions her narration of the story as an act of intervention. Above all, her political (and activist) perspective subverts the dominant Anglo patriarchal law as she speaks as an empowered woman from the domain of the kitchen. It also shows her how politics can take place in the reterritorialized space of the restaurant, as well as in the political arena of the nation. She knows well the exploitation of migrant and undocumented workers. Nonetheless, the allegory here has a double function: on the one hand, it bestializes the migrant in order to show the dictatorial torture of the Migra; on the other hand, it humanizes the chicken in order to highlight the dehumanized conditions that migrants have to experience when entering the U.S. This story can be decoded with the following reading and interpretation: the signifiers and the narrative of the chicken are duplicated in the story of the undocumented migrants up to a point that the audience has no difficulty in identifying with the chicken. Nor is there any difficulty in reading the not-said of the story. Though the spectator must decode another system of meaning, registered through parody and irony, s/he must distance her/himself from the story. Once the allegory is understood in its different levels of meaning, the spectator can respond with laughter and understand the ridiculous but nonetheless inhumane policing at the border. It is precisely humor that allows the spectator to assume a political position as well as to identify with Rosita's allegory of the abused chicken.

Nevertheless, the allegory, when seen as the embedded discourse that structures political acts within the space of the kitchen and the restaurant, still situates the spectator within the discursive realm of the recipe. Rosita closes the allegory with the final instructions to cook the chicken: "So you boil the chicken un rato hasta que the meat's bien soft. Next you start making the green chile sauce. I use tomatillo, a little jalapeño, with a bit of serrano" (8). As a result, her allegorical and parodic story contains a political act that cannot be detached from her art of cooking and from the discursive formation of the kitchen.

Food for Thought

In this chapter, we have seen many examples of embedded discourse that underscores the power of the community of women being celebrated in these plays and performances. These works revel in echoing the last lines of Denise Chávez's *Novena narrativas* (1986), where the protagonists exclaim, "Ay! Qué familia de mujeres, no? What dreams! What hopes! It makes me want to sing!" (100). Such is the action of las nuevas tamaleras, who insist: "we should drink a toast to our mothers . . . tías . . . abuelitas, and to all the women who ever made tamales" (Mena, *Las nuevas tamaleras,* 175). Such celebration in each of these plays and solo performances moves the dramatic action from the oral tradition to the printed page, from simply recipes to the embedded stories and gossip, from allegory to political action, from the stage to the page and back again. It is therefore no surprise that at the end of *Doña Rosita's Jalapeño Kitchen* the protagonist can claim with all certainty that, indeed, "The pen is mightier than the sartén" (28). With this exclamation, the audience leaves in no doubt that these Chicana playwrights and their protagonists have indeed taken la sartén por el mango.

SEVEN

HOMING THE STAGE

STAGING THE DISCOURSES OF HOME IN U.S. LATINA THEATER

Globalization, with its concomitant parallels of deterritorialization and migration, has inevitably changed our views of home as an anchored concept in time and space. In this sense, home can no longer be the bourgeois conceptualization maintained during the various reigns of imperial presence in many regions of the globe. In a postcolonial world, where subjects are always in transit and identities are relentlessly mobile, "home" is intrinsically portable and mutable. Cultural theorist bell hooks has lucidly captured the discursive formation of home in a postmodern world. In her assessment, the very meaning of home is altered with the "experience of decolonization, of radicalization. At times home is nowhere. At times one knows only extreme estrangements and alienation. Then home is no longer just one place. It is locations. Home is that place which enables and promotes varied and ever changing perspectives, a place where one discovers new ways of seeing reality, frontiers of difference" (hooks 1990:148). Crucial to hooks's point of view is how home becomes the very "house of difference" (Lorde 1994:226) for deterritorialized subjects. The process of decolonization, implying conscientización or Chela Sandoval's "oppositional consciousness" (1991) permits those in the margins to position themselves in the interstices of various locational identities. If we have learned from feminist and postcolonial theorists both in cultural studies and geography to address the issues of the politics of location, we must take those lessons and apply them to the construction of home in Latina theater. But before we can do that, it is necessary to map these discursive practices of home as they are manifested in this current theory.

Just as identities of people are fluid and always in the making, so, too, are those of places, or locational identities. In a world of constant displacements and dislocations, refugees, exiles, migrants, sojourners, even CEOs, and others articulate their identities in relation to place; the identity of places are therefore constructed in relation to the people—and to the power relations between them—who inhabit that place. Thus, we see a dialectical relationship between people and places, the identities of both of which are constantly conflictive, unfixed, and becoming. Furthermore, in this process of articulation, there is always space for contradiction, ambiguity, and ambivalence. This state is what Homi Bhabha has called interstitiality, which is central to the relationship between people and place. He writes: "These spaces provide the terrain for elaborating strategies of selfhood and communal representations that generate new signs of cultural difference and innovative sites of collaboration and contestation" (1994a:269). For us, Bhabha's theorization of the interstice echoes what we have been calling la transfrontera, and the denizen of the transfrontera is the transcultural subject.

These postcolonial theories have called into question essentialist, universalized, ahistorical notions of home, requiring them to undergo drastic revision. Home—once the unchallenged territory of patriarchal, imperial, and heterosexual national communities as well as of burgeoning Eurocentric expansions—now also belongs to those previously disregarded colonized subjects. In this sense, traditional definitions of home register it as "familiar, safe [with], protected boundaries," according to Biddy Martin and Chandra Mohanty (1986:196). They go on to suggest "home was an illusion of coherence and safety based on the exclusion of specific histories of oppression and resistance. . . . Because these locations acquire meaning and function as sites of personal and historical struggles, they work against the notion of an unproblematic geographic location of home" (196). In this final chapter, our understanding of home is informed by these critical theories that conceive of it as a dynamic, improvisational, and negotiable site.

Pinning down a concrete definition of home always seems to be a slippery enterprise because home is not only a material and physical space and location, but also an abstract idea, a sentimentalized repository of sensory images and memories. It is not until a subject leaves home and is at a distance from it that s/he can enunciate the narration of home and initiate her/his relation to that place called home. Such a process shows how home is not a neutral construction, but rather a politicized and fictionalized space (George 1996:11). Here, Doreen Massey's illuminating definition of space, constructed in terms of the relations of power in it, is useful to our discussion. According to her, a space must be thought of in terms of "the articulation of social relations which necessarily have a spatial form in their interactions with one another. . . . One way of thinking about place is as particular moments in such intersecting social relations, nets of which have over time been constructed, laid down, interacted with one another, decayed and renewed" (1994:120). Massey's proposal lands us exactly where we want to be: at the intersection of the politics of identity and the politics of location. In these terms, home is therefore not where you come from, but where you are at,[1] and, as Angelika Bammer has proposed, it "is the imaginary point where here and there . . . are momentarily grounded . . . in the virtual space between loss and recuperation." Thus, in Bammer's appraisal, home is "neither here nor there" but rather a "hybrid, it is *both* here *and* there" (1992:ix).

In spite of that instability, individuals always try to freeze their notion of home into a single unit of memory. This tendency is especially true with migration and diaspora, where identities are uprooted and need to reestablish themselves in new relations to place, space, and power. It is at this crux that the possibility of resistance and creativity emerges, according to hooks. As hooks repeatedly encourages her readers to enter that marginal space where intervention may occur, she assures them that it is the site of story making, of recovering something, of reclaiming history; most important, it is a space open to "pleasures, delights and . . . desires" as the dualist category of colonizer/colonized is dismantled and destabilized (1990:149 and passim). It is no coincidence that this space of politicization and creativity is the precise location that Chicana/o border theorists have been formulating for the last three decades as la transfrontera. Indeed, the recovery and reformulation of home at la transfrontera is the dominant paradigm from which to articulate the discourses of home for deterritorialized and diasporic Latina/o communities. The paradigm of la transfrontera applies to these migratory subjectivities in the sense that home is constantly elusive.

At the border, as well as in diaspora, loss and memory combine with nostalgia and desire to become the overlapping and intersecting discursive axes that redo and undo the concept of home. For example, in the case of Chicanas/os inhabiting la frontera, home is a strategic site that comprises the questioning of nation, the search for utopia (the recovery of Aztlán), and loss of a homeland after U.S. occupation. For other Latina/o migrants, regardless of the cause of their migration, home is a memory, and a desire for what was left behind. In each of these cases, for their children and for their children's children, home becomes at once more distant and more transcultural. These succeeding generations negotiate between their parent's nostalgia and their own desire for an ancestral homeland. Such a mediated memory contains traces of nostalgia, for they participate in their parents' nostalghía while at the same time attempting to articulate a home here and now. This agonizing process for self-definition and for positionality cannot be understood solely as indicating a reactionary posture. Again, bell hooks helps to clarify the difference between a "politicization of memory" and nostalgia as a "useless act." For her, that longing for "something to be . . . as once it was" is always political and is exactly what "transform[s] the present" (1990:147); in its capacity for political mutability, transculturation manifests itself as a *usable* and not a nostalgic act.

In order to understand the function of nostalgia, it is useful to recur to its etymology. Anthropologist Nadia Seremetakis, tells us that the Greek term *nostalghía* literally signifies "the desire or longing with burning pain to journey." She adds: "It also evokes the sensory dimension of memory in exile and estrangement; it mixes bodily and emotional pain and ties painful experiences of spiritual and somatic exile to the notion of maturation and ripening. In this sense, *nostalghía* is linked to the personal consequences of historicizing sensory experience which is conceived as a painful bodily and emotional journey" (1996:4). Relying on the Greek helps us to see "the transformative impact of the past as unreconciled historical experience" in contrast to its use in English, which "freezes the past in such a manner as to preclude it from any capacity for social transformation in the present, preventing the present from establishing a dynamic perceptual relationship to its history" (Seremetakis 1996:4). In these terms, problematizing nostalgia turns it into a processual, transformative, dialectical condition that connects the present with the past, the personal with the political, the border with the nation, and stagnation with mobilization. In la transfrontera, a selective picking and choosing takes place, a remembrance and forgetting, that returns us once again to the "toma y daca" of Latin American theories of transculturation.

From the above perspective, if any construction or trope of home is based on positionality, challenging any and all fixity, then we can argue that the transcultural home resides in that provisionality. This home is precisely what provides transcultural individuals with the freedom to inhabit multiple spaces simultaneously, to cross both invisible and real boundaries, and, most important, to imagine themselves differently. Within those imaginings lies this transcultural home, which differs from the one that preceded and succeeded it in given moments of history. Because home can never be repeated and because home, too, is a "doing and a thing done," we can therefore conceive of home as a performance—that is, as a transcultural performance.[2]

Although evocations of a desired, nostalgic, utopian, or nationalist home are not new to U.S. Latina/o literary productions, home on the stage has served a younger generation of U.S. Latina playwrights as a central discursive site where transcultural subjects exercise their agency. In the following pages, we examine how these playwrights articulate and negotiate the cultural, ethnic, and symbolic construct of home, and how it acquires a new definition in their struggle to define it. Home—in each particular case, either through leaving it, returning to it, questioning it, or redefining it for the stage— constitutes more than a mere family drama; rather, it reveals the dynamic interplay of postcolonial subjectivity and transculturation to the second power. If at face value it appears that Latina playwrights are merely representing well-rehearsed generational conflicts and gaps in addition to the unquestioned condition of inevitable assimilation, in fact these plays offer audiences new and innovative ways of looking at space and subjectivity, being and belonging, transnationalism and transculturation. Within the realm of home—or, as we have named it, the *transculturated home*—we analyze a series of plays whose protagonists juggle transculturated memory at the same time that they accom- modate the geographical past of dispossession and colonization. In this sense, home is always a geopolitical arena whose transversal boundaries are con- stantly in tension between inside and outside, here and there, and a sense of place and dislocation. It is this transculturated home that sets the transcul- turated memory into action (the dramatic action per se) and through which the deterritorialized subject gains her agency. Being mostly bilingual and bicul- tural, the protagonists of these plays survive the ravages of colonialism and neocolonialism by everyday acts of reterritorialization. Although each attempt to find a home is a partial and provisional endeavor, when we read these plays together, a sense of a collective home is achieved through the theater, and this imaginary space empowers the community at large. The whole production then becomes a kind of home both for the audience and the protagonists so that going to the theater is indeed "going home," as we see in the plays by Migdalia Cruz, Josefina López, Janis Astor del Valle, Silvia Gonzalez S., and Elaine Romero.

Latina playwrights' innovative ways of doing theater have inaugurated a new paradigm, which we call a *home play,* in which the main protagonist either leaves or returns home (or both) in order to negotiate, accommodate, and reconcile her sense of herself as a person of interwoven, overlapping, transcultural identities. These new protagonists must define themselves in relation to traditional concepts of gender, sexuality, race, class, education, and, of course, la familia. As the plays unfold, old models of social action encounter resistance and rejection from this younger generation whose political viewpoints now challenge such issues as misogyny, homophobia, racism, classism, imperialism, and domestic colonialism. Hence, each play provides an example of what we call transitional politics, whereby the play itself serves as the transcultural bridge between the traditional way of doing things and the new hybrid way for the protagonists to see their multitextured world.

In home plays, bringing home to the stage while simultaneously staging transcultural homes involves an "inside out" process. That is, what was once private, familial, domestic, and expected now in the theater becomes public, controversial, and open for scrutiny. The multiple staged spatial and metaphoric representations of home defy any specific notion or definition of it. Each protagonist (and playwright) fashions a personal rendition of home—whether house or prison, security or myth, exile or pain, culture or safety, family or history, imagined community or nationalist desire—dependent on her or his own particular location, experience, and historicopolitical moment.

We propose that three dominant paradigms emerge in these Latina plays: (1) home as an inescapable prison; (2) home as a site of difference actualized through the lesbian body and through the creation of a lesbian home; and (3) home as a mythical and allegorical journey. While unraveling the concept of home, we encounter a series of confrontations that reveal how homing the stage activates and mobilizes our central thesis: the construction of transcultural identities depends entirely on the given moment of history and cultural location of the subject. This is to say, few protagonists can actually leave home without having to resist the patriarchal authority figure, which, in turn, leads to a series of dramatic actions as they embrace feminist or queer agendas or both. The dynamics between identity and space configure home as a place of entrapment and confinement in Migdalia Cruz's *The Have-Little* and *Another Part of the House*. Cruz portrays home as a dead-end situation that paralyzes her characters, preventing them from developing their own agency in their gendered space of confined domesticity. Whether the setting is the South Bronx of 1976 or Cuba of 1895, Cruz locates the dramatic action between the four walls of the house and in the impossibility of leaving it. In Josefina López's play *Simply Maria, or The American Dream*, a young woman is offered the opportunity to leave home through the catalyst of an education. The empowerment she derives from that opportunity allows her to dismantle the patriarchal tradition of her family while simultaneously developing a sense of herself through a newly acquired feminist consciousness.

Gloria Anzaldúa's 1987 prophetic rendition of home, "carr[ied] . . . on my back" (21) like a turtle, resonates deeply with playwrights whose lesbianism simultaneously exiles them from a patriarchal domain while it provides them with an alternative home, shaped by the linkage between sexual identity and orientation. In this manner, Janis Astor del Valle's play *I'll Be Home para la Navidad* stages the return home of a lesbian protagonist who has come out to her family. Before initiating such a bold move as a return home, the playwright ensures that her protagonist has a home, albeit utopian at times, elsewhere. In other words, her marginality as a lesbian has already initiated her into the vicissitudes of inhabiting an alternate space. Indeed, reclaiming the lesbian body as home, a home exiled and excluded from dominant culture, entails a reterritorialization in these plays that can only be read as a political act.

For playwrights Silvia Gonzalez S. and Elaine Romero, whose Chicana roots delve deeply into their theatrical worlds, the concept of home is both allegorical and mythical. Gonzalez's play *Alicia in Wonder Tierra* occasions an encounter with history and identity with the assistance of the master narrative of Dorothy in *The Wizard of Oz*. A series of mythical and animated objects serve as her spiritual, cultural, and linguistic guides in her journey to the Aztec temple, the symbolic rendition of Aztlán. In Romero's *Walking Home,* home encompasses the whole geographic territory of Aztlán, across which her protagonist treks and where she confronts her history and its ghosts. In both of these works, the Chicana playwrights stage epiphanies as their protagonists come face to face with their ever-evolving Chicana concientización.

Home as Prison

The most uncomfortable notion of home that a spectator can encounter at the theater shows it as a place of such negativity that the most the transcultural subject can do is merely to learn coping strategies and survival techniques under the grimmest circumstances. Migdalia Cruz's character Lillian in *The Have-Little* inhabits a home whose contested space reveals the intricacies of her entrapment. Like so many characters in Latina plays, she—and her friend Michi—are girls on the verge of womanhood. In their South Bronx neighborhood, home is not merely a place; it must be a safe harbor from the chaotic and violent world outside. The fact that home is always "safe" masks the irony of the play, which is that this particular safe harbor is precisely what imprisons the characters. They express their desire and urge either to get as far away as possible or to make a home that is safe from the terrors of the ghetto. Lillian, like her mother before her, falls victim to a female passivity

I N T A R
Hispanic American Arts Center

Max Ferrá   *Eva Bruné*
Artistic Director   *Managing Director*

presents

The Have-little

written by
Migdalia Cruz

directed by
Nilo Cruz

May 29 - June 30, 1991

INTAR on Theatre Row
420 West 42nd Street NYC (212)695-6134

that leaves her pregnant as a teenager. At that young age, her future becomes circumscribed solely by motherhood and domesticity. Michi, Lillian's closest friend, sees herself as "somebody that's going somewhere" (*The Have-Little,* 1991 unpublished version, 48) precisely because she envisions a college education.

Because Lillian comes from a home where parental role models include domestic and substance abuse, her concept of home is akin to a broken dream. To compensate for that loss, she longs for an ideal, utopian space where she and her newborn son can be safe and happy, "a fine house" (48), "a house for me and him, so he don't have to walk around at night" (25). Her desire to relocate outside the barrio requires a new concept of space not conceived as an apartment, but as the ideal promoted by the American Dream, a middle-class house. As a single mother with little self-confidence and even less education, her prospects for upward mobility remain unpromising. As she imagines a new house and home, the possibility of her actually leaving the Bronx becomes ever more unattainable. The fact that home is either a prison or nonexistent leads her to fantasize about an ideal home far away from her current reality. As she imagines this new space, she acknowledges that the fantasy can in fact substitute for reality, just as it had for Don Quixote and Dorothy, her two literary models: "When I close my eyes, I can go somewhere. So I don't need to go nowheres, because it's all . . . in one place. It's my place. It's our place" (61). Obviously, Lillian lacks the resources that would lead to her own empowerment and agency, both of which would enable her to leave the barrio. Thus, like so many female protagonists throughout the history of literature whose entrapment has no solution, she takes refuge in her inner life, whose modes of fantasy offer her some control over her outer life.

Equally revealing of Lillian's remarks is the notion that a place called home may not exist at all. Although raw survival tactics motivate Lillian's actions, she is incapable of addressing larger issues of home in her conversations with Michi. This gap enables Michi to distance herself and to problematize the notion of home, specifically their South Bronx home. Even in the short span of their young lives, their neighborhood has been so drastically transformed that getting out becomes Michi's top priority:

---

12. Advertisement for Migdalia Cruz's *The Have-Little* at INTAR, New York City (1991). Photograph by James M. Kent. Advertisement courtesy of INTAR.

It's this place. It's dirt. It's like a place where people die. I passed by my old building the other day and it was gone. Just like that. Like we never played there. There was a pile of broken stone and glass where my house used to be. And the schoolyard's now a monument-making factory. Row after row of tombstones for sale. I bet it costs more to buy one there [than] any other place in America. People here are proud of their funerals. Gotta have a nice stone . . . it shows what your priorities are. Get the fuck out was my priority. And you should get out too. (57)

Michi's consciousness about home reveals that there is no longer a home possible in this particular space. Education has given her the perspective to distance herself from a place she calls "this dump" (23), the freedom to move on and imagine a new home for herself, unlike Lillian, whose imaginings are grounded in fantasy, dreams, and Disney. Lillian's displaced, misguided, and severely limiting notions discard Michi's hellish vision of the Bronx precisely because she does not possess Michi's survival instincts and tactics. Ultimately, then, in this apparent site of entrapment and imprisonment, Lillian's survival depends on the slim interstices where resistance resides. Despite no possibility of a college education for her, the play offers a hopeful outcome for Lillian in that she gains a sense of empowerment through motherhood, for her baby son's future interrupts the negative cycle where she feels entrapped.

If in *The Have-Little* the identity of the individual is determined by her location, confinement, and limitations, Cruz's *Another Part of the House,* a contemporary rendition of Lorca's classic tragedy, goes a step further. In this retelling of *The House of Bernarda Alba,* the action takes place during Cuba's War of Independence in 1895. Whereas Lorca repressed and silenced female voices as well as their inner passion, sexuality, and desire, Cruz unleashes them in her play. Bernarda's authority and control over her five daughters causes the house to implode with passion, drama, and the desire for jouissance from the youngest to the oldest members of her family. Like the characters of *The Have-Little,* these women are also entrapped within the four walls of the patriarchal house. Although the potential for transgression, rebellion, and, ultimately, liberation does not exist within the walls of the house, the protagonists create new physical and mental spaces in which to express their repressed sexuality. The best example is María Josefa, Bernarda's mother, whom Bernarda has consigned to the attic. Throughout the play, Cruz's strategy is to decenter the main characters of the original play while giving a freer rein to secondary ones. In this manner, Josefa becomes a central pro- tagonist and symbol of the play. Likewise, Poncia, the maid in the original, plays a more central role by revealing her love affair with el difunto (the deceased), Bernarda's dead husband, as well as by suggesting that she is Bernarda's half sister. These two characters betray Bernarda by carrying on illicit affairs with Bernarda's two now-deceased husbands. In so doing, they confront and wound Bernarda in the deepest possible way, thus contesting her despotism.

Cruz's title places the action in a specific location that decenters the house as solely Bernarda's. By relocating the dramatic action in "another part of the house," Cruz enables characters to speak the unspoken, to witness the unseen, to listen to the silences in Lorca's text from the vantage point of their own space. Underscoring Poncia's speech in the original, "Do you hear the silence? Well, there's a storm brewing in every room" (*Another Part of the House* 1) as an epigraph, Cruz encapsulates the internal dynamics, both social and spatial, of her own play. In this new version of Lorca, breaking that silence means liberation, freedom from taboos, and an explicit sexual desire. That silence, which in Hispanic culture is imposed by "el que dirán," speaks more loudly than the enforced abeyance to social mores. As the audience witnesses the most dramatic enactment of that code with the stoning of the young woman who has a child out of wedlock, it can also anticipate Adela's tragic ending for daring to express her sexuality. The enclosure that the house imposes on its inmates and that Bernarda demands of her daughters is meant to serve as a protection against the powerful tongues of el que dirán. In this way, the audience knows more than any of the characters because they/we witness the dialogic relationship between the domestic world of the house and what goes on outside of it. In this sense, space is articulated in given so- cial relations of power wherein individuals are consigned to their prescribed spaces within patriarchy and heteronormativity. Thus, we see that el que dirán regulates social action, moral behavior, and identity formation both inside and outside the house.

If this social code is the central paradigm and unifying structure of the work, its coordinates become desire, sexuality, and secrecy. Each character, whether her desire is present or past, harbors a secret that only one other member of the household—or the audience—shares. In almost all cases, these secrets are sexual actions that transgress the code of el que dirán and that therefore must be silenced and punished. Beginning with María Josefa, Ber- narda's mother, the secrets of the house abound. Having reached her eightieth birthday on the day the action takes place, she reviles the secrecy that has kept her imprisoned by her daughter. On the contrary, she takes pleasure in sexuality and advises her young granddaughter Adela to live and love openly. Ironically, her imagined lover, Pepe the lamb, happens to be Pepe el Romano, who is Angustias's betrothed, but Adela's lover. The model of rivalry, adultery, shamelessness, and transgression that María Josefa has established echoes in her legacy to her granddaughters.

As for Bernarda, her secret lies in her confession to her deceased husband's portrait that she never loved him. If she has been successful in camouflaging this truth, her final disclosure may be less private than she wishes. By announcing at the end of the play that her pregnant daughter Adela died a virgin, she reveals the extent to which el que dirán controls her thinking and the actions within her household. In a similar way, Poncia has also strayed from the rules by having an extramarital relationship with Bernarda's second husband, Antonio. At this point, the play alludes to Poncia's own genealogy: she is the illegitimate offspring of Bernarda's father and an Afro-Cuban woman, thus making her and Bernarda half sisters. Her biracial heritage reveals the extent to which el que dirán functions as the silencer of a colonial and mulatto/mestizo legacy. As if sibling rivalry and master-servant relations were not enough, Cruz delivers yet another scandalous liaison within the troubled household. Two of Bernarda's daughters, Amelia and Magdalena, explore their passions and satisfy their sexual desires in an incestuous lesbian relationship with each other. Under such drastic circumstances, Cruz reveals just how the power relations in a home are manifested within the norms of patriarchy, colonialism, and racism. Her protagonists discover a particular form of resistance that leads to new identity formations wherein desire, pleasure, and eros have a place.

Certain discursive commonalities develop between Cruz's two works that permit us to read them intertextually. In both, the playwright explores the world of women where the father is absent. If in *The Have-Little* the father's presence is tangential to the story line, in *Another Part of the House* the action takes place immediately following the father's death. In both plays, the women are constantly undoing the effects of a male presence on their lives. Bernarda supplants the patriarchal order by her own rule, equally or more repressive than the original. Lillian's boyfriend, like Pepe el Romano, demonstrates his male dominance as an intrusion. Lillian's early teenage pregnancy traps her into single motherhood and a future that parallels her own mother's life. In Adela's case, her secret affair with Pepe, which also

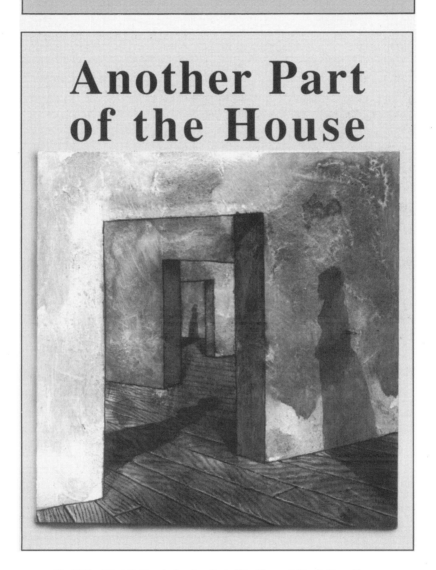

PLAYBILL®

CLASSIC STAGE COMPANY

Another Part of the House

13. Playbill for Migdalia Cruz's *Another Part of the House* at Classic Stage Company, New York City (1997). Used by permission of Playbill®. Playbill® is a registered trademark of Playbill, Inc. All rights reserved.

culminates in pregnancy, leaves her equally futureless at the moment that they are discovered. If in *The Have-Little* Michi is the only character to get out alive and with a college education, in *Another Part of the House* the only escape is death, the path both Adela and her grandmother choose. Nevertheless, such a choice underscores the fact that despite their imprisonment, these two characters exercise their own agency by choosing the only liberation available to them. Their intergenerational female bonding bypasses Bernarda's strict patriarchal rule, the representation of the law of the father. By allowing the Imaginary to rule, rather than the Symbolic Law of the Father, Cruz imbues her characters with an energy, liveliness, and subjectivity that demonstrate their creativity in their respective interstitial spaces.

Finding a way out of the house is the core of the essential dramatic action for the protagonists in both works. In this sense, it would seem that Lillian's imprisonment in early motherhood is a hopeless situation. Yet Cruz also allows her a space outside of the confines of the play by enacting her imagination with given master narratives of escapism. In contrast, Adela and María Josefa in *Another Part of the House* go beyond the official Lorquian tragic ending of the play by upstaging the final act. Audiences well schooled in Lorca find themselves surprised by an ending that is both celebratory and salvific, even in death. Cruz has found that alternative space outside the house where imagination, fantasy, and liberation reign. Once they leave the house behind, Adela and her grandmother speak from their new cosmic home. Whereas in real life the house is imploding with unfulfilled sexual desire, in their new incarnations Adela and María Josefa "taste a new beginning. One filled with light" (98). This new "house" is nothing short of the cosmos, a house with many rooms where the characters are "somebody different in every room" (98). This new space occupied by these two women registers Cruz's deep feminist agenda: in creating a women-only space, they redefine male absence by deauthorizing Bernarda's imposed patriarchal rule. When Adela inquires whether they will join her father, María Josefa emphatically replies that "Men and women don't go to the same place" (97). Escaping from patriarchy into a gender-specific space allows these women to place themselves with determination in a position of power.

In each of these examples of home as an apparent imprisonment with no way out, Cruz supplies an exit for her characters via education or fantasy or both. It is noteworthy that in neither play does she propose marriage as a viable solution for women. Although Angustias in *Another Part of the House* longs for marriage as her way out, the possibility of achieving it, given the laws of primogeniture and the customs of mourning, are slim indeed. If there is any escape, the women must effect it on their own. What becomes obvious is that home for each of these characters is much less a physical space than a state of mind: for Lillian, it's safety for her new baby; for Michi, it's an education; for Adela, it's sexual expression; and for María Josefa, it's the comfort of the ocean. In none of these cases do the characters conceive of home as a utopian or nostalgic space. Rather, because home is repression, imprisonment, ghetto, or "a dump," these characters must fashion their own home within their own psyches. Thus, when Adela declares, "We are to be prisoners in our own home!" (13), she contests the patrilineal, patriarchal dynamic that moves the action forward.

Desires for a new home, however, are not limited to Adela and María Josefa. Another sister, Magdalena, attributes her own liberation to Cuban patriotic hero José Martí, for he embodies the only possibility for a new revolutionary political system that advocates education and professions for women. If her sister and grandmother fantasize about sexuality, Magdalena's fantasies and dreams allow her to imagine herself as one of Martí's disciples. When Magdalena dreams of accompanying him to New York, Cruz not only sets in motion the politics of home and displacement, migration and colonialism, but also problematizes the issues of imperialism, independence, and nation building of the Caribbean diaspora. Cruz reveals her own Caribbean diasporic roots when Magdalena pronounces: "Maybe he'll take us to New York. That's where he does all his best writing" (25). Likewise, by placing Martí in the "face of the monster" (25), Cruz questions both *for* whom she and he are writing and *from* where they are writing. When we take into consideration that Cruz herself is a Nuyorican, we can see that she also regales Martí as the precursor of a U.S. Latina/o identity. At work here is the transcultural condition that the playwright projects in her reclaiming of Martí for Latina/o writers in the U.S.

◆　◆　◆

As we chart the imagery and conceptualization of home in Latina theater, Josefina López's play *Simply Maria, or The American Dream* (1992) offers a theatrical model in which the protagonist must leave home in order to construct her new feminist transcultural identity. Just like Michi *(The Have-Little),* who left home for a college education, Maria stumbles through the labyrinthine system of minority politics in order to procure a college scholarship for herself, despite her parents' protestations. The play, constructed through a series of vignettes that dramatize moments of her life, functions as a staged bildungsroman in that the protagonist experiences the rite of passage from childhood to womanhood, from the movements of migration to the illusory safety of home, from the pains and vicissitudes of her fractured sense of identity to a transcultural self-fashioning. What is at stake is not mere escape or dream or fantasy, but rather a negotiation through the political conscious-ness of being a Latina feminist. Maria must straddle and juggle the nonformal education and values learned at home with her budding feminist conscious-ness and destabilization of patriarchy, which is misinterpreted by her parents as her disdain of mexicanidad, indicated in her father's admonishment: "I don't want you to forget you're a Mexican. There are so many people where I work who deny they are Mexican. When their life gets better, they stop being Mexican! To deny one's country is to deny one's past, one's parents. How ungrateful!" (López, *Simply Maria,* 129).

Maria's need to break away from patriarchal law and house with all their attendant rules and regulations for codified gender behavior compels her to search for an identity that will accommodate both her mexicanidad and her feminism. Her father's conception of a woman's role is circumscribed by traditional gender behavior that for him is the essence of Mexicanness. Just as in Cruz's plays where home is a prison, the young daughter's future must be centered around the male figures of father, husband, and son. When Maria opts to study acting rather than obtain a husband, she not only transgresses her father's dictum, but also must endure his misogynist tirade about her choice of future profession: "I didn't know you had to study to be a whore" (129). Maria's father is not alone in his condemnation of a gringo lifestyle in which women talk back. In her submissive role as transmitter and perpetuator of traditional culture, Maria's mother echoes and promotes her father's confla-tion of gender roles with cultural models as she worries about the omnipre-sent el que dirán, musing, "It doesn't look right. ¿Qué van a decir?" (125).

While pursuing her education, Maria not only subverts her father's pa-triarchal horizon of expectations of her as the good little Mexican daughter, but also seeks and discovers a route to her own and her mother's liberation. Throughout the play, Maria's feminism contrasts with the passive role and compulsory heterosexuality that subjugates women. A series of dreams func-tions as an enabling learning tool that permits Lopez to parody, allegorize, and question gender roles in her culture. These visions consist of mini-actos, reminiscent of the agit-prop style of El Teatro Campesino.[3] The first vision, "The Making of a Mexican Girl," in which three angelic girls do an inventory of Maria's prescribed behavior, lists the obligations of marriage: "nice, forgiving, considerate, obedient, gentle, hard-working, gracious. [She] is to like dolls, kitchens, houses, cleaning, caring for children, cooking, laundry, dishes. [She] is not to be independent, enjoy sex, but must endure it as [her] duty to [her] husband, and bear his children" (119). Indeed, the ideological platform of the play confronts Mexican womanhood; Maria's cultural unconscious, imbued with feminism, satirizes the woman who conforms too easily. If her parents view themselves as strictly Mexican, their daughter knows herself to be a transcultural subject whose home is the borderlands. In her resistance to her parents, even her dreams are caught in the unconscious of these borderlands. Maria's sense of dislocation does not impede her from knowing that she is anchored in El Norte, however. Once again, the straddling of two cultures implies placing herself at the intersection of geography and ethnicity. She explains: "Mother, we are in America. Don't you realize you expect me to live in two worlds. How is it done?" (130).

In her negotiation of precisely "how it's done," we witness a subjectivity-in-process, a searching for a new cultural model that will permit her to give full rein and expression to her multiple transcultural self. The "American Dream" of the title is not a matter of total assimilation, as her parents fear, but rather an example of how she believes in the empowerment implicit in the proverbial American Dream. In her second vision, Maria's multiple identities (Maria, Maria 2, Mary) take shape to embody different philosophies or ways of seeing and doing. Maria 2 represents the Mexican superego who subscribes to the law of the father. Mary, on the other hand, materializes as the Anglo self who will liberate her as she undoes traditional gender scripts. Thus, the dramatic tension is set into action as Maria must discern which aspects of each model will serve her in her new transcultural positionality. The confrontation Mary poses is precisely the cultural dilemma of la transfrontera and the literature of resistance that it produces. The sexual, economic, and social independence that Mary promulgates requires Maria to challenge her parents' values. Not only that, the institutions of marriage and church come under special scrutiny in Maria's dreamworld. There, the presence of a priest at her mock wedding triggers the satire that forms the ideological crux of López's play: resistance. By conflating wedding, church, and social values, López's character gains enough agency to intervene in her own future. Such ceremonies are tantamount to an open refusal to participate in gender discrimination. The ultimate irony of this scene symbolizes the enslavement of women when Maria is given a golden dog collar in lieu of a wedding ring.

The purpose of the next dream, the soap opera "Happily Ever After," is to interrupt the rules and laws of primogeniture. In this vision, a soap opera star anchors a woman's fixity in the home-as-prison, where she can function only within the reproductive confines of "receptacle" and producer of male off-spring. In the next dream, "The Reproducing Machine," the audience begins to witness subversion and resistance as the actress produces three girl children whose names are Sacrifice, Abnegation, and Frustration. We are here re-minded of Bernarda's daughters' names: Angustias and Martirio (Affliction and Martyrdom). Women cannot control the laws of primogeniture or even the genetic odds of producing male or female offspring, so the playwright López satirizes the patriarchal code by gendering each of the three children as female. The final dream, a nightmare, conflates the cultural icons of the Aztec calendar and a tortilla into one giant symbol of oppression that requires Maria to stand up for herself. As the dream progresses, Maria finds herself in a situation where the only possible solution is transgression and rebellion, claiming, "I hate all housework because it offends me as a woman! This is not the life I want to live; I want more" (137–38). Such remarks cannot be uttered with impunity, and as a result of them she is taken to trial for subver-sion. The role of the prosecutor in this dream is central to the action and the ideological platform of the play because it reinstalls man as a "king of his castle" (139) and reinscribes home as a prison for woman. At the end of the trial, Maria is found guilty, with her father as a witness for the prosecution contributing to her conviction: "She was very obedient when she was young, but when she came to the United States, she began to think of herself as 'American'" (139).

Such a statement brings the play full circle in the negotiation of trans-cultural identity and feminist practices. If Maria's dreams resist, satirize, de-construct, parody, and undo questions of identity, by the play's end she will be required to take the necessary steps to build a new subjectivity. It is here that the play's somewhat awkward title gains currency. If we analyze each part of the equation, *Simply Maria, or The American Dream* on its own, we begin to see the tools of the protagonist's process of identity construction. "Simply Maria" is López's English translation of the title of the famous Latin American soap opera *Simplemente María,* which presents a cultural model of woman-hood that keeps women fettered to patriarchal law and that Maria's parents prefer. "The American Dream" is at least a double entendre as a political project that intersects a personalized feminist agenda in Maria's own dream life. Maria's liberation is not limited only to her own future, but rather encompasses her mother's tolerance of her husband's womanizing. In this sense, she joins the protagonists of other plays by Latinas, such as *Botánica, Real Women Have Curves,* and *The Fat-Free Chicana and the Snow Cap Queen,* where a younger generation finds a strategy that liberates an older generation of women as well. Furthermore, these protagonists are en route to abandoning the patriarchal confines of their parents' homeland and to carving out a transcultural space of their own.

Maria's decision to leave home, pursue an education, seek adventure, and think freely derives from many factors, not least of which is her parents' angry confrontation with each other the previous night. The play closes with Maria's farewell letter to her parents in which she constructs and delivers her transcultural message: "I want to create a world of my own. One that combines the best of me. I won't forget the values of my roots, but I want to get the best from this land of opportunities. I am going to college and I will struggle to do something with my life. You taught me everything I needed to know. Goodbye" (140–41). The three Marias, whose fleeting appearances throughout the play signal the protagonist's transformation, serve as a reminder that identity is indeed not fixed, monolithic, or immobile. Neither is home, nor is any *one* location. If at the beginning they promoted passivity and submission, at the end they represent Maria's plural selves: they are bilingual and bicultural. "Nunca los olvidaré" ("I will never forget you"); "Mexico is in my blood"; "America is in my heart" (141). As Maria utters these final words, she galvanizes the dialectical process that constitutes her multiple identity. Literally standing in the borderlands with one metaphorical foot in each culture, Maria signals the process of identity construction that both begins and ends with her transnational home.

The Lesbian Body and Home

If *Simply Maria* center stages the process of leaving home, Janis Astor del Valle's *I'll Be Home para la Navidad* represents the circuitous path of returning home. Here, homecoming is intricately linked to the formation of a lesbian identity that affects the traditional family dynamic, where homophobia is still an acceptable social practice. Thus, in this play, unlike in the previous ones, where most of the characters cannot leave home, the protagonist, Cookie, has already left, giving her the opportunity to construct an imagined Latina lesbian community. Now the central paradigm is a new set of values and alternative ways of seeing that revolve around respect, tolerance, and dignity. Being away from home has enabled the protagonist to explore her sexuality, to overcome fear of rejection, to come out, and to return home to challenge and negotiate homophobia within the family. Implicit is the understanding that the process of declaring sexual orientation or preference would have been impossible had she remained "home." In her imagined lesbian community, the protagonist embraces both Latino family values *and* her radical, transgressive sexuality, all of which constitute her constant interaction in and straddling of Latino and Anglo cultures. The articulation of Cookie's lesbian subjectivity-in-process, although central to the work, is not a crisis, but rather a given and a point of departure. As a result, the play does not center on the trauma of discovering one's gayness or coming out to one's family. Although sexuality is one of the discursive coordinates of the play, other issues such as racism, ethnicity, class, and transnational identity intersect in the development of the dramatic action, revealing Cookie's concientización.

I'll Be Home para la Navidad places the characters at the Christmas table in a series of exchanges in which the mounting tension between them comes to a crescendo at the moment the meal is served. The fact that the protagonist has already established a secondary home that includes a large, "chosen" gay and lesbian extended family (Weston 1991) permits her to question the patriarchal values, homophobia, and prejudices of her original home. Her bold actions are met with shock and scandal as she blatantly disregards el que dirán cherished by her parents. Having an alternative space with a chosen family provides Cookie with a space of safety, comfort, and honesty. Thus, honoring her "incumbency of space" (Douglas 1991:305) positions her so that she can incorporate her new sexual transcultural identity within her past, her puertorriqueñidad, her familia de origen, and her racial consciousness. Thus, in the deepest sense, this is a play of resistance and subversion.

The title of Astor del Valle's *I'll Be Home para la Navidad* inscribes the protagonist's bilingual and bicultural condition. The pronoun *I* defines the subjectivity of its protagonist, and the future tense projects her subject position both in space and in time. That she hovers in a present that is "not home" indicates a past in which leaving home was part of the process of sexual identity formation. Implicit in her future declaration is also her agency in an announcement that will allow her family time to adjust to the fact that "I" is really "we" and "home" is really "out." In other words, the title could be translated to "We'll Be Out for Christmas." In her family's cultural and ethnic system of values, Cookie has selected the most significant religious and cultural holiday of the year at which to perform her lesbian identity. In this sense, the title contains all the elements of the plot, which can be summarized as: a Puerto Rican lesbian introduces her (black) lover to her upwardly mobile family in Connecticut during Christmas. The dramatic action that ensues revolves around the reactions she receives from the various members of her family, who, with their presence, must confront their worst fears: blackness and queerness have invaded their home and their family history.

Although the play's ostensible theme is a comment on homophobia, its opening lines introduce the hydra head of racism. As the protagonist, Cookie, describes her girlfriend to her mother, the playwright center-stages a spectrum of blackness that contains models from Anglo, Caribbean, and U.S. Latino cultures, thereby registering the playwright's deep commitment to trans-cultural, liberatory identities. As the conversation unfolds, a chain reaction of expectations, stereotypes, and prejudices marks the flow of the dialogue. For this reason, it is crucial to unpack the underlying racism that reveals itself in the subtext:

MAMI: Which friend is this? The one you met at school?
COOKIE: Lena. We met in dance class.
MAMI: How do you spell it?
COOKIE: L-e-n-a!
MAMI: Oh, like Lena Horne.
COOKIE: Yes, except—
MAMI: That's a black name.
COOKIE: Ma! Anyhow, it's pronounced Ley-nuh! Short for Magdalena.
MAMI: Oh. She's Spanish?
COOKIE: Half—her mother's Dominicana, her father's black.
MAMI: He's a black Dominicano?
COOKIE: No, he's black African American.
MAMI: What is your friend?
COOKIE: I just told you!
MAMI: No, I mean, is she—tú sabes?
COOKIE: What?
MAMI: Morena o negra?
COOKIE: She's about as dark as Titi Luisa.
MAMI: Your father's sister?
COOKIE: No, your sister.
MAMI: That's dark.
COOKIE: Mira, mami, don't start—

MAMI:	Who's starting what? I'm not starting nothing! Where did you put the green peppers? All I said was she must be pretty dark.
COOKIE:	I can't believe you! (motioning) In the fridge, by the carrots. Who were you engaged to before Papi?
MAMI:	Miguel Gonzalez.
COOKIE:	And he passed for black.
MAMI:	But he wasn't black. His mother was Puertorriqueña and his father was Dominicano—or was it the other way around? Anyway, he was dark, but he wasn't black. (*I'll Be Home,* 1993 unpublished version, 2–4)

In this swift-moving yet comfortable conversation between mother and daughter, the name *Lena* serves as a signifier that unleashes a chain reaction depending on whether it is pronounced "Ley-nuh" (Spanish) or "Lee-nuh" (English). Indeed, the language factor is more than merely casual, for it reveals the mother's degree of assimilation (she insists on the English pronunciation) and the daughter's reversal of that position, indicated by her acts of decolonization and reterritorialization, as we see as the play progresses. If the conversation is initially a casual misreading of the mother's understanding of Cookie's girlfriend's name, once Cookie explains Magdalena's heritage, her mother immediately activates the racist fears that sent her to the suburbs in the first place. As Cookie equates her girlfriend's color to her own aunt's color, she reveals the racial heterogeneity, the plurality of pigmentation, and the classification of blackness in the Caribbean. Cookie's insistence on establishing a new Caribbean identity that reclaims and refuses to deny its black and indigenous roots places the mother's remarks within a racist and nationalist ideological framework. The shifting paradigms of the mother's idealized identity manifest themselves as she invents colors and races for the people in her life, according to her affect. Furthermore, the mother's insistence on differentiating between "moreno" and "negro" (dark and black), "dominicano" and African American, shows how these classifications function on a national level of categorizing the racial other or attempting deracination. For the mother, race is not defined by race per se; rather, her remarks reveal how nationality and ethnicity are, for her, racialized.

For Cookie, her mother's concept of Puerto Ricanness is antiquated, essentializing, and anachronistic. Her mother's failure to recognize the inherent racial component of Puerto Ricans signals the practices of amnesia and denial. For example, the mother indicates that *Puerto Rican* is a category of its own based solely on a nationalist agenda. For Cookie, however, reconciliation with a mixed racial past helps her to negotiate her new transcultural Latina self, a process through which she also must deal with constructs of race, sexuality, and class. If on the island identity is simply "Puerto Rican," once Cookie's parents migrate to the mainland, they and all Puerto Ricans are categorized by race alone and consequently as a minority. What is essentialized after migration causes a series of confrontations and dislocations in which the Puerto Rican national imagined community no longer remains in a fixed position in the U.S. As Cookie explains to her mother that "We've got black blood in us. All Puerto Ricans do!" (4), she exemplifies the ways in which race and ethnicity are conflated. In this bold act of contestation and in her desire to reinvent herself as a new Latina conscious of her ethnic and cultural heritage, Cookie may be overlooking the fact that there are indeed Puerto Rican families who have "protected" their whiteness. Cookie understands the process of transculturation as a racial mélange. But more importantly, she demonstrates the politics of affinity of a new Latina consciousness. Furthermore, by adding that all Puerto Ricans have Taíno roots, she firmly and squarely places her ethnic identity at the crossroads of the races that have composed the island's populations, no matter how mythical those origins may be. In this regard, her political act of renaming herself as a member of a culturally and racially mixed group resembles the acts of naming that we have come to associate with the Chicana works of Gloria Anzaldúa, Cherríe Moraga, and Ana Castillo.

In the same way that Cookie must instruct her mother on issues of race, so, too, must she guide her on questions of sexuality. As they wade their way through the mother's conservative politics and religious background, Cookie learns that her mother trivializes her sexuality as an issue of "lifestyle" (7) or even sinfulness (8). Whatever her mother's objections, Cookie manages to return the discussion to an issue of autonomy, self-affirmation, and defiant resistance to heteronormativity. For the mother, however, Cookie's sexuality is a "disease" that could have been "cured" if only they had taken her to a doctor at an earlier time. Implicit in her mother's remarks is the ideological stance of the political and religious right as well as the class privilege that reveals that visits to psychiatrists would have been within their economic means.

Without a doubt, this opening scene stages the political and cultural dislocations between the various members and generations of Cookie's family. As the action unfolds, all of the previous confrontations erupt into a full-scale crisis during the meal. But before that happens, Janis Astor del Valle gives all the characters the opportunity to express themselves in all their prejudices, phobias, absurdities, and accommodations. And her sassy protagonist has an answer for every single objection that the family can invent. In this process of exchanges, accusations, and partial reconciliation, a new politics of identity emerges up to the point that the whole concept of familia and home undergoes assessment and redefinition.

Cookie's reason for returning home for the most symbolic day of the year entails her desire to be part of her family of origin as well as to incorporate her new alternative familia into the picture. The thesis of the play revolves, then, on the integration of this new familia-in-process with her parents' concept of familia. As Cookie and her mother take inventory of Cookie's previous girlfriends' visits to the family home, both mother and daughter reveal their diverging concepts of familia. For the mother, Cookie's failure to disclose the true nature of their relationship was a betrayal. After all, she took each one into the house as familia (9). Yet, for Cookie, there is no contradiction here: each one of these girlfriends *was* familia to her. In this manner, Cookie's sense of family expands and includes both her girlfriend and those members of her community who accept her for who she is. Cookie's self-assurance provides her with the ready answers to confront her mother and family with an ultimatum: either they accept her girlfriend, or she and her girlfriend will leave and spend the holiday in the city, at their own home.

The mother's outrage at the threatened abandonment of the family is matched only by Cookie's assertion that Lena is indeed her familia (13). The redefinition and new constituency of familia at work here echoes Cherríe Moraga's notion of making "familia from scratch" (1986b:58). Once the protagonist puts into practice the "specific histories of oppression and resistance" (Martin and Mohanty 1986:196), she acquires the agency to make her own familia and home, independent of her parents. Her education has not only given her the retorts to her mother's protestations, but also presumably the means by which to establish her own home, to earn her own living, and indeed to question the values with which she was raised.

Cookie's mother's instruction and consequential bonding with her daughter on issues of sexuality take place in the privacy of the kitchen, but the education of the other members of her family defines the subsequent action of the play. Of all of them, her father and brother show the greatest resistance to and abhorrence of lesbianism. Repeatedly, members of the family sidestep the father's machismo, racism, and homophobia. When he is confronted with the relationships that each of his children brings to the Christmas table, for him the most problematic one is Cookie's, the lesbian. Her sister Yolanda's erring, gambling, and womanizing husband is welcomed into the family without hesitation. The same applies to their brother, Hector, who, unlike Cookie, did not need to ask his father's permission to invite *his* girlfriend home for the holiday. In Cookie's case, however, permission, negotiations, and cajoling play an important role in the act of bringing her girlfriend home. Not only does the father feel his masculinity threatened by a homosexual daughter, but he increases his comfort level by attributing his wife's family with genetically transmitting the "disease" to Cookie through Luisa Vazquez, his wife's sister. Now that he has outed Titi Luisa and, in so doing, revealed his undisguised machismo and homophobia, he is unprepared for the by-product of this confrontation, which is that his wife sides with Cookie, claiming that their home is also hers. As the mother becomes more empowered, the figure of the father becomes more absurd, just as we have seen in other plays.

Although Cookie is willing to come out, she is still careful about how to perform her lesbianism in front of her family. For this reason, the moment Magdalena gets off the train, Cookie entreats her to remember that they are not alone and not at home. Although Magdalena's family embraces her sexual choices, Cookie's is still learning to deal with the news of her lesbianism. Lena's activism and lesbianism are contrasted with Cookie's desire to meet her family "half way" (6). Thus, although Cookie's lesbianism is a shock and affront to the family, Cookie's politics seem tame and conciliatory when contrasted with Lena's. This positioning places Cookie's identity at the borders and periphery of sexuality and ethnicity. Thus, as she negotiates her way through the paradigms of her new Latina transcultural identity, she is forging a path for herself and her new familia.

As the play develops, race and sexuality are continually offered to the family on the same platter. Each member of the family must react to the series of scenes set before them. The presence of the two "outsiders" continually activates and circulates the issues center-staged in the first scene of the play: Who is white? Who is black? Who is Puerto Rican? Who is Dominican? Who is African American? Who is Indian? Who is lesbian? The family's implicit and explicit racism is superseded only by their less than implicit homophobia. If the meeting between Yolanda and Lena produces hostility, another scene takes place when Cookie meets Kathleen, her brother's girlfriend, with whom, it turns out, Cookie attended school. Now it is Hector's turn to become hysterical when he learns that Cookie and Kathleen experimented with lesbian sexuality in middle school. His blatant homophobia is registered in his line, "Fuckin' dykes!" (2). As Cookie later recounts the episode to Magdalena, she explains how and why race and sexuality converge for her. As the only two girls of color in a white school, the bond that Cookie and Kathleen forged reveals a budding politics of racial affinity that transcended sexuality but also placed them within a lesbian continuum.

At the disastrous family meal that ensues, all previous hostilities and animosities find a place at the Christmas table. Once again, Madgalena's racial heritage is questioned, affirmed, denied, or erased depending on the speaker addressing her. Significantly, though, it is the mother who has processed the term *Latina* as a newly claimed identity. In doing so, she bonds totally with her daughter's generation and new politics of representation, identity, and home. The clearest indication of the mother's understanding of her daughter occurs when she leaves her safe Connecticut home, following her disgruntled daughter, who abruptly leaves the table. As the mother trudges her way to Washington Heights, she not only celebrates the holiday with her daughter and her daughter's familia, but she also challenges and resists some of the effects of her husband's homophobia and racism at the meal.

Once back in their own apartment, Cookie and Magdalena analyze the day's events as they affirm their need for truthfulness. That truthfulness entails not living a lie, being free to touch each other, not living by the rules imposed by a homophobic establishment. In this way, they establish the primacy of their own home as the real home. It is in this space where the multiple coordinates of identity may flourish. First, as they claim their home as their own space, they are being truthful to themselves. Second, that their home is located in Washington Heights circumscribes its ethnic component as a barrio dominicano, including its class signifiers. Third, the fact that they choose a Dominican neighborhood in which to enact their new Latina lesbian identity points to the extent to which sexuality, race, and ethnicity conflate in the play. Fourth, as Cookie's mother comes to terms with her daughter's new life choices, she also unsilences the paths of migration that she herself followed, paths that led her from Puerto Rico, to Harlem, to Connecticut. If the mother's choices tried to whiten the family history at each stopping point in their ascendance and assimilation, the daughter's process is just the reverse. Here, Latina subjectivity has as its foundation a racialized space where its inhabitants learn to juggle multiple identities. As they uncover and unravel family and national histories, they embrace all the components of their Latina transcultural positioning manifested in given relations of power both within the home and within the society at large.

For all of these reasons, the concept of home in *I'll Be Home para la Navidad* is a floating signifier, for the family home can no longer be home for the protagonist. As she disengages from the ravages of the family meal and from the verbal abuse of certain members of her family, she reestablishes her own alternative home in the city. That her entire family except her father joins her there at the end of the play shows the extent to which they have accepted her new life. At this point, where the dramatic conflict comes to its conclusion, we must reread the title of the play. If in the beginning it means that Cookie will be at her parent's home for Christmas, at the end it means that she has effected a complete reversal in that home is now her own apartment with Magdalena, her lover. Likewise, the title encodes another level of signification when we consider that the father is the only member of the family to stay home. For his intolerance and intransigence, his title of the play might be "I'll Be Home (Alone) para la Navidad." Yet, as all the other members of her family join Cookie and Magdalena for an ad hoc Christmas meal, they share a new operative model of family, which undoes traditional performances of ethnicity, race, and queer identity.

Home as Myth and Allegory

In Chicana theater, the construction of a mythical and allegorical home entails a deep engagement with history, which in exchange is used to create a future full of potentiality and agency, enabling the edification of a transcultural home. Both home and identity are determined by a sophisticated negotiation of cultural memory and utopian desire. Two plays, *Alice in Wonder Tierra* and *Walking Home,* stage a journey back home that centers on the protagonists' recovery of a historical, ethnic, and cultural past. In the unfolding of this personal odyssey, a double narrative emerges. The first narrative deals with the trials and tribulations of constructing and articulating a transcultural identity. The second narrative frames that cultural identity within the mythical and allegorical narrative of Aztlán, moving the personal experience into the collective cultural imaginary, while at the same time connecting the deterritorialized home of the familia to the utopian home of la raza. In this way, reterritorialization makes possible the momentary landing of Chicana/o transcultural subjects within the mythical realm of Aztlán.

Alicia in Wonder Tierra by Silvia Gonzalez S. takes place in various rooms of a Mexican curio shop, each of which serves a specific function in the play. While Alicia visits the store with her mother, her ignorance of Mexican culture, the Spanish language, and her own ethnic history collides with the icons exhibited in the front room of the shop. These artifacts have no meaning or value for Alicia, who lacks the tools to differentiate between them and the purposes they serve. She comments: "There's nothing here from the mall. Aztec instruments, a new flamenco comb, here are Mexican dolls. It looks like a village on this counter. Useless stuff" (1996 published version, 3). Her remarks reveal not only the degree to which Alicia is deterritorialized from her own culture but also the extent of her assimilation into Anglo consumerism. As the plot develops, she must unlearn Anglo hegemonic culture seeped in capitalism in order to recover and reclaim the value system of her Mexican ancestors. That process of reterritorialization constitutes a journey that begins in the back room of the curio shop, where, according to the shopkeeper, the "magia" resides. Once Alicia enters this magical, liminal domain, she begins a rite of passage; her separation from Anglo social reality permits her to reenter her own transcultural space.

The play begins with Alicia's specific questions about the pottery in the back room of the shop and her desire to meet the "pottery maker." She initiates her journey with an accident: tripping and stumbling over pottery and crashing it to the ground transport her to a magical realm of unconsciousness. Ironically, it is the master narratives of the dominant culture, specifically *Alice in Wonderland* and *The Wizard of Oz,* that place her in the suspended realm of liminality. At work here is not only assimilation and amnesia, but also her adoption and adaptation of that master narrative in order to configure her own hybrid history. As we have seen in previous chapters, it is precisely the role of transculturation that permits this process to take place. In contrast to Lillian in *The Have-Little,* who uses these narratives as a form of escape or utopian location, Alicia employs those dominant discourses to find a new way home. Lacking a narrative of her own reveals itself in the play as her inability to speak Spanish and her ignorance of Mexican/Chicano history.

It is no wonder, then, that her first confrontations in this journey relate to these two absences in her life. Just as we have seen many protagonists negotiate their way in unknown territory, Alicia, too, embarks on just such a journey. She enlists the assistance of various characters along the way, which is a common element in folkloric tales; these magical helpers—the Mexican doll, the sugar skull, the puppet, the horny toad, and the pottery maker—serve as culture guides for Alicia. Although they appear to be a fragmented representation of Chicano culture, in fact their presence gives body to a mythical narrative essential to identity formation. Because they are always in a partial relationship with the mother tongue and the culture, they function mainly through synecdoche. Undoubtedly, "partial" representations are often viewed as incomplete, fragmented, schizophrenic, and confusing by those who claim a monolithic national identity. For transcultural subjects such as Alicia, just the opposite is true. Instead of an incomplete identity, she finds logic and truth in the synecdoches that represent the Other. In this way, Alicia deauthorizes and dismantles dominant stereotypical images of Chicano culture such as the piñata, the cactus, and the mariachis that adorn the front room of the shop, making visible what was once *in*visible. The magical helpers serve as the agents who remove la cultura from its position in "cold storage" and marginality.

During each stage of the journey, these mythical protagonists provide riddles for Alicia to answer or obstacles for her to overcome. The Elvira sisters, for example, are a mocking group that continually attempt to strip Alicia of any sign of cultural identity. Alicia's rite of initiation takes the form of challenging, ontological questions designed to heighten her awareness. Taunting remarks such as "where are you from, and what is your sense of history?" (12) operate as directives to push her along her way closer to a decolonized, transcultural self. But the puppet who serves as Alicia's guide informs her that only the Aztec temple will provide her with the proper answers. The issue is not only defining a transcultural identity, but also creating a new transculturated memory. Doing so, Alicia could recover the symbolization of such formidable cultural icons as the sugar skull, the cultural performances of such holidays as the Day of the Dead, and the instructive legacy of her grandmother. As she enters the "Distorted Memory Forest" (18), where "memory becomes real, but in a stranger way" (18), Alicia begins her recollection of the culinary traditions of her childhood that will give the play its subtitle, *I Can't Eat Goat Head.* As one of her father's favorite foods, the goat head symbolizes full integration into Mexican culture in the play. In refusing to eat it, Alicia stages her own agency and willingness to negotiate with her past, forging a future that she alone constructs. In validating this past, though, she simultaneously triggers a transculturated memory that serves her own purpose as well as the audience's.

No process of constructing a new transcultural future, which consists of learning and mythologizing Chicano culture, can take place without the simultaneous act of decolonizing and deconstructing assimilation. In the play, Alicia must decode the meanings of such stereotypes as "[the heads of] Pancho Villa, a mambo king, a pachuco, Charo, and a Hispanic Yuppie" (20), all of whom perpetuate one-dimensional images of Latinas/os in the U.S. She must learn to distinguish between the stereotypes and cultura, no small task for this second-generation Chicana whose parents thought they would protect her against discrimination by *not* teaching her Spanish. So extensive is her alienation from her own culture and so intense is her hunger for it that she even appropriates the tourist-driven velvet paintings of Tijuana as legitimate representations of Mexican art. The fact that Tijuana plays so largely in the plot indicates the extent to which Alicia is unable to distinguish between Mexican culture, U.S.–imposed commodification of stereotypes of Mexican culture, and a new paradigm of transcultural, transnational border identity. It is only within the interstices of these multiple cultural locations that Alicia is able to engage in the discursive heterogeneity of transcultural straddlers.

The closer Alicia and her helpers get to the Aztec temple, the more urgent her education becomes. The puppet concentrates seriously on teaching Alicia to roll her Rs (41) and to learn Spanish (42), and he is most particularly outraged by her lack of historical knowledge. Entrance to the temple itself signifies entering history, which is synonymous with entering cultura. Alicia's first lesson consists of a revision of the plundering hands of the conquest and subsequent colonization of Mexico: "If you're from Spain, you better keep your hands in your pockets. I remember the last time. Who was that guy? Oh, yeah, called himself Cortez" (47). Having lost their treasures once, the inhabitants of *this* Aztec temple practice caution against dispossession by the greedy impulses of imperialism. Implicit here is the determination that an Aztec identity and, by extension, a Chicana/o identity condemns any further invasions, exploitation, or pillaging. The new Aztlán can be accessed only through a "decolonization" of the mind so that the reterritorialization processes may be set into motion.

As Alicia's rite of passage continues within the chambers of the temple, she meets souls waiting for deliverance. Such an encounter reflects the liminal condition that those souls inhabit while it also reveals Alicia's own liminality. As part of her initiation into a Latina identity—that is, a transfrontera identity—Alicia must solve the riddles placed before her by the puppet, the foremost of which is: "What is always better when it is broken?" (53). The fact that she answers correctly, "a piñata," indicates that she retains some vestiges of cultural memory despite her Anglofication. Ashamed not to know her cultura, she excuses her ignorance in spite of having solved this difficult riddle: "There's so much to know. I see the tradition, but from afar. It is not mine, but it is. I'm expected to know the meaning of everything because of who I am. But I don't know. I have to look it up like every one else" (53). As the correct answer qualifies her to continue on her mission to meet the pottery maker, her quest resumes. All along the way, her immersion into cultura consists of fundamental ethnic determinants such as music, food, icons, myth, genealogy, cultural heroes, and language. They also become the tools and building blocks to edify and reclaim her Latinidad and her specific ethnic transcultural positioning.

Alicia's quest, like many typical folktales, not only entails guides and helpers, but also enemies and obstacles. Such is the function of the Elviras in this play. If at the beginning the Elviras taunted her with labels such as "coconut, wetback, gringa, Mexican-American, Latina, Chicana, pocha" (8), at the conclusion they are no longer capable of intimidating her or of erasing her Mexican roots. Alicia's self-confidence and self-affirmation after the trip indicate the level at which her identity has undergone a transformation through the initiation process. At the beginning of the play, she has no knowledge of her ancestral homeland and what it might mean to her, but by the end she is a bilingual, bicultural daughter of Aztlán. Now, in order to return home, Alicia revisits the cultural sites of her past and her childhood, sites that map cultural locations: a forest of mangoes, piñata land, tortilla garden, church, pinto bean garden, coffee bean farm, Spanish Echo tunnel (75). In this final encounter, the puppet reminds her: "You know who you are" (77). With these words, Alicia returns home with a new transculturated memory that facilitates her awareness of who she is and the role she can play. The part of herself that was denied now surges forward as she responds: "I always knew, but I never really wanted to acknowledge it" (77).

Once she has reincorporated herself into reality, the audience can see how the allegorical journey functions as a pretext. The equation of broken pottery and fragmented identity is only too visible to audiences whose own bilingual and bicultural experiences mirror Alicia's. Her guilt complex, which in the beginning of the play registers a sense of inadequacy and failure, disappears by the end of the play as she achieves a sense of her self, regardless of how multiple, dispersed, porous, and heterogeneous her identity is. Not only that but her new mestiza consciousness locates her in relation to other ways of constructing and articulating identity in all its difference and even contradiction. In these terms, the moral of the play is consolidated in the following didactic lesson contained in the phrase that compares identity with Mexican blankets: "See how no two Mexican blankets are the same? That's like all of us. We are all like one another, but we have our differences. And that's what makes it beautiful. So why run away. You only run into yourself" (76). At this point, Alicia concludes the rite of passage by incorporating her new mestiza self into a decolonized, geopolitical space.

What was a mass of disconnected objects strewn around the shop without any meaning are at the closing connected by a cultural thread. As the play moves from allegory to reality in its final remarks, Alicia's awakening is both literal and metaphoric because she has now learned to recognize and utilize all the items of her cultura and history. This new Alicia awakens giving a bilingual account of her new appreciation and understanding of her experience: "I was lost but then I found my way" (78). The "way" that she has found is, of course, a way back home. Equipped now with cultura, she understands that there is no place like home because home *is* culture, memory, and history. After visiting the heart of Aztlán, Alicia has a new sense of place, identity, and be(long)ing. A mutual exchange has taken place: as she searches for her cultura, the locational identity of Aztlán empowers her and places her in the much-desired home that the name implies. Finally, instead of succumbing to the "geography of power" (Massey 1994:161) implicit in global border arrangements such as the North American Free Trade Agreement, Alicia, in an innovative and creative negotiation, discovers that ethnic memory is the key to realizing a new transnational self.

The geography of Aztlán also dominates and gives meaning to the locational identity of Elaine Romero's *Walking Home,* a play whose coordinates of "home" once again include memory, myth, and allegory. The title inscribes the protagonist's process of returning home and finding her way both literally and figuratively as she wanders through the border states. After a suicide attempt, the protagonist, Maria, enters a mythical world inhabited by lost souls like herself. Entering this liminal space, which traverses the entire length of Aztlán and again stages a rite of passage as in *Alicia in Wonder Tierra,* she, like Alicia, must chart a new geography of the Southwest in order to construct *her* transfrontera identity. In *Alicia in Wonder Tierra,* the helpers and guides are allegorical figures, and here the main assistant, Woman in the Sand, a mythical and timeless Chicana mentor and guide, initiates Maria into transculturation by introducing her to a collectivity of women, all of whom represent a different historical moment of Chicana identity.

Liminality functions in the play on various levels. Geographically, the action takes place at the border. Maria concretely travels through each border state in a westward direction, the liminal site par excellence, the blurred and hybrid contact zone of "doublings and redoublings" (Gupta and Ferguson

1992:10). The border also embodies the space between life and death, a mythical place, the between-and-betwixt condition of transcultural identities. Most importantly, the play concretizes a space between the homeless condition of Woman in the Sand and the path Maria must follow if she is to find her way and a place called home. In this way, location not only informs identity but also defines its parameters. This gendered, liminal border space where Maria encounters Woman in the Sand and other spirits is constituted through these characters who straddle present and past, myth and reality, life and death in a movement that once again has the politics of identity functioning dialectically with the politics of location, each mutually dependent on the other. For this reason, Woman in the Sand returns from the dead at a moment when Maria, representative of her entire generation, experiences the crisis of cultural transition: a time when suicide looks better than attempts to articulate an identity, which until then meant wandering aimlessly through that space. Once Maria enters this interstitial state in dialogue with Woman in the Sand, she activates her cultural memory, which in turn permits her to begin her existentialist and ontological journey. At the completion of the rite of passage, this mythical wandering will empower Maria to such a degree that suicide is no longer the only alternative: instead of walking into homelessness and death, she reverses the process by walking into Aztlán or by "walking home." In this sense, walking functions as a metaphor for becoming; each step takes her closer to her goal of reimagining her Self and reterritorializing its historical connection with the land.

The close of the play could not take place without the deep underpinnings of a Chicana feminist consciousness. Maria does not walk alone through history. Rather, the apparition of key historical women to accompany her is central to the play's thesis. Woman in the Sand, Maria's main helper, assists her in the construction of her Chicanidad. Woman in the Sand's mythical proportions thus enable Maria to enter history, displacing amnesia and oblivion with ethnic and geographic memory and its infinitesimal cultural archives. Under these circumstances, women who were once anonymous in the pages of official history, both in Anglo and Chicano versions, contest male-centered spaces and thus rewrite and decenter the historical process. This political intervention transgresses and subverts a more traditional view of Aztlán. Now that women have genderized that Chicano space and have thereby given themselves legitimacy, they gain agency and historical depth. The first woman Maria encounters, Señora Flores, feels so strongly about her Mexican citizenship that she prefers execution to forfeiting it.

14. Elaine Romero's *Walking Home* at Planet Earth Multi-Cultural Theatre, Phoenix, Arizona (1996). *Bottom, left to right:* Mary Kay Zeeb and Kim Baker Davis. *Top:* Anna Luera. Photograph by Molli Kellog Cirino.

This is quite a lesson for Maria, whose own citizenship is questioned and questionable in the occupied territory of Aztlán. Ironically, it is Señora Flores who tells Maria: "It takes courage to save your life" (*Walking Home,* 1996 unpublished version, 25). Her solution to save Maria is to listen to her heart. If men have constructed Western history through dualisms and binary oppositions of mind and body, theory and practice, reason and emotion, here a woman-centered history unhinges that official history by overlapping those dualisms. It is not coincidental in these terms that at the precise moment that Maria enters Aztlán, she is instructed to listen to the lessons of her own heart: that is to say, her own body speaks to her through sensory memory. Implicitly, as she searches for her heart in a mythical, paradigmatic journey like that in *The Wizard of Oz,* she unveils the transcultural process through her act of reterritorialization. Romero appropriates the master narrative of Anglo dominant culture, relocating Maria within a Chicana geography and discursive domain. What is more important is that her repositioning establishes a dual track in which race and ethnicity are both the catalyst and the final product: on the one hand, that process empowers her to write her own history of decolonization, and, on the other, the final result is a feminized Chicana space that interrupts and disrupts the male-centered dominance of Aztlán.

As the journey proceeds westward into New Mexico, Maria encounters Valentina Valdez, a meeting that positions her at the historical moment of 1848. In spite of her college education, Maria has a scanty knowledge of Chicana/o history, which she must relearn here as geography continually defines her identity. Decolonizing herself entails a thorough knowledge of how her people were dispossessed and their lands stolen, catapulting them into homelessness and amnesia. Thus, Maria equates their plight and her own, thereby connecting individual experience with the collectivity. Precisely at this infamous moment of U.S. imperialism, Maria not only questions the premises of Manifest Destiny, but more importantly she establishes the primacy of a silenced parallel Chicana/o history that deconstructs and undermines the official Anglo one.

At this moment, it is crucial to identify the three historical strands that compose Maria's journey: (1) a personal life story, (2) Chicana history, and (3) Anglo imposition. Undoubtedly, these simultaneous discursive formations are fraught with fragmentation, disjuncture, and contradiction, and consequently do not fit into a neat linear narration. For this reason, Woman in the Sand's presence is continually required in her multiple roles as counselor, guide, and shaman, a thread that connects all the discrete parts, a voice that suggests what has been silenced. As they continue their walk, a walk whose purpose is to retrieve and activate memory, more historical women appear to Maria to tell her their own stories. Although each feminist ethnography is essential in order to get rid of the general cultural amnesia from which Maria suffers, the genealogy that most captivates her—and the audience—is, in fact, the story of Woman in the Sand herself. As someone who was a successful suicide, her eerie presence in the play is meant to deter Maria from making the same mistake. Each woman who appears not only tells her story, but also moves the plot along farther west. Repeatedly, we learn that an alternative version of an official history is available to the woman who will listen to it. Even Woman in the Sand informs Maria, "I had no choice, but you do" (71). Here, a personal suicide intersects with cultural suicide after assimilation and deterritorialization. In this way, Maria's decision to live also implies her reappropriation of her history and her land as well as legitimization of her cultura—an act of decolonization.

But such acts of determination never go unchallenged. The damaging effects of life along the border for a Mexican woman, "despised" (61) and devalued, are counteracted in the play by the presence of Juanita, the curandera who teaches Maria the legacy of the abuelitas: "We all learn a little about medicine from our great-grandmothers, and then our grandmothers. There's always new *curanderas* who teach the next generation" (65). Although Maria has an education, she must not forget the oral traditions, values, and folkways of her people. Similarly, Juanita is able to place Maria's suffering within a historical context that lessens its devastating effect. Her advice—"Every person has a time to speak, a time to be silent, a time to suffer" (65)—places Maria in a historical continuum of learning, seeking, and finding. Juanita is also the first character to indicate a new way of being, which she calls the "change" (69) and which we have been calling transculturation. As she addresses Maria with the questions "Where are you going? Where've you been? Why it's so hard for you to let yourself get there?" (68), she is really addressing a new generation of Chicanas/os who have traveled with Maria on this journey of genealogical recovery and geographical repossession.

When Maria completes the final stage of her cultural odyssey, Woman in the Sand, assuming Maria's readiness for independence, announces her own departure, but not before reminding Maria to choose life over death. Setting her agency into motion, Maria moves toward her destination, this time without the spiritual guides that had paved the way for her previously. At this historic juncture, Maria's agency and identity unite with those of so many Latina protagonists whose journeys we have analyzed in this book. A politics of identity and location have to be firmly in place in order for her to reclaim her mestizaje, her cultural past, her unspoken history, and her future of promise. That future is imagined precisely because in the articulation of her new transcultural identity as a Latina, she positions herself within a praxis of decolonization and reterritorialization. If during the length of her mythical journey Maria was guided by an imaginary mother and grandmother who took her from the throes of suicide to the depths of her own inner core, as she reenters and reintegrates into the real world, she must be prepared for the inevitability of facing her father. In these terms, both the playwright and her protagonist realize that the work of identity formation is not done until it incorporates a Chicano inclusiveness, one that no longer relegates men to the margins. Unlike the collectivity of feminist plays of the 1980s, in which all the characters are women, these protagonists are ready, willing, and able to confront their mythical, historical, and actual fathers.

The final act for Maria and her generation is to negotiate their relationship and reconcile their differences with their fathers, however symbolic this act may be. It signifies coming to terms both with a patriarchal colonial past of abuse, rape, and deterritorialization as well as with the absent father in female-headed households. In these terms, Maria is able to rewrite her own history as it pertains to her childhood, speaking almost the same monologue she gives in the opening of the play: "I'm seeing him. In the past. I'm just a child. Really tiny. He's enormous. The biggest man in the world. We walk together. By the tide pools. It's easy to lose your balance there because the rocks are rugged and the pools are wet and slick. He tries to help. He offers me his hand, but I won't take it because I'm an independent little girl. And I don't need his help" (1). In the narrative revision, what has changed is that Maria can no longer reject her father's helping hand. "My father tries to help. He offers me his hand. And I take it" (80). The reversal that she effects in her final words signals a change in political strategy and ideological maneuvers. If an earlier generation condemned the absurd, macho, ridiculous figure of the father symbolized in the crisis of patriarchy, now we see a younger generation who reaches out to engage with this male presence. That she does so on her own terms is an act of intervention that puts her feminist agenda to work from the inside out. Even within the familia, there is a politics of affinity: survival depends on community, and community means everyone. Implicit in these actions is the emergence of a feminism that heals the wounds of gender separation in the understanding that the new strategies of oppositional consciousness include a politics of reconciliation.

＊　＊　＊

However different these plays are from one another, their common denominator of home reveals the extent to which the protagonists' transcultural identities are contingent upon their negotiations with a place called home. In the articulation of identity formation that these negotiations necessarily imply, they must transact and maintain a lively engagement with the politics of space. The dramatic action depends on the dialectical relationships between subjectivities and locational identities that are produced by the discourses of home. For the new denizens of la transfrontera, home is neither nostalgic nor utopian, but rather situational, ritualistic, and processual in given geocultural and political discursive locations. The spatial foundation of their newly discovered transcultural homes serves as a provisional site, always informed by ethnic memory and producing continual performances of identity. Each transcultural performance not only reconciles present and past, but also vectors to an uncharted future in the making that anticipates new constructions of home along with original and creative Latina identity formations.

NOTES

Introduction

1. In the mid 1990s, there were some stirrings toward a chronological grouping of Latina plays (Huerta 1996; Marrero 1996), but these review essays offered a linear development of Latina playwriting without relating one play to another. Alicia Arrizón's recent book (1999) goes a long way to redressing that absence.

2. Una Chaudhuri has commented on this pedagogical function of minority theater: "Among the figures that organize the drama of multiculturalism is one that has a long history and a complex meaning: the figure of pedagogy. The spectacle of one person teaching or trying to teach another some signal truth, usually a technique for survival as a minority in America, is multiculturalism's thematization of its vital social and political function. The ethnic theater had from its earliest incantations, served a dual pedagogical function, teaching immigrants about their native cultures while at the same time exposing them to the new one" (1995:216).

Chapter 1

1. Martí's famous phrase "Viví en el monstruo y le conozco las entrañas" (our translation: "I lived inside the monster, and I know him from the inside out") is from his 1885 "Carta a Manuel Mercado" in Martí 1970:177. Darío, in his introduction to *Cantos de vida y esperanza,* states: "Si en estos versos hay política, es porque es universal. Y si encontráis versos a un presidente, es porque son un clamor continental. Mañana podremos ser yanquis (y es lo más probable); de todas maneras, mi protesta queda escrita" (1946:21). (Our translation: "If there are politics in this, it is because it is universal. If you find verses to refer to a president, it is because there is a continental clamor. Tomorrow we could be Yankees [and it is very probable]; however, let my protest be written.") No doubt, Nancy Morejón was also inspired by her compatriot, Martí, when she referred to U.S. imperialism as "las garras devoradoras de la hegemonía capitalista yanqui" (1982:272).

2. The term *transcultural subject* was used by Julie Munich in her excellent honor's thesis "The Space between the Borders: Transcultural Subjectivity in Latina Lesbian Prose and Performance," Smith College, May 1999.

3. See also Inderpal Grewal's excellent essay (1994) on this subject.

4. Generally speaking, when Latin Americans say "América," they refer to all of the Americas. In order to accomplish this same goal in English, we must use the plural, "Americas."

5. Translation by Harriet de Onís: "the concept of transculturation is fundamental and indispensable for an understanding of the history of Cuba, and, for analogous reasons, of that of America in general" (Ortíz 1947:103).

6. Harriet de Onís's translation: "the process of transition from one culture to another, because this does not consist merely in acquiring another culture, which is what the English word 'acculturation' really implies, but the process also necessarily involves the loss or uprooting of a previous culture, which could be defined as a *deculturation.* In addition, it carries the idea of the consequent creation of new cultural phenomena, which could be called *neoculturation*" (Ortíz 1947:102–3)

7. Vasconcelos's concept of the cosmic race is so appealing in theory that few contemporary scholars actually look closely enough at its racist bias to realize that his plan calls for the elimination of blacks by a gradual whitening process.

8. Our translation: "means constant interaction, change, between two or three cultural components whose unconscious goal is to create a third cultural ensemble, that is to say a new and independent culture, although its bases and roots rest on their forebears. The reciprocal influence determines everything. No one element overpowers the other; on the contrary, they change until they form a third element. Neither one remains unchangeable. They all change to grow in a give and take that will engender a brand new texture."

9. Our translation: "The double condition of exploitation that Black Cuban citizens suffer: they are workers whose situation in the social life of the country is limited by the color of their skin."

10. Harriet de Onís's translation: "Interdependence is mutual. Cuba, together with Mexico, is the closest of the Latin American nations in which the 'good-neighbor policy' should be set up with all the intelligence, foresight, and generosity of which statesmen and even the captains of finance of the United States are sometimes capable" (Malinowski 1973, xv).

11. Jean Franco writes, "Un nuevo libro por un importante crítico de la cultura norteamericana o europea, habría recibido inmediatamente la atención merecida; mientras que éste, escrito por el crítico más importante de América Latina, no provocó discusión, diálogo o comentario alguno" (1984:68). (Our translation: "A new book by an important critic of Europe or North America would have immediately received its well-deserved attention, whereas this book, written by the most important critic of Latin America, did not provoke any discussion, dialogue, or commentary at all.")

12. Rama puts it quite succinctly when he calls the boom "el club más exclusivista que haya conocido la historia cultural de América Latina, un club que tiende a aferrarse al principio intangible de sólo cinco sillones" (1979:26). (Our translation: "the most exclusive club ever known in the cultural history of Latin America, a club that tends to abide by the intangible principle of only five seats.")

13. See Kathy Perkins and Roberta Uno's *Contemporary Plays by Women of Color* (1996). Likewise Nao Bustamante performed her piece *Indiguirrito,* a de-

construction of the moment of colonization, in Santa Monica, California, in January 1994. Coco Fusco's video *The Couple in the Cage: A Guatinaui Odyssey,* performed by Fusco with Gómez-Peña in many European and North American locations, had a second appearance as a video in 1993.

14. See Angel Rama's *La ciudad letrada* (1984).

15. For an especially chilling account of this expansion, see Eduardo Galeano, *Las venas abiertas de América Latina* (1971).

16. In spectacular headline news, the migration of a twelve-year-old boy from Honduras to New York, on his own and in search of his father, garnered front page news in the *New York Times,* but on the very same day the story of a Cuban raft that appeared in Miami was relegated to the back pages of the paper. In the latter story, a graphic photo of the Coast Guard violently trying to prevent the raft from landing and thus procuring refugee status stands in counterpoint to the tender story of the hurricane-torn Honduran adolescent in search of his father. See Sachs 1999.

17. The center-periphery paradigm that Appadurai sees as anachronistic for transnational historical moments was the dominant theoretical conception of Latin America during the 1960s and 1970s, and was known by social scientists as the theory of dependence. See Cardoso 1972 and 1977.

18. As José David Saldívar has written, "While the Cuban-Marxist work of Fernández Retamar is indispensable for analyzing theory in terms of location and the dialectics of difference, it needs modification when extended to our global Borderland context. His supremely mutable polemics of marginality and centrality, of the same and the other, cannot entirely account for the hybrid appropriations and resistances that characterize the travel of theories and theorists who migrate between places in our 'First' world and 'Third' world" (1991b:xvii).

19. Phyllis Peres (1997) notes that Luso-African writers also rely on reconversion in their works. Similarly, Amilcar Cabral (1973) conceives of reconversion as an act of resistance.

20. Definitions of the border have proliferated in postcolonial theory as well as in Latin America. Two useful definitions are: "The term does not indicate a fixed topographical site between two other fixed locales (nations, societies, cultures), but an interstitial zone of displacement and deterritorialization that shapes the identity of the hybridized subject" (Gupta and Ferguson 1992:18). And "The frontier does not merely close the nation in on itself, but also immediately opens it to an outside, to other nations. All frontiers, including the frontier of nations, at the same time as they are barriers are also laces of communication and exchange . . . places of separation and articulation (Sarup 1994:98).

21. In this sense, the suggestive work of Antonio Cornejo Polar on Latin American heterogeneity provides a fruitful point of departure for the continent. Unfortunately, his untimely death left some issues unresolved. In developing his theory of heterogeneity, Cornejo Polar leans heavily on Rama's theory of transculturation, even

when he vehemently disagrees with it. Both Rama's and Cornejo's theoretical apparatus allows for a postmodern definition of a Latin American identity. Both intellectual giants are concerned uniquely with a Latin American identity within Latin America, which excludes Latina/o subjectivity within the U.S. For further discussion, see Cornejo Polar (1994, 1998) and Moraña 1997.

22. Lowe's definition of hybridization concurs with Canclini's and stands in opposition to the definitions developed by Homi Bhabha. Whereas all three see hybridization as the result of violences done to the colonial subject, for Lowe (1996) and Canclini (1995a, 1995b) the hybrid develops strategies of resistance in opposition to the colonizer. For Bhabha (1994b), the relationship between colonizer and colonized is almost symbiotic at a discursive level—with unequal relations of power—and the hybrid is as much the colonizer as it is the colonized. For Lowe and Canclini, the term *hybrid* refers more specifically to the colonized. In that Lowe and Canclini see the hybrid as a creative, vital, surviving cultural force, their cultural contribution must always be read as counterhegemonic. In this, Bhabha would be likely to concur.

23. Such a view would correspond to that espoused by postcolonial theorist Homi Bhabha, who complicates the notion of hybridity by showing that both colonizer and colonized are affected, however unequally, by the contact zone. However, although Bhabha's work is universalized as postcolonial criticism par excellence, Canclini's remains of interest to anthropologists and literary critics of Latin America. In this regard, postcolonial writing has a global reception, whereas theories of transculturation seem to remain local.

24. As Rita de Grandis notes, "dentro de los procesos de 'reconversión cultural' íntimamente vinculados con desplazamientos geográficos y culturales—desterritorialización—que dan como resultado nuevas formas y prácticas culturales, las que a su vez surgen de un proceso de reacomodamiento, es necesario restituirle al objeto no sólo las condiciones de enunciación (su contexto), sino toda su complejidad y su articulación interna" (1997:46). (Our translation: "within the processes of 'cultural reconversion' intimately linked with geographic and cultural displacements—deterritorializations—that result in new forms and cultural practices, which at the same time come about as a process of reaccommodation, it is necessary to return not only to the conditions of the enunciation to the object, but to all its complexity and internal articulation.")

25. Code-switching is an integral element in the poetry of Chicanos/as and Nuyoricans, and is a metaphor of resistance as well as a symbol of their creativity as transcultural subjects.

26. Rich writes: "the need to begin with the female body—our own—was understood . . . as locating the grounds from which to speak with authority *as* women. Not to transcend this body, but to reclaim it" (1986:213). Caren Kaplan examines Rich's essay and politics in her own lucid remarks in "The Politics of Location as Transnational Feminist Critical Practice" (in Grewal and Kaplan 1994). As she argues for

"critical practices that mediate these most obvious oppositions, interrogating the terms that mythologize our differences and similarities" (138), she seems simultaneously to be addressing the issues of transculturation that we outline in this chapter.

27. Transcultural subjects who are also biracial often find that their "authentic identity" undermines their racial affiliation. In terms of ethnicity, Puerto Rican mulattoes, for example, conflict over their affiliation as Latinos or as Afro-Caribbeans. They do not see themselves in racial terms, like African Americans do, but rather in nationalist, ethnic terms as Puerto Rican. A transcultural subjectivity permits both of these identities to manifest themselves simultaneously into a single new identity formation. Equally, the transcultural location of gender places a female subjectivity anywhere from a "beautiful señorita" to a labor organizer. Yet, in both realities, we see subjects who are transculturated.

Chapter 2

1. Some examples are TENAZ XVI Festival Latino Guadalupe Center of the Arts, November 1992; Teatro Pregones, Teatro Festival, July 1993; First Annual Festival Latino of New Plays, Teatro Misión, San Francisco, 1993. The annual Hijas del Quinto Sol Festival held in San Antonio featured Latina theater and performance as its main theme for the 1999 conference.

2. See the pioneering work of Yvonne Yarbro-Bejarano and Yolanda Broyles-González. Broyles-González's well-known work uncovered the role of women in Teatro Campesino in many publications.

3. Although this definition also applies to Brazilians who live within the boundaries of the U.S., until now most Brazilians have preferred not to be called Latinos, opting instead for retaining their uniquely Brazilian identity.

4. A vast and extensive bibliography exists on the debate over labels and terminology. On this debate, see Gimenez 1989; Hayes-Bautista 1980; Hayes-Bautista and Chapa 1987; Oboler 1992; Padilla 1984; Yankauer 1987.

Also of interest is Bruce-Novoa 1990; Choldin 1986; Nelson and Tienda 1985; and Melville 1988. See also Tienda and Ortíz 1986; Shorris 1992; and D. Gonzalez 1992.

5. The concept of hispánica for native speakers of Spanish entails and celebrates their cultural, ethnic, and linguistic heritage from Spain. Many Latin Americans still see Spanish culture as a paradigm of their identity and use the term *hispano*. Hispania (Spain) accounts for their cultural epicenter. In consequence, Latin Americans can name Spanish-speaking countries in Latin America as Iberoamérica or Hispanoamérica, terms that exclude the cultural and linguistic diversity in the Americas.

6. Most recently, the revival and new definition of the term *criollo/a* has gained some currency in Latino circles.

7. For examples of this "betrayal," see Mohr 1989:111–16 and Tato Laviera's poignant poem "Nuyorican" (1985:53).

8. See Midgalia Cruz and Hilary Blecher's opera *Frida* (2000); Dolores Prida's play *Botánica* (2000); and Diana Sáenz's play, *A Dream of Canaries* (1992).

9. Marga Gomez in performance. Iron Horse Music Hall, Northampton, Mass., April 1999.

10. An emerging theater of Dominican Americans and Colombian Americans is visible on stages in New York.

11. Such is the case of Yolanda Broyles-González's revisionary reading of the Teatro Campesino in her 1994 book.

12. This phenomenon is not unique to the theater; writers such as Sandra Cisneros, *The House on Mango Street* (1985), Gloria Anzaldúa, *Borderlands/La Frontera* (1987), and Rosario Morales, *Getting Home Alive* (1986) exemplify this process in fiction and poetry.

13. For an analysis of Puerto Rican theater in the U.S., see Sandoval-Sánchez 1993.

14. For a useful distinction between Cuban and Cuban American, see Rivero 1989. Rivero places writers who have a "niche" on the island in the category of Cuban. Those who identify with the condition of marginality assigned to most Latinos would qualify as Cuban American. Also, see one of the anthologies devoted to "Cuban American" theater, such as Cortina 1991 or González-Cruz and Colecchia 1992.

15. Another manifestation of this theater is the legacy of the comic sketches known as teatro bufo, which originated on the island.

16. This contrast becomes a palpable difference in the entertainment world when we note the cultural identity of Celia Cruz compared to that of Gloria Estefan, for example. In music, they represent the differences between the generation of those exiled and the second generation born in the U.S. Cruz sings only in Spanish, whereas Estefan is bilingual. Estefan considers home to be the U.S. For her, the cultural past is not an exercise in nostalgia as it is for the exiles, but rather an integral foundation for the articulation of her identity in the U.S. In these terms, Estefan's record *Mi Tierra* ("the highest debuting Spanish album in U.S. music history" [*Hispanic Business*, July 1994, 35]) constitutes a recovery of her roots in her historical present.

17. See, respectively, *The Rooster and the Egg, The Greatest Performance, Beautiful Señoritas, Siempre Intenté Decirte Algo (S.I.D.A.),* and *A Park in the House.*

18. See Efraín Barradas 1979. For the term *tropicalized,* see Aparicio and Chávez-Silverman 1997.

19. See Aurora Levins Morales and Rosario Morales's suggestively titled text *Getting Home Alive* (1986) for an account of how one family deals with this issue intergenerationally. Julia Alvarez discusses the ramifications of home and the island in her novel *How the García Girls Lost Their Accents* (1991).

20. See, respectively, *Emplumada* (1981); *Getting Home Alive* (1986); *Dreaming in Cuban* (1992); *Borderlands/La Frontera* (1987); and *How the García Girls Lost Their Accents* (1991). On the other hand, Latino male writer Richard Rodríguez

articulates a desire to get away from home in his book *Hunger of Memory* (1982). Rubén Martínez, however, a much younger Latino, claims his roots in Mexico, Central America, and Los Angeles in his book *The Other Side* (1992).

21. Interview with Monica Palacios, Smith College, March 28, 1994.

22. Teresa de Lauretis analyzes plot and narration to show how female characters are simply the object of desire for the male protagonist: "she (it) is an element of plot-space, a topos, a resistance, matrix and matter" (1984:119). While she ("female-obstacle-boundary-space" [1984:121]) is the other, the male character is the subject. When we apply this theory to Latina theater, women are no longer distracted by male desire. Consequently, they move from objectivity to subjectivity. As the action develops, they become the agents of their own needs and desires, the tellers of their own stories.

23. Personal interview, May 1993, South Hadley, Mass. (Cruz 1993).

24. This phenomenon has not been limited to Latinas. Even Broadway and off-Broadway have had to welcome solo performances by artists such as Whoopi Goldberg, Eric Bogosian, Guillermo Gómez-Peña, and John Leguizamo.

Chapter 3

1. For a discussion on feminist revisionism, see Adrienne Rich's classic essay, "When We Dead Awaken: Writing as Re-Vision." Rich writes that "Re-vision—the act of looking back, of seeing with fresh eyes, of entering an old text from a new critical direction—is for women more than a chapter in cultural history: it is an act of survival" (1979:35).

2. Among these women's theater groups, the most prominent ones are Las Cucarachas (*Chicana* 1974) and Valentina Productions of San Jose (*Voz de la Mujer* 1981). Teatro Raíces of San Diego (1971), Teatro de la Esperanza (originally of Santa Barbara, then San Francisco), Teatro Visión of San Jose, Su teatro, Ahora Teatro Hispano, Teatro La Causa (Denver), Teatro Aguacero (New Mexico), Teatro Libertad and Teatro del Sol (Tucson), Teatro Vivo (Los Angeles), and Brava (San Francisco) have all played a very important function in the dramatic representation of positive roles for women and in the development and representation of women's theater in Latina/o communities.

3. See our article "Revisiting Chicana Cultural Icons: From Sor Juana to Frida" (Sandoval-Sánchez and Saporta Sternbach forthcoming).

4. Both of these works dramatically honor and retell the story of Puerto Rican pro-independence activist and political prisoner Lolita Lebrón.

5. In the Southwest, both Denise Chávez in Las Cruces, New Mexico, and Silviana Wood in Tucson, Arizona, have made great contributions to their communities.

6. In her article on Chicano murals, "The Story of Chicano Park," Eva Cockcroft distinguishes between the two trends she sees in muralism, the "cosmic" and the "politico-historical" (1984). From her definition of the cosmic, as well as our back-

ground in Latin American literature, we see the "mythopoetic" as a poetic use of cultural myth, incorporating, in this case, Aztec cosmology and the importance of Aztlán to Chicanas/os. For one of the earliest articles on Chicano literature, see Sommers 1977.

7. In 1980, WIT singled out the needs of women in the theater to include every kind of artistic endeavor. The group understood early on the vital role that women play as producers, directors, actresses, and playwrights in the production of theater.

8. One such article, María Teresa Marrero's "In the Limelight: The Insertion of Latina Theater Entrepreneurs, Playwrights, and Directors into the Historical Period," although praising Nicolás Kanellos's *A History of Hispanic Theater in the United States: Origins to 1940* (1990), points out the lack of information about Latinas in the theater; only a few names appear sporadically in Kanellos's study: La Chata Noloesca, Virgina Fábregas, Carmen Soto de Vásquez, Pilar Arcos, Marita Reid. To fill this void, Marrero proposes that given the invisibility owing to the lack of published material, fieldwork rather than archival research is needed. She states: "Researchers today must develop numerous interdisciplinary skills, from archival recovery to journalistic and anthropological techniques of field work" (1996:78). One such example of this kind of field work would be Marguerite Waller's "Border Boda or Divorce Fronterizo" (1994).

9. One exception is the work of the Colorado sisters, Native Americans and Chicanas, born and raised in New York City, where they have performed on many occasions.

10. Here is the complete text of Pottlitzer's report in the section entitled "The Role of Women in U.S. Hispanic Theater":

"In New York, the names Marta Moreno Vega and Miriam Colón are synonymous with leadership in Hispanic Arts. Vega has been instrumental in bringing New York State and New York City legislative attention to Hispanic Arts, and Miriam Colón has worked at both the state and national levels to promote and defend the rights of Hispanic artists. Both women founded and direct their own arts organizations: Colón, the Puerto Rican Traveling Theatre; and Vega, the Caribbean Cultural Center.

"In Miami, Cuban-American Olga Garay-Ahern, now assistant director of the Metro-Dade Cultural Affairs Council, plays a major role in efforts to strengthen Miami-based Hispanic theaters. Other Hispanic women who have made important contributions to Hispanic theaters in New York include Magali Alabau, Silvia Brito, Lourdes Casals, Alba Olms, Elsa Ortiz, Ilka Tanya Payán, and Margarita Toraic. In addition, Hispanic theater in the United States boasts a substantial number of women playwrights, including Lynne Alvarez, Maria Irene Fornes, Dolores Prida, and Ana Maria Simo in New York; Milcha Sánchez-Scott and Edit Villarreal in Los Angeles; Denise Chávez in Las Cruces, New Mexico; Estela Portillo Tramblay in El Paso, Texas; and Silviana Wood in Tucson, Arizona. Their plays cover a wide range of styles and themes. Unfortunately, there is little communication among them. One of the goals of WIT had been to build a network of women playwrights, starting with those who were TENAZ members. A meeting of women writers planned by TENAZ in the early 1980s never materialized" (1988:29–30).

11. See Honan 1992, which features Miriam Colón and her efforts to overcome financing cutbacks for the Puerto Rican Traveling Theatre.

12. Brochure for DramaDIVAS, San Francisco, Teatro Brava.

13. No better tribute could be mounted than María Delgado and Caridad Svich's homage to Fornes in their book *Conducting a Life* (1999), celebrating her accomplishments.

14. Fornes's way of doing theater leaves some critics wondering if, in fact, her debt to and influence by Europe limits her work and its audience. The exotic aura of her plays seems to address radical chic intellectuals of New York, but may leave a Latina/o audience questioning her roots. Concerning her Latin American identity, here is what she says: "In many ways, I still think like a Cuban, or maybe just a Latin, or maybe like a European. In 1945 Cuba was much closer to Europe than to the United States—in the sense of values, the order of things, what you were and were not allowed to do. I have a strong accent, and I think it's because there's a part of me I don't want to eradicate" (qtd. in Osborn 1987:47).

Considering Fornes's strong ties to Europe, her involvement with and commitment to a Latino/a theater—that is, a theater politically and culturally committed as well as community based—seemed until recently to take a second place in her work. Rather, her plays uphold an international theater form, and their surreal content hardly seems consonant with a U.S. Latino working- or middle-class population and its concerns with migration, assimilation, ethnic identity, and resistance. One of her more recent plays, *Sarita,* however, breaks from this norm and gets closer to Latino/a theater in that its main character is a Latina. The play takes its rightful place alongside other Latina/o plays, for it alludes to issues such as discrimination, racism, oppression, ethnicity, affirmation of cultural heritage, and bicultural identity.

Nor does Lynne Alvarez, a playwright whose subject matter mirrors her middle-class values and experience as a white person, seem to identify with the Latino community. She says: "I found myself in a peculiar situation as a playwright. My experience with Hispanic culture was in Mexico, but I wasn't Mexican. I had nothing to say about regular daily life in the United States, or about the clash between cultures experienced by immigrant families. I had no stories to tell about that. I couldn't speak as a Mexican, so the Hispanic theaters didn't want to put my plays on. I couldn't be an Argentinian, I'd never been to Argentina. And I couldn't speak about the urban Hispanic-American experience. It was hard to get productions" (qtd. in Osborn 1987:4).

15. Fornes's collection *Maria Irene Fornes Plays* appeared in 1986 and includes the plays *Mud, The Danube, The Conduct of Life,* and *Sarita.* In her introduction to

this collection, Sontag specifies the type of audience that will enjoy a Fornes plays: intellectual and middle class. Although Sontag reaches out to include Fornes in the bicultural community, she also strongly identifies Fornes with her Cuban roots: "Her imagination seems to me to have, among other sources, a profoundly Cuban one. I am reminded of the witty, sensual, phantasmagorias of Cuban writers such as Lydia Cabrera, Calvert Casey and Virgilio Piñera" (7). It is interesting to point out that Fornes recognizes just how much her work is informed by her Cuban roots, for the music of Olga Guillot served as inspiration and background while she was writing *Fefu and Her Friends*. In fact, even when it is least expected, a muted transculturated text reveals itself in Fornes's confession of her sensorial, ethnic memory: "I wrote the whole play listening to Olga Guillot. . . . There was one record, *Añorando el Caribe*, that particularly seemed to make my juices run" (qtd. in Robinson 1999:217).

16. Caridad Svich and María Teresa Marrero's book *Out of the Fringe: Contemporary Latina/Latino Theatre and Performance* (2000) constitutes one such example, as does Carmelita Tropicana's collected works (2000). In terms of criticism, Yvonne Yarbro-Bejarano's forthcoming book on Cherríe Moraga as well as Lillian Manzor and Alicia Arrizón's anthology *Latinas on Stage* (2000) will do much to fill the lacunae in this area.

17. In some cases, however, the existence of the plays does not assure the production of them. Because there is a scarcity of Latina/o students in university drama departments that feel the actors must also be Latinas/os, the plays may run the risk of being put aside. Often, fears of stereotyping the "other" and political correctness prevent Anglo drama departments from taking theatrical risks. Therefore, the plays are never or rarely produced. Some notable exceptions should be mentioned: Smith College produced Sánchez-Scott's *Roosters* in 1990, and the University of Massachusetts New World Theater produced Sáenz's *A Dream of Canaries* in 1993. Although there appears to be an underrepresentation of Latina/o plays in drama departments, Latina organizations at universities sometimes take it on themselves to produce a play written by a Latina. For example, at Mount Holyoke College, La Unidad produced Dolores Prida's *Beautiful Señoritas* in 1984 and Denise Chávez's *Novena narrativas* in 1993.

18. Some sources on the bildungsroman include: Aizenberg 1985; Amrine 1987; Baym 1981; Fuderer 1990; LeSeur 1986; O'Neale 1982; Pratt with White 1981; J. Smith 1987; and Turner 1979.

19. Also see Braendlin 1979.

20. For a definition of *rite of passage,* we rely on Victor Turner (1977, 1982, 1983)—following Arnold van Gennep—and his tripartite processual structure consisting of these stages: separation, margin or limen, and reaggregation. The first stage detaches the individual from her or his previous places and status in society; the last installs that individual, inwardly transformed and outwardly changed, in a new place in society. During the intermediate stage, the initiate experiences a threshold situa-

tion, wavering between two worlds, a potentiality that is "neither/nor." Also see van Gennep 1993.

21. Anzaldúa describes the new mestiza in the following manner: "The new *mestiza* copes by developing a tolerance for contradiction, a tolerance for ambiguity. She learns to juggle cultures, she has a plural personality, she operates in a pluralistic mode—nothing is thrust out, the good, the bad and the ugly, nothing rejected, nothing abandoned. Not only does she sustain contradictions, she turns the ambivalence into something else" (1987:79).

22. Our concept of the term *the politics of difference* is informed by the theoretical work of Stuart Hall and Cornel West. In "New Ethnicities," Hall writes: "What is at issue here is the recognition of the extraordinary diversity of subjective positions, social experiences and cultural identities which compose the category 'black'; that is, the recognition that 'black' is essentially a politically and culturally constructed category, which cannot be grounded in a set of fixed trans-cultural or transcendental racial categories and which therefore has no guarantees in Nature. What this brings into play is the recognition of the immense diversity and differentiation of the historical and cultural experience of black subjects" (1988:27). In "The New Cultural Politics of Difference," West attributes black diasporic women such as Toni Morrison with the creation of a new cultural politics of difference by "bury[ing] the innocent notion of the essential Black subject . . . with the termination of the Black male monopoly on the construction of Black subjects. In this regard, the Black diaspora womanist critique has had a greater impact than the critiques that highlight exclusively class, empire, age, sexual orientation or nature" (1990:29). For a contrasting view of the issue, see Carby 1990.

23. First a community of artists working together, then a political agenda contribute to a politics of solidarity. These coalitions have emerged with a theater that promotes a socioagenda for change. This process is what we call a politics of affinity, based on the work of cultural critic David Román, who develops the concept of a politics of affinity among Latinos/as in "Teatro VIVA! Latino Performance, Sexuality, and the Politics of AIDS in Los Angeles" (1995b). For Román, this politics of affinity works through the political formation of alliances and coalition building that take difference into consideration. Also see Alberto Sandoval-Sánchez's "Staging AIDS: What's Latinos Got to Do with It?" (1994), where he demonstrates how a politics of affinity is a survival strategy in two Latino plays in which the protagonists have been diagnosed with AIDS: Louis Delgado's *A Better Life* and Pedro Monge Raful's *Noche de Ronda.*

Chapter 4

1. Witness the prolific flourish of Latina poetry, fiction, autobiography, and essay in publications by Gloria Anzaldúa, Sandra Cisneros, Julia Alvarez, Rosario Morales, Cristina García, Judith Ortiz Cofer, Lorna Dee Cervantes, Ana Castillo, Helena María Viramontes, and Cherríe Moraga. And the list goes on.

2. The conceptualization of a foundational discursive site in this chapter derives from Michel Foucault's theorization of discourse: "Whenever one can describe, between a number of statements, such a system of dispersion, whenever, between objects, types of statement, concepts, or thematic choices, one can define a regularity (an order, correlations, positions and functionings, transformations), we will say for the sake of convenience, that we are dealing with a *discursive formation*" (1972:38, emphasis in original). In these terms, we approach Latina theater as a set of discursive formations and practices in a specific historical moment and location in given relations of power. It is within these discursive sites that individuals, as they socially interact, are subjected, become speaking subjects, and assume subject positionings in relation to institutions and systems of power.

3. *Giving Up the Ghost* was first performed as a stage reading in 1984 and published in 1986. Teresa de Lauretis has observed: "the play itself has moved away from any simple opposition of 'lesbian' to 'heterosexual' and into the conceptual and experiential continuum of a female, Chicana subjectivity from where the question of lesbian desire must finally be posed. The play ends with that question—which is at once its outcome and its achievement, its *éxito*" (1988:175).

Moraga, however, was no newcomer to issues of critical and theoretical importance, having coedited and authored such landmark texts as *This Bridge Called My Back* (Moraga and Anzaldúa 1983) and *Loving in the War Years* (Moraga 1983).

4. Although the earliest publication we can find of this play is 1972, Portillo herself, on the back cover of *Sor Juana and Other Plays,* puts the date as 1971, which we consider the date it was written.

5. Significantly, the grandmother in *La casa de Bernarda Alba* is also named doña Josefa. In chapter 6, we continue the analysis of Lorca with another playwright, Migdalia Cruz, and her adaptation of the Bernarda Alba story in *Another Part of the House.*

6. Ginetta Candelario's suggestive work on the racial and gendered construction of beauty in Dominican culture has greatly informed our work. See her excellent article "Hair Race-ing," in *Meridians: feminism, race, transnationalism* (2000).

Chapter 5

1. As David Román has observed, "the diversity of performance styles within Latino performance says as much about the different subject positions of Latino performers as it does about the diversity and flexibility of the medium" (1997:157). He adds, "These performers insist on the visibility and coherence of Latino identity even as they refuse to stabilize that identity as any one image, role, stereotype, or convention. . . . These performers extend the stage and continue to reverberate in the public world, where Latinos enact their daily lives" (163–64).

2. Carmelita Tropicana, monologue, unpublished ms. In "Performance Art Manifesto," Carmelita parodies definitions of performance by Laurie Anderson and

Holly Hughes. Despite the humor, she attests that "Performance art changes the way you look at the world. Your perceptions are changed: An object is no longer what it seems to be" (Tropicana, "Performance Art Manifesto," 177). In this way, performance cannot be disassociated from identity formation.

3. Goldberg understands performance art as the genre that "came to fill the gap between entertainment and theatre and in certain instances actually revitalized theatre and opera" (1988:162). Her definition is a springboard to understanding performance art, though in the case of Latinas the genre embodies its own characteristics. Nevertheless, we are grateful to Goldberg for her useful definition, which we quote in its entirety: "Unlike theatre, the performer *is* the artist, seldom a character like an actor, and the content rarely follows a traditional plot or narrative. The performance might be a series of intimate gestures or large-scale visual theatre, lasting from a few minutes to many hours; it might be performed only once or repeated several times, with or without a prepared script, spontaneously improvised, or rehearsed over many months" (1988:8).

This definition is complemented by Philip Auslander, who sees performance as "the cultural practices . . . which include experimental theater, performance art, and stand-up comedy. The now notorious collapse of distinctions between media and between 'high art' and 'popular culture' . . . characterizes the postmodern" (1994:3).

4. See Diana Taylor's excellent article on this piece, "A Savage Performance" (1998).

5. Cherríe Moraga and Ana Castillo "read" their respective works *Giving Up the Ghost* and *The Mixquihuala Letters* at Smith College in 1987 in a simultaneous "performance" that showed the interconnectedness of themes that confronted Chicanas at that time. For a panoramic view of Latino/a performance in its historicity and contextualization, see David Román's "Latino Performance and Identity" (1997).

6. For a historical account of carpas, see Tomás Ybarra-Frausto, "I Can Still Hear the Applause. La Farándula Chicana: Carpas y tandas de variedad" (1984). It is interesting to note that Ybarra-Frausto's carpa resembles today's performance art: "Performance strategies were anchored on the broadly realistic representations of character types in semi-improvised, spontaneous clowning situations. . . . *Carpa* performances were fluid, open, semi-structured presentational events with direct audience interaction and feedback" (47).

7. In contrast to our earlier assertions of eschewing the term *Latin,* we use it here as it was employed in its historical context of the 1940s and 1950s by such entertainers as Carmen Miranda and Desi Arnaz.

8. See Kanellos 1984. For an overview of La Chata herself, see Tomás Ybarra-Frausto, "La Chata Noloesca: Figura del Donaire" (1983). Alicia Arrizón has devoted part of a chapter of her book (1999) to La Chata and recognizes the performativity of las soldaderas during the Mexican Revolution. Her important contribution asserts a praxis of Latinidad that allows for the recovery of important historical figures under-

stood within new theoretical paradigms. Arrizón's work creates a genealogy of performance and inscribes it within a social practice and historical context that refashions Latina identity today.

9. Nicolás Kanellos also considers the pelado as the precursor of such characters as Cantinflas. For a complete definition, see "Two Centuries of Hispanic Theatre in the Southwest" (1983:19). Also see Kanellos 1990.

10. Arturo Madrid's paper "Forming the Imagined Latino Community of the U.S.: The Challenge for the Twenty-First Century" (delivered at Mount Holyoke College, October 1999) is an excellent analysis of an imagined Latino/a community. Here, Madrid exhorts his audience to "imagine themselves" as a creative, "collective project central to U.S. society and its institutions." Central to Madrid's thesis is the idea that if Latinos do not imagine themselves (both in the present and in the future), others will do the imagining for them.

11. According to Chin, "Much of what passes for performance art, experimental film, and 'advanced' visual art is more like an audition, a trial-run, a mock-up for work in television, commercial movies or advertising" (1991:19–20). For further discussion of the commodification of performance art, see Auslander 1994.

12. Performed by Eileen Galindo at the American Place Theatre, spring 1999.

13. Teatro Pregones, New World Theatre, University of Massachusetts, spring 1999.

14. Such is the case of Robert Houston's review, where he criticizes and faults the novel for its theatricality: "A number of chapters appear to be performance pieces with marginal relevance, not yet integrated into a plot" (1994:20).

15. Teresa de Lauretis defines this butch-femme aesthetic in the following way: "butch-femme role-playing is exciting not because it represents heterosexual desire, but because it doesn't; that is to say, in mimicking it, it shows the uncanny distance, like an effect of ghosting, between desire (heterosexually represented as it is) and the representation; and because the representation doesn't fit the actors who perform it, it only points to their investment in a fantasy—a fantasy that can never fully represent them or their desire" (1991:250–51). Also see Case 1989 and Dolan 1988a, 1993b.

16. See Eliana Ortega and Nancy Saporta Sternbach, "At the Threshold of the Unnamed" (1989:3).

17. When we refer to Marga Gomez as stage performer and writer, we use "Gomez." In our allusions to "Marga," we are referring to the persona/character that she creates in these performance pieces. When the distinction is either unclear or refers to both, we call her Marga/Gomez.

18. In the 1980s, after moving to San Francisco, Gomez worked with Lilith, a feminist theater collective. Later, she collaborated with Culture Clash, a Latino comedy performance group. She has also worked with the San Francisco Mime Troupe, which is known for its agit-prop work and political consciousness.

19. Marga Gomez's theatrical career began with her parents in a comedy sketch called "La familia cómica."

20. This was true in the workshop performance that Marga Gomez did for the New World Theater in October 1994, Amherst, Massachusetts. The show no longer carries this subtitle. We are grateful to Irene Pinn for pointing this out to us.

21. In Marga Gomez's words, "I'm in between a lot of worlds. I'm Latin yet I'm assimilated. I don't dance or speak Spanish and I'm not a big family person but I'm still Latin. . . . I'm in a relationship with a woman but I question the need to identify as straight or gay—I think that need comes more out of the society being homophobic. . . . I'm also a misfit as far as performing. I'm in theatre but I still have that vaudeville thing from my past" (Uno 1994:5).

22. Obviously, the entire trilogy invites a Lacanian analysis, as each text (performance) could be read as one of Lacan's stages (the Imaginary, the Mirror, and the Symbolic) in the formation of a child's identity. In this way, *Memory Tricks* represents Marga's continual struggle to return to the Imaginary, a precondition for the functioning of the individual in a world with language and desire. Up until that time, the child identifies solely with the mother's body and does not view itself as a separate entity until it contemplates itself in the mirror. The subject (in this case, Marga) must see itself in the mirror in order to enter the domain of language. Such is the case in *Marga Gomez Is Pretty, Witty, and Gay,* where Marga performs in front of a mirror as she articulates her lesbian sexuality. This act leads to her transition from the world of the mother to that of the father in *A Line around the Block.* In the first piece, a world without language and therefore before desire, Marga lacks the language to speak of her sexuality. It is not until *A Line around the Block,* which would correspond to her entry into the Symbolic Order, that she weaves together the intersection of sexuality and ethnicity, having fully entered the cultural domain of the Father, language, and the patriarchy.

Chapter 6

1. We are not the first to turn our attention to the Latin American/Mexican kitchen. Readers of Sor Juana Inés de la Cruz will fondly remember her ironic statement about writing and cooking: "Si Aristóteles hubiera guisado, mucho más hubiera escrito" (1985:839; translation: "had Aristotle prepared victuals, he would have written more" [Peden 1982:113]). In the late 1980s and the 1990s, with the advent of a feminist critical imprint on the Latin American canon, Sor Juana's now famous text has been restored to its rightful foundational place in a tradition that underestimated and misunderstood its author. Such revisionary practices have recovered the works of women writers with new interpretive approaches. One area that has particularly benefited from this attention is the metaphor of cooking as writing, begun by Sor Juana and articulated throughout the ages by Juana Manuela Gorriti, Rosario Castellanos, Rosario Ferré, and Laura Esquivel (as well as by the critics of their work). A major term of the debate has always been whether or not cooking, recipes, and other so-called women's genres could be considered real literature, high art, or anything but a "subgenre," peripheral to dominant canons of literature.

We distinguish between this kind of theater and the so-called kitchen sink dramas, which, in the words of Dolores Prida, deal with "drugs and welfare" (Prida 1988:82).

2. We include here Rodrigo Duarte Clark's play because it was written as a performance piece for a specific woman, Ruby Nelda Pérez.

3. We share Barbara Smith's view on the importance of kitchens, as when she describes why she chose the name Kitchen Table Women of Color Press: "We chose our name because the kitchen is the center of the home, the place where women in particular work and communicate with each other. We also wanted to convey the fact that we are a kitchen table, grass roots operation, begun and kept alive by women who cannot rely on inheritances or other benefits of class privilege to do the work we need to do" (Smith 1989:11).

4. Genaro Padilla's excellent article (1991) discusses Cleofas Martínez Jaramillo's "whispers" of resistance to Anglo dominance in her historic cookbook, *The Genuine New Mexico Tasty Recipes.*

5. See Susan Leonardi's definition: "*recipere* implies an exchange, a giver and a receiver" (1989:340).

6. Fray Bernadino de Sahagún's *The General History of the Things of New Spain*—a.k.a. *The Florentine Codex*—is an excellent source for a description of what have become ancestral heritage foods as well as the place of the cook in serving them. Further in his ethnography, Sagahún notes: "The good cook is honest, discreet . . . one who likes good food—an epicure, a taster . . . clean, one who bathes herself," whereas "The bad cook [is] dishonest, detestable, nauseating, offensive to others—sweaty, crude, gluttonous, stuffed, distended with food" (1961:53).

7. Echoing Roland Barthes's discussion of the mythology of wine and its semiotic importance in French culture, we stress how the tamal, too, holds a place of reverence in Mexican and Chicano culture, replete with its own mythology.

8. The same applies to many other plays, such as *Botánica* by Dolores Prida, *Real Women Have Curves* by Josefina López, *When the Cucui Walks* by Roy Conboy, *The House of Ramón Iglesia* by José Rivera, and *I Don't Have to Show You No Stinking Badges* by Luis Valdez.

Chapter 7

1. This expression is a paraphrase of the title of Paul Gilroy's excellent article "It Ain't Where You're from, It's Where You're At . . . : The Dialectics of Diasporic Identification" (1990–91:3).

2. We thank Angelika Bammer for the brilliant, offhanded way she suggests that one can look at "home as a performance" (1994:ix).

3. It is not coincidental that it was El Teatro Campesino that took this play on tour. The trademark "actos" of El Teatro Campesino are visible in López's play.

BIBLIOGRAPHY OF LATINA PLAYWRIGHTS

Acosta, Belinda. *2 Girls and Clorox.* Unpublished manuscript, 1990.

Alvarez, Lynne. *Collected Plays.* Lyme, N.H.: Smith and Kraus, 1998.

——. *Eddie Mundo Edmundo.* In *New Plays, from A.C.T.'s Young Conservatory,* edited by Craig Slaight, 1–51. Lyme, N.H.: Smith and Kraus, 1996. Also in *Collected Plays,* 327–74. Lyme, N.H.: Smith and Kraus, 1998.

——. *The Guitarrón.* In *On New Ground: Contemporary Hispanic-American Plays,* edited by M. Elizabeth Osborn, 1–43. New York: Theatre Communications Group, 1987. Also in *Collected Plays,* 1–43. Lyme, N.H.: Smith and Kraus, 1998.

——. *Hidden Parts.* In *Collected Plays,* 45–84. Lyme, N.H.: Smith and Kraus, 1998.

——. *On Sundays.* In *Plays in One Act, Antaeus* 66, edited by Daniel Halpern, 44–52. New York: Ecco, 1991. Also in *Collected Plays,* 375–84. Lyme, N.H.: Smith and Kraus, 1998.

——. *The Reincarnation of Jaime Brown.* In *Women Playwrights: The Best Plays of 1994,* edited by Marisa Smith, 51–116. Lyme, N.H.: Smith and Brown, 1995. Also in *Collected Plays,* 263–326. Lyme, N.H.: Smith and Kraus, 1998.

——. *Thin Air: Tales from a Revolution.* In *Collected Plays,* 213–62. Lyme, N.H.: Smith and Kraus, 1998.

——. *The Wonderful Tower of Humbert Lavoignet.* New York: Broadway, 1990. Also in *Collected Plays,* 85–123. Lyme, N.H.: Smith and Kraus, 1998.

Aragon, Cecilia J., and Heide K. Montemayor. *Rio Seco.* Unpublished manuscript, 1996.

Arce, Elia. *My Grandmother Never Past Away: A Stream of Consciousness and Unconsciousness.* In *Latinas on Stage,* edited by Alicia Arrizón and Lillian Manzor, 138–47. Berkeley: Third Woman, 2000.

Arizmendi, Yareli. *Nostalgia Maldita: 1–900–Mexico.* In *Puro Teatro: An Anthology of Latina Playwrights, Performance, and Testimonios,* edited by Alberto Sandoval-Sánchez and Nancy Saporta Sternbach, 228–38. Tucson: University of Arizona Press, 2000.

——. *Penny Envy/La envidia del penny.* Unpublished manuscript, n.d.

Astor del Valle, Janis. *El bloque de la escritora/The Writer's Block.* Unpublished manuscript, 1994.

——. *Fuchsia.* In *Puro Teatro: A Latina Anthology,* edited by Alberto Sandoval-Sánchez and Nancy Saporta Sternbach, 194–226. Tucson: University of Arizona

Press, 2000. Also in *Intimate Acts: Eight Contemporary Lesbian Plays,* edited by Nancy Dean and M. G. Barnes, 65–110. New York: Britto and Lair, 1997.

——. *Gyn.* Unpublished manuscript, n.d.

——. *I'll Be Home para la Navidad.* Unpublished manuscript, 1993.

——. *I'll Be Home para la Navidad* (excerpts). In *Amazon All Stars: Thirteen Lesbian Plays,* edited by Rosemary Keefe Curb, 19–33. New York: Applause Theatre, 1996. Also in *Torch of the Heart: Anthology of Lesbian Art and Drama,* edited by Sue McConnell-Celi, 97–113. Red Bank, N.J.: Lavender Crystal, 1994.

——. *Mi casa es tu casa.* Unpublished manuscript, 1995.

——. *The San Diego Street Padres.* Unpublished manuscript, 1999.

——. *Transplantations: Straight and Other Jackets para Mí.* In *Action: The Nuyorican Poets Café Theater Festival,* edited by Miguel Algarín and Lois Griffith, 373–94. New York: Touchstone, 1997.

——. *Where the Señoritas Are* (excerpt). In *Torch of the Heart: Anthology of Lesbian Art and Drama,* edited by Sue McConnell-Celi, 83–96. Red Bank, N.J.: Lavender Crystal, 1994.

——. *The Writer's Retreat, the Androgynous Zone.* Unpublished manuscript, n.d.

Barrera, Marisela. *Los de Abajo Have Nowhere Left to Fall.* Unpublished manuscript, 2000.

——. *Weeping Woman Cry Alone.* Unpublished manuscript, 2000.

Benavidez, María Elena. *Y cantaron mariachis.* Unpublished manuscript, 1998.

Bonet, Wilma. *Good Grief, Lolita!* In *Puro Teatro: A Latina Anthology,* edited by Alberto Sandoval-Sánchez and Nancy Saporta Sternbach, 239–56. Tucson: University of Arizona Press, 2000.

Bustamante, Nao. *Indigurrito.* Performance piece, 1997.

Calvet, Koala. *Conducting.* Unpublished manuscript, 1995.

——. *Foreigner's Biopsy.* Unpublished manuscript, 1995.

——. *The Green Madonna.* Unpublished manuscript, 1986.

——. *Pa' protejerte mejor.* Unpublished manuscript, 1995.

——. *Pest Control.* Unpublished manuscript, 1995.

Chávez, Denise. *Hecho en Mexico.* Unpublished manuscript, n.d.

——. *Nacimiento.* Unpublished manuscript, 1992.

——. *Novena narrativas.* In *Chicana Creativity and Criticism: Charting New Frontiers in American Literature,* edited by Maria Herrera-Sobek and Helena María Viramontes, 85–100. Houston, Texas: Arte Público, 1988. Also in *Goddess of the Americas/La Diosa de las Américas: Writings on the Virgin of Guadalupe,* edited by Ana Castillo, 153–69. New York: Riverhead, 1996.

——. *Plaza.* In *New Mexico Plays,* edited by David Richard Jones, 79–106. Albuquerque: University of New Mexico Press, 1989.

——. *Rainy Day Waterloo.* Unpublished manuscript, 1992.

——. *Sí, hay posada.* Unpublished manuscript, 1992.

Chavez, Theresa. *L.A. Real.* Unpublished manuscript, 1993.

Chicana. Performed by Las Cucarachas, 1974.

Colorado, Elvira, and Hortensia Colorado. *1992: Blood Speaks.* In *Contemporary Plays by Women of Color,* edited by Kathy E. Perkins and Roberta Uno, 79–89. New York: Routledge, 1996.

———. *A Traditional Kind of Woman: Too Much, Not 'Nuff—A Journey within and Without.* Performance piece. 1994.

Cruz, Migdalia. *Another Part of the House.* Unpublished manuscript, 1997.

———. *¡Che, Che, Che! (A Latin Fugue in 5/8 Time).* Unpublished manuscript, 1997.

———. *Cigarettes and Moby-Dick.* Unpublished manuscript, 1993.

———. *Dreams of Home.* In *The Best American Short Plays 1991–1992,* edited by Howard Stein and Glenn Young, 23–48. New York: Applause Theatre, 1992.

———. *Las flores de Miriam.* Princeton, N.J.: Libretas, 1987.

———. *Fur.* In *Out of the Fringe: Contemporary Latina/o Theatre and Performance,* edited by Caridad Svich and María Teresa Marrero, 71–114. New York: Theatre Communications Group, 2000.

———. *The Have-Little.* Unpublished manuscript, 1991.

———. *The Have-Little* (excerpt). In *Contemporary Plays by Women of Color,* edited by Kathy E. Perkins and Roberta Uno, 106–26. New York: Routledge, 1996.

———. *How!?* Unpublished manuscript, 1992.

———. *Latins in La-La Land.* Unpublished manuscript, 1994.

———. *Lolita de Lares.* Unpublished manuscript, 1995.

———. *Lucy Loves Me.* Unpublished manuscript, 1987.

———. *Lucy Loves Me.* In *Latinas on Stage,* edited by Alicia Arrizón and Lillian Manzor, 22–69. Berkeley, Calif.: Third Woman, 2000.

———. *Mariluz's Thanksgiving.* Unpublished manuscript, 1998.

———. *Miriam's Flowers.* Plays in Process. New York: Theatre Communications Group, 1990. Also in *Shattering the Myth: Plays by Hispanic Women,* edited by Linda Feyder and Denise Chávez, 51–84. Houston: Arte Público, 1992.

———. *Running for Blood: No. 3.* Unpublished manuscript, 1991.

———. *Rushing Waters.* Unpublished manuscript, 1993.

———. *Salt.* Unpublished manuscript, 1996.

———. *So . . .* Unpublished manuscript, 1995.

———. *Telling Tales.* In *Telling Tales: New One-Act Plays,* edited by Eric Lane, 1–16. New York: Penguin, 1993.

———. *Yellow Eyes.* Unpublished manuscript, 2000.

———. *Welcome Back to Salamanca.* Unpublished manuscript, n.d.

Cruz, Migdalia, and Hilary Blecher. *Frida.* In *Puro Teatro: A Latina Anthology,* edited by Alberto Sandoval-Sánchez and Nancy Saporta Sternbach, 337–90. Tucson: University of Arizona Press, 2000.

Davila, Flores Olivia. *Que, como, y cuando.* In *Chicano Theater,* edited by Juan Villegas and Julie Foraker, 47–64. Irvine: Ediciones Teatrales de Gestos, 1987.

Delmar, Linda. *Shadows.* Unpublished manuscript, 1997.

Esparza, Laura. "Battle-Worn." Testimonio. In *Puro Teatro: A Latina Anthology,* edited by Alberto Sandoval-Sánchez and Nancy Saporta Sternbach, 287–99. Tucson: University of Arizona Press, 2000.

——. *Border Boda.* Performance piece, 1990.

——. *Chicanatalk.* Unpublished manuscript, 1989.

——. *Flaco, Paco, and Esperanza.* Unpublished manuscript, 1994.

——. *I Dismember the Alamo.* Unpublished manuscript, 1991.

——. *I Dismember the Alamo.* In *Latinas on Stage,* edited by Alicia Arrizón and Lillian Manzor, 70–89. Berkeley, Calif.: Third Woman, 2000.

Feliciano, Gloria. *Between Blessings.* In *Action: The Nuyorican Poets Café Festival,* edited by Miguel Algarín and Lois Griffith, 237–55. New York: Touchstone, 1997.

——. *Zapatos viejos.* Unpublished manuscript, 1995.

Fernandez, Alicia. *Big, Bad, Beautiful.* Unpublished manuscript, 1997.

Fernández, Evelina. *How Else Am I Supposed to Know I'm Still Alive?* In *Contemporary Plays by Women of Color,* edited by Kathy E. Perkins and Roberta Uno, 158–67. New York: Routledge, 1996.

——. *Loving Rage.* Unpublished manuscript, 1994.

Feyder, Linda, ed. 1992. *Shattering the Myth: Plays by Hispanic Women.* Houston: Arte Público.

Fontes, Synidie M. *Butterfly in the Ashes.* Unpublished manuscript, 2000.

Fornes, Maria Irene. *The Conduct of Life.* In *On New Ground: Contemporary Hispanic-American Plays,* edited by M. Elizabeth Osborn, 45–72. New York: Theatre Communications Group, 1987. Also in *Telling Tales: New One Act Plays,* edited by Eric Lane, 32–53. New York: Penguin, 1993.

——. *The Danube.* In *Maria Irene Fornes Plays,* 41–64 .New York: PAJ, 1986.

——. *Dr. Kheal.* In *Promenade and Other Plays,* 127–35. New York: PAJ, 1992.

——. *Enter the Night.* In *Plays for the End of the Century,* edited by Bonnie Marranca, 121–79. Baltimore: Johns Hopkins University Press, 1996.

——. *Fefu and Her Friends.* New York: PAJ, 1978 (reprinted in 1980 and 1990).

——. *Fefu y sus amigas.* In *TEATRO: 5 autores cubanos,* edited by Rine Leal, 1–47. New York: Ollantay, 1995.

——. *Maria Irene Fornes Plays.* New York: PAJ, 1986.

——. *Molly's Dream.* In *Promenade and Other Plays,* 89–116. New York: PAJ, 1992.

——. *Mud.* In *Maria Irene Fornes Plays,* 13–40. New York: PAJ, 1986.

——. *Promenade.* In *Promenade and Other Plays,* 1–45. New York: PAJ, 1992.

——. *Sarita.* In *Maria Irene Fornes Plays,* 89–145. New York: PAJ, 1986.

——. *Springtime.* In *Amazon All Stars: Thirteen Lesbian Plays,* edited by Rosemary

Keefe Curb, 93–108. New York: Applause Theatre, 1996. Also in *Plays in One Act, Antaeus* 66, edited by Daniel Halpern, 81–90. New York: Ecco, 1991.

———. *The Successful Life of 3.* In *Promenade and Other Plays,* 47–68. New York: PAJ, 1992.

———. *Tango Palace.* In *Promenade and Other Plays,* 69–88. New York: PAJ, 1992.

———. *Terra Incognita. Theater* 2.1 (1993): 99–111.

———. *A Vietnamese Wedding.* In *Promenade and Other Plays,* 117–25. New York: PAJ, 1992.

———. *What of the Night?* In *Women on the Verge: Seven Avant Garde Plays,* edited by Rosette C. Lamont, 157–235. New York: Applause Theatre, 1993.

Fox, Ofelia, and Rose Sánchez. *About "The Change."* Unpublished manuscript, n.d.

———. *I Always Meant to Tell You Something.* Unpublished manuscript, 1989.

———. *Of Barbers and Other Men.* Unpublished manuscript, 1988.

———. *Siempre Intenté Decirte Algo (SIDA).* Unpublished manuscript, n.d.

Fusco, Coco, *Pochonovela: A Chicano Soap Opera.* Videocassette. Chicago: Art Institute of Chicago, Cabrona Soy Productions, 1995.

Fusco, Coco, and Nao Bustamante. "Stuff." *Drama Review* 41.4 (winter 1997): 63–82. Also in *Out of the Fringe: Contemporary Latina/o Theatre and Performance,* edited by Caridad Svich and María Teresa Marrero, 43–68. New York: Theatre Communications Group, 2000. Also excerpted in *Corpus Delecti,* edited by Coco Fusco, 61–62. New York: Routledge, 2000.

Fusco, Coco, and Guillermo Gómez-Peña. "Norte: Sur." In *English Is Broken Here: Notes on Cultural Fusion,* by Coco Fusco, 169–78. New York: New Press, 1995.

———. *Radio Pirata: Colón Go Home!* In *English Is Broken Here: Notes on Cultural Fusion,* by Coco Fusco, 179–95. New York: New Press, 1995.

Fusco, Coco, and Paula Heyedia. Video recording. *The Couple in the Cage.* Authentic Documentary Productions, 1993.

García Crow, Amparo. *Appeal.* Unpublished manuscript, 1993.

———. *Cocks Have Claws and Wings to Fly.* Unpublished manuscript, 1993.

———. *Nuestro barrio.* Unpublished manuscript, 1992.

———. *A Roomful of Men.* In *Puro Teatro: A Latina Anthology,* edited by Alberto Sandoval-Sánchez and Nancy Saporta Sternbach, 257–80. Tucson: University of Arizona Press, 2000.

———. *Under a Western Sky.* Unpublished manuscript, 1997.

García, Anne Romero. *Immigrant Interludes.* Unpublished manuscript, 1997.

———. *Santa Concepción.* Unpublished manuscript, 1998.

Gasteazoro, Eva. *Amor de mis amores.* In *Action: The Nuyorican Poets Café Theatre Festival,* edited by Miguel Algarín and Lois Griffith, 315–23. New York: Touchstone, 1997.

Gómez, Magdalena. *Chopping.* Unpublished manuscript, 2000.

———. *A Joyful Grieving.* Unpublished manuscript, 2000.

——. *You Don't Look It.* Unpublished performance piece, 1999.

Gomez, Marga. *A Line around the Block.* Video, n.d. Used by permission of the artist.

——. *Marga Gomez Is Pretty, Witty, and Gay* (excerpt). In *Out, Loud, and Laughing,* edited by Charles Flowers, 85–95. New York: Anchor, 1995.

——. *Marga Gomez Is Pretty, Witty, and Gay.* Video, n.d.

——. *Memory Tricks.* Video, n.d.

——. *Memory Tricks; Marga Gomez Is Pretty, Witty, and Gay;* and *A Line around the Block* (excerpts). In *Contemporary Plays by Women of Color,* edited by Kathy E. Perkins and Roberta Uno, 191–98. New York, N.Y.: Routledge, 1996.

Gomez, Terry. *Inter-Tribal.* In *Contemporary Plays by Women of Color,* edited by Kathy E. Perkins and Roberta Uno, 199–214. New York: Routledge, 1996.

González, Gloria. *Café con leche.* Unpublished manuscript, 1983.

Gonzalez S., Silvia. *Alicia in Wonder Tierra (or I Can't Eat Goat Head).* Unpublished manuscript, 1995.

——. *Alicia in Wonder Tierra (or I Can't Eat Goat Head).* Woodstock, Ill.: Dramatic, 1996.

——. *Border.* Unpublished manuscript, 1992.

——. *Boxcar.* Unpublished manuscript, 1991.

——. *Fiesta!* Unpublished manuscript, 1995.

——. *Gang Girls.* Unpublished manuscript, 1991.

——. *La Llorona llora.* Unpublished manuscript, 1992.

——. *Los matadores.* Unpublished manuscript, 1992.

——. *The Migrant Worker's Son.* Unpublished manuscript, 1992.

——. *The Shrinking Wife.* Unpublished manuscript, 1995.

——. *Squeezed Avocados.* Unpublished manuscript, 1995.

——. *T.* Unpublished manuscript, 1992.

——. *U Got the Look.* Unpublished manuscript, 1995.

——. *Waiting Women.* Unpublished manuscript, 1993.

Iizuka, Naomi. *Skin.* In *Out of the Fringe: Contemporary Latina/Latino Theatre and Performance,* edited by Caridad Svich and María Teresa Marrero, 159–99. New York: Theatre Communications Group, 2000.

Llamas, Lorraine. *After School with Dad.* Unpublished manuscript, 1990.

——. *Black Jack.* Unpublished manuscript, 1991.

——. *Me! Me! Me!* Unpublished manuscript, 1992.

——. *Stretch and Lex.* Unpublished manuscript, 1988.

——. *This Quarter Is Worn on One Side.* Unpublished manuscript, 1987.

Loomer, Lisa. *Bocón.* In *Aplauso!* edited by Joe Rosenberg, 34–71. Houston: Arte Público, 1995.

——. *The Waiting Room.* In *American Theatre* 11.10 (1994): 31–51.

López, Eva. *Marlene.* In *Nuestro New York: An Anthology of Puerto Rican Plays,* edited by John Antush, 495–504. New York: Penguin Group, 1994.

López, Josefina. *Confessions.* Unpublished manuscript, 1996.

——. *Confessions of Women from East L.A.* Unpublished manuscript, 1996.

——. *Food for the Dead.* Unpublished manuscript, 1989.

——. *La Pinta.* Unpublished manuscript, n.d.

——. *Real Women Have Curves.* Unpublished manuscript, 1998.

——. *Simply Maria, or The American Dream.* In *Shattering the Myth: Plays by Hispanic Women,* edited by Linda Feyder and Denise Chávez, 113–41. Houston: Arte Público, 1992.

——. "Unconquered Spirits." Unpublished manuscript, 1992.

Lopez, Melinda. *God Smells Like a Roast Pig.* Performance piece, 2000.

——. *The Order of Things.* Unpublished manuscript, 2000.

Mar, María. "Dancing with the Voice of Truth." Testimonio. In *Puro Teatro: A Latina Anthology,* edited by Alberto Sandoval-Sánchez and Nancy Saporta Sternbach, 300–312. Tucson: University of Arizona Press, 2000.

——. *Temple of Desire.* Performance piece, 1994.

——. *What If . . . ?* Unpublished manuscript, n.d.

Márquez, Rosa Luisa. *Son Corazón/Heartstrung.* Unpublished manuscript, 1996.

Mena, Alicia. *Las nuevas tamaleras.* In *Puro Teatro: A Latina Anthology,* edited by Alberto Sandoval-Sánchez and Nancy Saporta Sternbach, 149–75. Tucson: University of Arizona Press, 2000.

——. *There Comes a Time.* Unpublished manuscript, 1993.

Moraga, Cherríe. *Giving Up the Ghost.* Los Angeles: West End, 1986. Also in *Heroes and Saints and Other Plays,* 1–35. Los Angeles: West End, 1994. Also in *Gay and Lesbian Plays,* edited by Eric Lane and Nina Shengold, 380–416. New York: Penguin, 1995.

——. *Heart of the Earth: A Popul Vuh Story.* In *Puro Teatro: A Latina Anthology,* edited by Alberto Sandoval-Sánchez and Nancy Saporta Sternbach, 46–88. Tucson: University of Arizona Press. 2000.

——. *Heroes and Saints.* In *Heroes and Saints and Other Plays,* 85–149. Los Angeles: West End, 1994. Also in *Contemporary Plays by Women of Color,* edited by Kathy E. Perkins and Roberta Uno, 230–61. New York: Routledge, 1996.

——. *The Hungry Woman: Mexican Medea.* In *Out of the Fringe: Contemporary Latina/o Theatre and Performance,* edited by Caridad Svich and María Teresa Marrero, 289–362. New York: Theatre Communications Group, 2000. Also excerpt of work in progress in *Latinas on Stage,* edited by Alicia Arrizón and Lillian Manzor, 158–61. Berkeley, Calif.: Third Woman, 2000.

——. *Shadow of a Man.* In *Heroes and Saints and Other Plays,* 37–84. Los Angeles: West End, 1986. Also in *Shattering the Myth: Plays by Hispanic Women,* edited by Linda Feyder and Denise Chávez, 9–49. Houston: Arte Público, 1992.

——. *Watsonville.* Unpublished manuscript, 1996.

Ortiz Cortes, Noelia, and Brenda Cotto Escalera. *Immaculate Infection.* Unpublished manuscript, 2000.

——. *MOTHERlands.* Unpublished manuscript, 1997.

Palacios, Monica. *Clock.* Unpublished manuscript, n.d.

——. *Confessions.* Unpublished manuscript, 2000.

——. *Deep in the Crotch of My Latino Psyche* (in collaboration with Luis Alfaro and Albert Araiza). Unpublished manuscript, 1992.

——. *Describe Your Work.* In *Puro Teatro: A Latina Anthology,* edited by Alberto Sandoval-Sánchez and Nancy Saporta Sternbach, 281–84. Tucson: University of Arizona Press, 2000.

——. *Greetings from a Queer Señorita.* Unpublished manuscript, 1995.

——. *Greetings from a Queer Señorita.* In *Out of the Fringe: Contemporary Latina/o Theatre and Performance,* edited by Caridad Svich and María Teresa Marrero, 365–91. New York: Theatre Communications Group, 2000.

——. *Latin Lezbo Comic.* In *Latinas on Stage,* edited by Alicia Arrizón and Lillian Manzor, 90–116. Berkeley, Calif.: Third Woman, 2000.

——. *Pilgrim Woman.* Unpublished manuscript, 2000.

——. *Tomboy.* In *Living Chicana Theory,* edited by Carla Trujillo, 306–9. Berkeley, Calif.: Third Woman, 1998.

Pérez, Ruby Nelda. Performer of *Doña Rosita's Jalapeño Kitchen.* Unpublished performance piece written by Rodrigo Duarte Clark, n.d.

——. *A Woman's Work.* Performance of Chicana poetry by Mary Sue Galindo, Enedina Casarez Vasquez, and Beverly Sánchez-Padilla. Unpublished manuscript, n.d.

Pérez, Judith, and Severo Pérez. *Soldierboy.* In *Necessary Theater: Six Plays about the Chicano Experience,* edited by Jorge Huerta, 20–75. Houston: Arte Público, 1989.

Portillo Trambley, Estela. *Autumn Gold.* In *Sor Juana and Other Plays,* 37–99. Ypsilanti, Mich.: Bilingual/Editorial Bilingüe, 1983.

——. *Blacklight.* In *Sor Juana and Other Plays,* 101–42. Ypsilanti, Mich.: Bilingual/Editorial Bilingüe, 1983.

——. *The Day of the Swallows.* In *El Espejo,* edited by Herminio Rios and Octavio Romano V., 149–93. Berkeley: Quinto Sol, 1972. Also in *We Are Chicano: An Anthology of Mexican-American Literature,* edited by Philip D. Ortega, 224–71. New York: Washington Square, 1973. Also in *Contemporary Chicano Theatre,* edited by Roberto J. Garza, 207–45. Notre Dame: University of Notre Dame Press, 1976.

——. *Puente Negro.* In *Sor Juana and Other Plays,* 1–35. Ypsilanti, Mich.: Bilingual/Editorial Bilingüe, 1983.

——. *Sor Juana.* In *Sor Juana and Other Plays,* 143–95. Ypsilanti, Mich: Bilingual/Editorial Bilingüe, 1983.

———. *Sor Juana and Other Plays.* Ypsilanti, Mich.: Bilingual Press/Editorial Bilingüe, 1983.

———. *Sun Images.* In *Nuevos Pasos: Chicano and Puerto Rican Drama,* edited by Nicolás Kanellos and Jorge A. Huerta, 19–42. Houston.: Arte Público, 1989.

Prida, Dolores. *Beautiful Señoritas.* In *Beautiful Señoritas and Other Plays,* 17–45. Houston: Arte Público, 1991. Also in *In Other Words: Literature by Latinas of the United States,* edited by Roberta Fernández, 508–31. Houston: Arte Público, 1994.

———. *Beautiful Señoritas and Other Plays.* Edited by Judith Weiss. Houston: Arte Público, 1991.

———. *The Beggars Soap Opera.* Unpublished manuscript, n.d.

———. *Botánica* (in English). In *Puro Teatro: A Latina Anthology,* edited by Alberto Sandoval-Sánchez and Nancy Saporta Sternbach, 7–45. Tucson: University of Arizona Press, 2000.

———. *Botánica* (in Spanish). In *Beautiful Señoritas and Other Plays,* edited by Judith Weiss, 141–80. Houston: Arte Público, 1991.

———. *Casa propria.* Unpublished manuscript, 1999.

———. *Coser y cantar.* In *Beautiful Señoritas and Other Plays,* edited by Judith Weiss, 47–67. Houston: Arte Público, 1991. Also in *The Hispanic Literary Companion,* edited by Nicolás Kanellos, 264–81. New York: Visible Ink, 1997. Also in *Tramoya* 22 (1990): 117–36.

———. *4 Guys Named José . . . and una Mujer Named María!* Unpublished manuscript, 2000.

———. *Garbash* (excerpt). In *Review: Latin American Literature and Arts,* edited by Alfred J. Mac Adam, 34–38. New York: Americas Society, 1992.

———. *Pantallas.* In *Beautiful Señoritas and Other Plays,* edited by Judith Weiss, 117–40. Houston: Arte Público, 1991.

———. *Savings.* In *Beautiful Señoritas and Other Plays,* edited by Judith Weiss, 71–116. Houston: Arte Público, 1991. Also in *Barrios and Borderlands: Cultures of Latinos and Latinas in the United States,* edited by Denis Lynn Daly Heyck, 164–203. New York: Routledge, 1994.

———. *Screens.* In *Cuban Theater in the United States: A Critical Anthology,* edited and translated by Luis F. González-Cruz and Francesca M. Colecchia, 123–50. Tempe, Ariz.: Bilingual/Editorial Bilingüe, 1992.

Prida, Dolores, and Victor Fragoso. *La era latina.* Unpublished manuscript, n.d.

Ramirez, Yvette M. *Family Scenes.* In *Recent Puerto Rican Theater: Five Plays from New York,* edited by John Antush, 227–55. Houston: Arte Público, 1991.

Rivera, Carmen. *La gringa.* Unpublished manuscript, n.d.

———. *Julia.* In *Nuestro New York: An Anthology of Puerto Rican Plays,* edited by John V. Antush, 133–78. New York: Penguin Group, 1994.

——. *Julia de Burgos: Child of Water.* Unpublished manuscript, 1999.

——. *The Next Stop.* Unpublished manuscript, 1999.

——. *Plastic Flowers.* Unpublished manuscript, n.d.

——. *To Catch the Lightning.* Unpublished manuscript, 1997.

Rodríguez, Diane. *The Path to Divadom.* Unpublished manuscript, 1995.

——. "Searching for Sanctuaries: Cruising through Town in a Red Convertible." Testimonio. In *Puro Teatro: A Latina Anthology,* edited by Alberto Sandoval-Sánchez and Nancy Saporta Sternbach, 313–18. Tucson: University of Arizona Press, 2000.

Rodríguez, Sandra, and Nueva Visión Theater Troupe. *Colors.* Unpublished manuscript, 1995.

Rodríguez, Sandra, and Grupo Bridges. *The Return of Margarita.* Unpublished manuscript, 1995.

Rodríguez, Sandra, with Grupo Moriviví and Nueva Visión Theater. *Tales from the Flats.* Unpublished manuscript, n.d.

Rodríguez, Yolanda. *The Cause.* Unpublished manuscript, 1994.

——. *Emigración: An American Play.* Unpublished manuscript, 1994.

——. *Rising Sun, Falling Star.* In *Nuestro New York: An Anthology of Puerto Rican Plays,* edited by John V. Antush, 363–420. New York: Penguin Group, 1994.

Romero, Elaine. *Baby Food.* Unpublished manuscript, 1995.

——. *Barrio Hollywood.* Unpublished manuscript, 1999.

——. *Before Death Comes for the Archbishop.* Unpublished manuscript, 2000.

——. *California Big and Small.* Unpublished manuscript, 1999.

——. *Curanderas! Serpents of the Clouds.* Unpublished manuscript, 1996.

——. *Dream Friend.* Unpublished manuscript, 1995.

——. *Ethnic Data.* Unpublished manuscript, 1990.

——. *A Family Tradition.* Unpublished manuscript, 1995.

——. *The Fat-Free Chicana and the Snow Cap Queen.* In *Puro Teatro: A Latina Anthology,* edited by Alberto Sandoval-Sánchez and Nancy Saporta Sternbach, 89–144. Tucson: University of Arizona Press, 2000.

——. *Fear of Extinction.* Unpublished manuscript, 2000.

——. *If Susan Smith Could Talk.* Unpublished manuscript, 1995.

——. *Living Dolls.* Unpublished manuscript, 1992.

——. *Lost.* Unpublished manuscript, 1998.

——. *Memorial Day.* Unpublished manuscript, 1988.

——. *Roadaphobia.* Unpublished manuscript, 1999.

——. *Secret Things.* Unpublished manuscript, 2000

——. *Shelly's Daughters.* Unpublished manuscript, 1998.

——. *Smashed.* Unpublished manuscript, 1987.

——. *A Still Small Voice.* Unpublished manuscript, 1998.

——. *Strangers.* Unpublished manuscript, 1991.

——. *Undercurrents.* Unpublished manuscript, 1990.

——. *Walking Home.* Unpublished manuscript, 1996.

——. *Walking Home. Ollantay Theatre Magazine* 4.1 (1996): 127–74.

Ruiz, Elizabeth. *Dating Dummies, or The Inevitable Extinction of the Homo Sapiens.* Princeton, N.J.: Libreti, 1997.

Sáenz, Diana. *Baby Goats.* Unpublished manuscript, 1988.

——. *A Dream of Canaries.* In *Shattering the Myth: Plays by Hispanic Women,* edited by Linda Feyder and Denise Chávez, 209–55. Houston: Arte Público, 1992.

——. *Frida, Self-portrait in Dance.* Unpublished manuscript, n.d.

——. *Orca at Viznar.* Unpublished manuscript, 1990.

——. *Oswald's Chin.* Unpublished manuscript, 1992.

——. *Phoenix Café.* Unpublished manuscript, 1988.

Sánchez-Scott, Milcha. *The Cuban Swimmer.* In *Plays in One Act, Antaeus* 66, edited by Daniel Halpern, 407–20. New York: Ecco, 1991.

——. *Dog Lady* and *The Cuban Swimmer.* New York: Dramatists Play Service, 1988.

——. *Evening Star.* New York: Dramatists Play Service, 1989.

——. *The Old Matador.* Unpublished manuscript, n.d.

——. *Roosters.* In *On New Ground: Contemporary Hispanic-American Plays,* edited by M. Elizabeth Osborn, 243–80. New York: Theatre Communications Group, 1987.

——. *Roosters.* Video broadcast on *American Playhouse,* PBS, 1989.

Sánchez-Scott, Milcha, and Jeremy Blahnik. *Latina.* In *Necessary Theater: Six Plays about the Chicano Experience,* edited by Jorge Huerta, 85–141. Houston: Arte Público, 1989.

Serrano-Bonaparte, Lynnette. *Broken Bough.* Unpublished manuscript, 1988.

Simo, Ana María. *Going to New England.* Unpublished manuscript, 1990.

——. *What Do You See?* In *The Sexuality of Latinas,* edited by Norma Alarcón, Ana Castillo, and Cherríe Moraga, 113–19. Berkeley, Calif.: Third Woman, 1993. Also in *Tough Acts to Follow: One-Act Plays on the Gay/Lesbian Experience,* edited by Noreen C. Barnes and Nicholas Deutsch, 112–20. San Francisco: Alamo Square, 1992.

Svich, Caridad. *Alchemy of Desire/Dead-Man's Blues.* In *Out of the Fringe: Contemporary Latina/o Theatre and Performance,* edited by Caridad Svich and María Teresa Marrero, 393–442. New York: Theatre Communications Group, 2000.

——. *Any Place But Here.* Unpublished manuscript, 1991.

——. *Away Down Dreaming.* Unpublished manuscript, n.d.

——. *Brazo Gitano. Ollantay Theatre Magazine* 6.11 (1998): 151–80.

——. "Home, Desire, Memory: There Are No Borders Here." Testimonio. In *Puro Teatro: An Latina Anthology,* edited by Alberto Sandoval-Sánchez and Nancy Saporta Sternbach, 319–24. Tucson: University of Arizona Press, 2000.

———. *Gleaning/Rebusca.* In *Shattering the Myth: Plays by Hispanic Women,* edited by Linda Feyder and Denise Chávez, 85–112. Houston: Arte Público, 1992.

———. *Pensacola.* Unpublished manuscript, 1996.

———. *Prodigal Kiss.* Unpublished manuscript, 1998.

———. *Scar.* Unpublished manuscript, 1994.

———. *Scar.* In *Latinas on Stage,* edited by Alicia Arrizón and Lillian Manzor, 148–56. Berkeley, Calif.: Third Woman, 2000.

Svich, Caridad, and María Teresa Marrero, eds. *Out of the Fringe: Contemporary Latina/Latino Theatre and Performance.* New York: Theatre Commnications Group, 2000.

Tatiana de la Tierra. *Biop-see.* Unpublished manuscript, 1998.

———. *This Is about Pleasure.* Unpublished manuscript, 1998.

Tropicana, Carmelita. *The Boiler Time Machine.* Unpublished manuscript, n.d.

———. *Chicas 2000.* In *I, Carmelita Tropicana,* 72–122. Boston: Beacon, 2000.

———. "The Conquest of Mexico as Seen through the Eyes of Hernan Cortes's Horse." In *I, Carmelita Tropicana,* 173–76. Boston: Beacon, 2000.

———. "Food for Thought." In *I, Carmelita Tropicana,* 187–90. Boston: Beacon, 2000.

———. *I, Carmelita Tropicana.* Boston: Beacon, 2000.

———. *Milk of Amnesia/Leche de amnesia. Drama Review* 39, 3 (1995): 94–111. Also in *O Solo Homo: The New Queer Performance,* edited by David Román and Holly Hughes, 17–47. New York: Grove, 1998. Also in *I, Carmelita Tropicana,* 52–71. Boston: Beacon, 2000. Also in *Latinas on Stage,* edited by Alicia Arrizón and Lillian Manzor, 118–37. Berkeley: Third Woman, 2000.

———. "Performance Art Manifesto." In *I, Carmelita Tropicana,* 177–178. Boston: Beacon, 2000.

———. "Radio Spot for WNYC." In *I, Carmelita Tropicana,* 179. Boston: Beacon, 2000.

———. "El recibo social/The Social Visit." In *I, Carmelita Tropicana,* 180–86. Boston: Beacon, 2000.

———. *Speech at the L.U.S.T. Conference.* In *The New Fuck You: Adventures in Lesbian Reading,* edited by Eileen Myles and Liz Kotz, 25–29. New York: Semiotext(e), 1995.

Tropicana, Carmelita, and Uzi Parnes. *Carnaval. Michigan Quarterly Review* 33 (1994): 733–47.

———. *Memories of the Revolution/Memorias de la revolucion.* In *Puro Teatro: A Latina Anthology,* edited by Alberto Sandoval-Sánchez and Nancy Saporta Sternbach, 391–424. Tucson: University of Arizona Press, 2000. Also in *I, Carmelita Tropicana,* 1–51. Boston: Beacon, 2000.

Tropicana, Carmelita, and Ela Troyana. *Sor Juana: The Nightmare.* In *I, Carmelita Tropicana,* 123–34. Boston: Beacon, 2000.

Troyano, Alina. *I, Carmelita Tropicana: Performing between Cultures.* Boston: Beacon, 2000.

Vélez Mitchell, Anita. *Nonsense.* Unpublished manuscript, n.d.

———. *The Rippling Mind.* Unpublished manuscript, 1990.

———. *The Salsamerican Connection.* Unpublished manuscript, n.d.

Villarreal, Edit. *Alone in the Water: A Hispano Farce at Sea.* Unpublished manuscript, n.d.

———. "Catching the Next Play: The Joys and Perils of Playwriting." Testimonio. In *Puro Teatro: A Latina Anthology,* edited by Alberto Sandoval-Sánchez and Nancy Saporta Sternbach, 330–33. Tucson: University of Arizona Press, 2000.

———. *Crazy from the Heart.* Unpublished manuscript, 1989.

———. *The Language of Flowers.* Unpublished manuscript, 1995.

———. *My Visits with MGM.* In *Shattering the Myth: Plays by Hispanic Women,* edited by Linda Feyder and Denise Chávez, 143–208. Houston: Arte Público, 1992.

Voz de la Mujer. Performed by Valentina Productions, 1981.

Walden, Lisa Cortez. *Tripas.* Unpublished manuscript, 2000.

Women of Ill Repute: REFUTE! Performance piece, 2000.

Wood, Silviana. *Amor de hija.* Unpublished manuscript, 1990.

———. *And Where Was Pancho Villa When You Really Needed Him?* In *Puro Teatro: A Latina Anthology,* edited by Alberto Sandoval-Sánchez and Nancy Saporta Sternbach, 176–93. Tucson: University of Arizona Press, 2000.

———. *Anhelos por Oaxaca.* Unpublished manuscript, 1986.

———. *Caras y mascaras: A Drunkard's Tale of Melted Wings and Memories.* Unpublished manuscript, 1992.

———. *El chiflo de oro.* Edited by Beatriz J. Rizk. *Tramoya: Cuaderno de Teatro* 22 (1990): 21–30.

———. *Cuentos de barrio.* Unpublished manuscript, 1982.

———. *The Dragon Slayer.* Unpublished manuscript, 1989.

———. *Surcos de oro.* Unpublished manuscript, 1999.

———. *Una vez, en un barrio de sueños.* Unpublished manuscript, 1984.

———. *Yo, Casimiro Flores.* Unpublished manuscript, 1997.

CRITICAL WORKS CITED & SECONDARY SOURCES

Ahmad, Aijaz. 1995. "Postcolonialism: What's in a Name?" In *Late Imperial Culture,* edited by Román de la Carpa, E. Ann Kaplan, and Michael Sprinker, 11–32. London: Verso.

Aizenberg, Edna. 1985. "El *Bildungsroman* fracasado en Latinoamérica: El caso de *Ifigenia* de Teresa de la Parra." *Revista Iberoamericana* 51: 539–46.

Alarcón, Norma. 1988. "Making 'Familia' from Scratch: Split Subjectivities in the Work of Cherríe Moraga." In *Chicana Creativity: Charting New Frontiers in American Literature,* edited by María Herrera-Sobek and Helena María Viramontes, 147–59. Houston: Arte Público.

——. 1994. "Cognitive Desires: An Allegory of/for Chicana Critics." In *Listening to Silences: New Essays in Feminist Criticism,* edited by Elaine Hedges and Shelley Fisher Fishkin, 260–73. New York and Oxford: Oxford University Press.

——. 1996. "Conjugating Subjects in the Age of Multiculturalism." In *Mapping Multiculturalism,* edited by Avery Gordon and Christopher Newfield, 127–48. Minneapolis: University of Minnesota Press.

Alonso, Carlos J. 1996. "The Burden of Modernity." *Modern Language Quarterly* 57.2 (June): 227–35.

Alvarez, Julia. 1991. *How the García Sisters Lost Their Accents.* Chapel Hill: Algonquin.

Amrine, Frederick. 1987. "Rethinking 'The Bildungsroman.'" *Michigan Germanic Studies* 13.2: 119–39.

Anderson, Benedict. 1991. *Imagined Communities: Reflections on the Spread of Nationalism.* Rev. ed. London: Verso.

Angus, Ian H. 1997. *A Border Within: National Identity, Cultural Plurality, and Wilderness.* Montreal, Buffalo: McGill-Queens University Press.

Anzaldúa, Gloria. 1987. *Borderlands/La Frontera.* San Francisco: Spinsters/aunt lute.

Aparicio, Frances, and Susan Chávez-Silverman, eds. 1997. *Tropicalizations: Transcultural Representations of Latinidad.* Hanover, N.H..: University of New England Press.

Apodaca, Sylvia P. 1993. "Milcha Sanchez-Scott." In *Notable Hispanic American Women,* edited by Diane Telgen and Jim Kamp, 367–68. Detroit: Gale Research.

Appadurai, Arjun. 1988. "How to Make a National Cuisine: Cookbooks in Contemporary India." *Comparative Studies in Society and History* 30: 3–24.

——. 1990. "Disjuncture and Difference in the Global Cultural Economy." *Theory, Culture, and Society* 7.2–3: 295–310.

——. 1996. *Modernity at Large: Cultural Dimensions of Globalization.* Minneapolis: University of Minnesota Press.

Apple, Jacki. 1994. "Performance Art Is Dead: Long Live Performance Art." *High Performance* 17.2: 54–59.

——. 1995. "Notes on Teaching Performance Art." *Performing Arts Journal* 50–51: 121–25.

Arizmendi, Yareli. 1994. "Whatever Happened to the Sleepy Mexican?" *The Drama Review* 38.1 (spring): 106–17.

Arrizón, Alicia. 1996. "Chicanas en la escena: Teatralidad y performance." *Ollantay Theater Magazine* 4.1: 21–32.

——. 1999. *Latina Performance: Traversing the Stage.* Bloomington: University of Indiana Press.

——. 2000a. "Conquest of Space: The Construction of Chicana Subjectivity in Performance Art." In *Latinas on Stage,* edited by Alicia Arrizón and Lillian Manzor, 352–69. Berkeley: Third Woman.

——. 2000b. "Mythical Performativity: Relocating Aztlán in Feminist Cultural Productions." *Theatre Journal* 52.1: 23–49.

Arrizón, Alicia, and Lillian Manzor, eds. 2000. *Latinas on Stage.* Berkeley: Third Woman.

Atkins, Pope G. 1998. *The Dominican Republic and the United States: From Imperialism to Transnationalism.* Athens: University of Georgia Press.

Auslander, Phillip. 1994. *Presence and Resistance: Postmodernism and Cultural Politics in Contemporary American Performance.* Ann Arbor: University of Michigan Press.

Avila, Kat. 1996. "The Genesis of Edit Villarreal's *MGM.*" *Ollantay Theater Magazine* 4.1: 52–57.

Bammer, Angelika, ed. 1992. "Editorial." *New Formations* 17: vii–xi.

——. 1994. *Displacements: Cultural Identities in Question.* Bloomington: Indiana University Press.

Barradas, Efraín. 1979. " 'De lejos en sueño verla . . .': Visión mítica de Puerto Rico en la poesía neorrican." *Revista Chicano-Riqueña* 7.3: 46–56.

Barthes, Roland. 1979. *Mythologies.* New York: Hill and Wang.

Baucom, Ian. 1991. "Dreams of Home: Colonialism and Postmodernism." *Research in African Literatures* 22.4: 5–27.

Baym, Nina. 1981. "Melodramas of Beset Manhood: How Theories of American Fiction Exclude Women Authors." *American Quarterly* 33.2: 125–39.

Belsey, Catherine. 1992. *Critical Practice.* London and New York: Routledge.

Berkman, Len. 1993. "An Interview with Amy González: 'All Ears, to Let My Ideas Transform.' " In *Upstaging Big Daddy: Directing Theater as if Gender and Race*

Matter, edited by Ellen Donkin and Susan Clement, 309–15. Ann Arbor: University of Michigan Press.

Berry, Pam. 1993. "Silvia Brito." In *Notable Hispanic American Women,* edited by Diane Telgen and Jim Kamp, 60. Detroit: Gale Research.

Bhabha, Homi K. 1990a. "DissemiNation: Time, Narrative, and the Margins of the Modern Nation." In *Nation and Narration,* edited by Homi K. Bhabha, 291–322. London and New York: Routledge.

———. 1990b. "Narrating the Nation." Introduction to *Nation and Narration,* edited by Homi K. Bhabha, 1–7. London and New York: Routledge.

———. 1992. "The World and the Home." *Social Text* 31–32: 141–53.

———. 1994a. "Frontlines/Borderposts." In *Displacements: Cultural Identities in Question,* edited by Angelika Bammer, 269–72. Bloomington: Indiana University Press.

———. 1994b. *The Location of Culture.* London and New York: Routledge.

———. 1996. "Culture's In-Between." In *Questions of Cultural Identity,* edited by Stuart Hall and Paul du Gay, 53–60. Thousand Oaks, Calif.: Sage.

Bissett, Judith. 1993. "Luisa Josefina Hernández y Estela Portillo Trambley: La expresión dramática de una voz femenina: ¿Semejante o distinta?" *Ollantay Theater Magazine* 1.2: 14–20.

Bonilla-Santiago, Gloria. 1993. "Miriam Colón." In *Notable Hispanic American Women,* edited by Diane Telgen and Jim Kamp, 108–9. Detroit: Gale Research.

Boone, Joseph A. 1996. "Queer Sites in Modernism: Harlem/The Left Bank? Greenwich Village." *Geographies of Identity,* edited by Patricia Yaeger, 243–72. Michigan: University of Michigan Press.

Bourne, Jenny. 1987. "Homelands of the Mind: Jewish Feminism and Identity Politics." *Race and Class* 29.1: 1–24.

Brady, Mary Pat, and Juanita Heredia. 1993. "Coming Home: Interview with Cherríe Moraga." *Mester* 22–23: 149–64.

Braendlin, Bonnie Hoover. 1974. "*Bildung* in Ethnic Women Writers." *PMLA* 89: 75–87.

———. 1979. "Alther, Atwood, Ballantyne, and Gray: Secular Salvation in the Contemporary Feminist Bildungsroman." *Frontiers* 4.1: 18–22.

Brown, Linda Keller, and Kay Mussell, eds. 1997. *Ethnic and Regional Foodways in the United States: The Performance of Group Identity.* Knoxville: University of Tennessee Press.

Broyles-González, Yolanda Julia. 1986. "Women in El Teatro Campesino: Apoco estaba molacha la Virgen de Guadalupe?" In *Chicana Voices: Intersection of Class, Race, and Gender,* edited by Ricardo Romo, 162–87. Austin: Center for Mexican American Studies.

———. 1989. "Toward a Re-Vision of Chicano Theatre History: The Women of El Teatro Campesino." In *Making a Spectacle: Feminist Essays on Contemporary Wom-*

en's Theatre, edited by Lynda Hart, 209–38. Ann Arbor: University of Michigan Press.

——. 1994. *El Teatro Campesino: Theatre in the Chicano Movement.* Austin: University of Texas Press, 1994.

Bruce-Novoa, Juan. 1978. "El Teatro Campesino de Luis Valdez." *Texto Crítico* 7.10 (May–August): 65–75.

——. 1980. "Interview with Estela Portillo." In *Mexican-American Authors: Inquiry by Interview,* 163–81. Austin: University of Texas Press.

——. 1990. *Retro-Space: Collected Essays on Chicano Literature.* Houston: Arte Público.

Brunner, José Joaquín. 1995. "Notes on Modernity and Postmodernity in Latin America Culture." In *The Postmodern Debate in Latin America,* edited by Michael Aronna, John Beverley, and José Oviedo, 34–54. Durham, N.C.: Duke University Press.

Buckley, Jerome. 1974. *Season of Youth: The Bildungsroman from Dickens to Golding.* Cambridge, Mass.: Harvard University Press.

Butler, Judith. 1988. "Performative Acts and Gender Constitution: An Essay in Phenomenology and Feminist Theory." *Theatre Journal* 40.4 (Dec.): 519–31.

——. 1990. *Gender Trouble: Feminism and the Subversion of Identity.* New York: Routledge.

——. 1993. *Bodies That Matter: On the Discursive Limits of Sex.* New York and London: Routledge.

Byers Pevitts, Beverly. 1987. *"Fefu and Her Friends."* Review of *Fefu and Her Friends,* by Maria Irene Fornes. In *Women in American Theatre,* edited by Helen Krich Chinoy and Linda Walsh Jenkins, 314–17. New York: Theatre Communications Group.

Cabral, Amilcar. 1973. *Return to the Source.* London: Monthly Review.

Calderón, Héctor, and José David Saldívar, eds. 1991. *Criticism in the Borderlands: Studies in Chicano Literature, Culture, and Ideology.* Durham, N.C.: Duke University Press.

Candelario, Ginetta. 2000. "Hair Race-ing: Dominican Beauty Culture and Identity Production." *Meridians: feminism, race, transnationalism* 1.1: 128–56.

Canning, Charlotte. 1995. "Contemporary Feminist Theatre." In *American Drama,* edited by Clive Bloom, 178–92. New York: St. Martin's.

Cantú, Norma. 1995. *Canícula.* Albuquerque: University of New Mexico Press.

Cao, Antonio F. 1994. "Elementos comunes en el teatro cubano del exilio: Marginalidad y patriarcado." In *Lo que no se ha dicho,* edited by Pedro Monge-Rafuls, 43–52. Jackson Heights: Ollantay.

Carby, Hazel V. 1990. "The Politics of Difference." *Ms.* (Sept.–Oct.): 84–85.

Cardoso, Fernando Henrique. 1972. "Dependency and Development in Latin America." *New Left Review* 74 (July–August): 83–95.

——. 1977. "The Consumption of Dependency Theory in the United States." *Latin American Research Review* 12.3: 7–24.

Carlson, Lance. 1990. "Performance Art as Political Activism." *Artweek* 22 (May): 23–24.

Carlson, Marvin. 1996. *Performance: A Critical Introduction.* London and New York: Routledge.

Carr, Cythnia. 1993. *On Edge: Performance at the End of the Twentieth Century.* Hanover, N.H.: University of New England Press.

Case, Sue Ellen. 1988. "Women of Colour and Theatre." In *Feminism and Theatre,* 95–111. New York: Methuen.

——. 1989. "Toward a Butch-Femme Aesthetic." In *Making a Spectacle: Feminist Essays on Contemporary Women's Theatre,* edited by Lynda Hart, 282–99. Ann Arbor: University of Michigan Press.

——, ed. 1990. *Performing Feminisms: Feminist Critical Theory and Theatre.* London and Baltimore: Johns Hopkins University Press.

——. 1992. Introduction to *The Divided Home/Land: Contemporary German Women's Plays,* edited by Sue Ellen Case, 1–23. Ann Arbor: University of Michigan Press.

——. 1994. "Seduced and Abandoned: Chicanas and Lesbians in Representation." In *Negotiating Performance: Gender, Sexuality, and Theatricality in Latin/o America,* edited by Diana Taylor and Juan Villegas, 88–101. Durham, N.C.: Duke University Press.

Case, Sue Ellen, and Janelle Reinelt, eds. 1991. *The Performance of Power: Theatrical Discourse and Politics.* Iowa City: University of Iowa Press.

Castillo, Ana. 1992. *The Mixquiahuala Letters.* New York: Doubleday.

——. 1993. "The Distortion of Desire." Review of *Roosters,* by Milcha Sánchez-Scott. In *The Sexuality of Latinas,* edited by Norma Alarcón, Ana Castillo, and Cherríe Moraga, 147–50. Berkeley: Third Woman.

Castillo, Debra. 1991. "The Daily Shape of Horses: Denise Chávez and Maxine Hong Kingston." *Dispositio* 16.41: 29–43.

Cervantes, Lorna Dee. 1981. *Emplumada.* Pittsburgh: University of Pittsburgh Press.

Chaudhuri, Una. 1995. *Staging Place: The Geography of Modern Drama.* Ann Arbor: University of Michigan Press.

Chávez, Denise. 2000. "The Spirit of Humor." Interview by Bridget Kevane and Juanita Heredia. In *Latina Self-Portraits: Interviews with Contemporary Women Writers,* by Bridge Kevane and Juanita Heredia, 33–44. Albuquerque: University of New Mexico Press.

Chin, Daryl. 1991. "From Popular to Pop: The Arts in/of Commerce, Mass Media, and the New Imagery." *Performing Arts Journal* 37 (Jan.): 5–20.

Choldin, Harvey M. 1986. "Statistics and Politics: The 'Hispanic Issue' in the 1980 Census." *Demography* 23.3 (Aug.): 403–18.

Cisneros, Sandra. 1985. *The House on Mango Street.* Houston: Arte Público.

Cockcroft, Eva. 1984. "The Story of Chicano Park." *Aztlán* 15.1: 79–103.

Colebrook, Claire. 1997. *New Literary Histories: New Historicism and Contemporary Criticism.* Manchester and New York: St. Martin's.

Colón, Miriam. 1989. "Statements by Producers." *Melus* 16.3: 47–50.

Colón-Lespier, Alvan. 1990. "Teatro Pregones: Finding Language in Dialogue." In *Reimaging America: The Art of Social Change,* edited by Mark O'Brien and Craig Little, 251–54. Santa Cruz, Calif.: New Society.

——. 1991. "El teatro boricua de Pregones en los Estados Unidos." *Conjunto* 88(July–Sept.): 47–49.

Colorado, Elvira, and Hortensia Colorado. 1996. "Talking with Vera and/or Hortensia Colorado." Interview by Michelle Macau. *Ollantay Theater Magazine* 4.1: 43–51.

——. 2000. "Storytelling as a Source of Healing." Interview by Michelle Macau. In *Latinas on Stage,* edited by Alicia Arrizón and Lillian Manzor, 216–33. Berkeley: Third Woman.

Conquergood, Dwight. 1992. "Ethnography, Rhetoric, and Performance." *Quarterly Journal of Speech* 78: 80–97.

Constantino, Roselyn. 2000. "And She Wears It Well: Feminist and Cultural Debates in the Work of Astrid Hadad." In *Latinas on Stage,* edited by Alicia Arrizón and Lillian Manzor, 368–421. Berkeley: Third Woman.

Cornejo Polar, Antonio. 1994. "Mestizaje, transculturación, heterogeneidad." *Revista de Crítica Literaria Latinoamericana* 20.40: 368–71.

——. 1998. "Mestizaje e hibridez: Los riesgos de las metáforas." *Revista de Crítica Literaria Latinoamericana* 24.47: 7–11.

Corrales, José. 1996. "A Walk over New Terrain." *Ollantay Theater Magazine* 4.1: 124–26.

Cortina, Rodolfo J., ed. 1991. *Cuban American Theater.* Houston: Arte Público.

Cotter, Colleen. 1997. "Claiming a Piece of the Pie: How the Language of Recipes Defines Community." In *Recipes for Reading: Community, Cookbooks, Stories, Histories,* edited by Anne L. Bower, 51–71. Amherst: University of Massachusetts Press.

Cruz, Migdalia. 1993a. Personal interview by Alberto Sandoval-Sánchez and Nancy Saporta Sternbach. South Hadley, Mass., May 5.

——. 1993b. "The Playwrights Speak: What It Means to Be a Hispanic Playwright, or Am I Latina or What?" *Ollantay Theater Magazine* 1.2: 40–42.

——. 2000. "Black Opium." Interview by Tiffany Ana López. In *Latinas on Stage,* edited by Alicia Arrizón and Lillian Manzor, 201–15. Berkeley: Third Woman.

Cruz, Miriam. 1994a. "Looking Back." *Ollantay Theater Magazine* 3.2: 48–59.

——. 1994b. "Recuentro de mi experiencia." *Ollantay Theater Magazine* 3.2: 86–95.

Cruz, Nilo. 1996. *A Park in the House.* Unpublished manuscript.

Cummings, Scott. 1985. "Seeing with Clarity: The Visions of Maria Irene Fornes." *Theater* 17.1: 51–56.

Cypess, Sandra M. 1989. "From Colonial Constructs to Feminist Figures: Re/visions by Mexican Women Dramatists." *Theatre Journal* 41.4: 492–502.

Daniel, Lee. 1996. "The 'Other' in *Teatro Chicano.*" *Ollantay Theater Magazine* 4.1: 103–8.

Darío, Rubén. 1946. *Cantos de vida y esperanza: Los cisnes y otros poemas.* Buenos Aires: Austral.

de La Cruz, Sor Juana Inés. 1985. "Repuesta de la poetisa a la muy ilustre Sor Filotea de la Cruz." In *Obras Completas,* edited by Francisco Monterde, 827–48. Mexico City: Porrúa.

De La Roche, Denise. 1995. *¡Teatro Hispano! Three Major New York Companies.* New York: Garland.

de Lauretis, Teresa. 1984. *Alice Doesn't: Feminism, Semiotics, Cinema.* Bloomington: Indiana University Press.

———. 1987. *Technologies of Gender.* Bloomington: Indiana University Press.

———. 1988. "Sexual Indifference and Lesbian Representation." *Theatre Journal* 40.2 (May): 155–77.

———. 1991. "Film and the Visible." In *How Do I Look: Queer Film and Video,* edited by Bad Object-Choices, 223–64. Seattle: Bay.

Delgado, Louis A. 1994. *A Better Life. Ollantay Theater Magazine* 2.2: 112–62.

Delgado, María M. 2000. "From the U.K.: A European Perspective on Latino Theatre." In *Out of the Fringe: Contemporary Latina/Latino Theatre and Performance,* edited by Caridad Svich and María Teresa Marrero, 451–61. New York: Theatre Communications Group.

Delgado, María M., and Caridad Svich, eds. 1999. *Conducting a Life: Reflections on the Theatre of Maria Irene Fornes.* North Lyme, N.H.: Smith and Kraus.

DeRose, David J. 1996. "Cherríe Moraga: Mapping Aztlán." *American Theatre* (October): 76–78.

Dewey, Janice. 1989. "Doña Josefa: The Bloodpulse of Transition and Change." In *Breaking Boundaries: Latina Writing and Critical Readings,* edited by Asunción Horno-Delgado, Eliana Ortega, Nina Scott, and Nancy Saporta Sternbach, 39–47. Amherst: University of Massachusetts Press.

Diamond, Elin. 1996. *Performance and Cultural Politics.* London and New York: Routledge.

———. 1997. *Unmaking Mimesis.* London and New York: Routledge.

Dilthey, Wilhelm. 1913. *Das Erlebnis und die Dichtung.* Leipzig and Bern: Teubner.

Dolan, Jill. 1985. "Carmelita Tropicana Chats at the Club Chandelier." *The Drama Review* 29.1: 26–32.

———. 1988. *The Feminist Spectator as Critic.* Ann Arbor: University of Michigan Press.

——. 1993a. "Geographies of Learning: Theatre Studies, Performance, and the 'Performative.'" *Theatre Journal* 45.4: 417–41.

——. 1993b. *Presence and Desire: Essays on Gender, Sexuality, and Performance.* Ann Arbor: University of Michigan Press.

Douglas, Mary. 1972. "Deciphering a Meal." *Daedalus* 101 (winter): 61–81.

——. 1991. "The Idea of Home: A Kind of Space." *Social Research* 58.1: 287–307.

Doyle, Jennifer, Jonathon Flately, and José Muñoz, eds. 1996. *Pop-Out: Queer Warhol.* Durham, N.C.: Duke University Press.

Duarte Clark, Rodrigo. n.d. *Doña Rosita's Jalapeño Kitchen.* Unpublished manuscript.

Durnell, Laura Elizabeth. 1994. "This Time of Truth and Talent: Latina Playwrights Conquer Center Stage." *The Creative Woman* 14.3 (autumn): 9–14.

Eagleton, Terry, Fredric Jameson, and Edward W. Said. 1990. *Nationalism, Colonialism, and Literature.* Minneapolis: University of Minnesota Press.

Elam, Harry J. 1995. "Of Angels and Transcendence: An Analysis of *Fences* by August Wilson and *Roosters* by Milcha Sánchez-Scott." In *Staging Difference: Cultural Pluralism in American Theatre and Drama,* edited by Marc Maufort, 287–300. New York: Peter Lang.

——. 1997. *Taking It to the Streets: The Social Protest Theater of Luis Valdez and Amiri Baraka.* Ann Arbor: University of Michigan Press.

Esparza, Laura. 2000. "Pocha or Pork Chop." Interview by Marguerite Waller. In *Latinas on Stage,* edited by Alicia Arrizón and Lillian Manzor, 248–59. Berkeley: Third Woman.

Espener, Maida Watson. 1988. "Teatro, mujeres hispanas, e identidad." In *Hispanos en los Estados Unidos,* edited by Rodolfo J. Cortina and Alberto Moncada, 285–96. Madrid: Ediciones de Cultura Hispánica.

Eysturoy, Annie O. 1990. "Denise Chávez." In *This Is about Vision: Interviews with Southwestern Writers,* edited by William Balassi, John F. Crawford, and Annie O. Eysturoy, 157–69. Albuquerque: University of New Mexico Press.

Feliciano, Wilma. 1994. "Language and Identity in Three Plays by Dolores Prida." *Latin American Theater Review* 28.1: 125–138.

——. 1995. "I Am a Hyphenated American." Interview with Dolores Prida. In *Latin American Theater Review* 29.1: 113–18.

Féral, Josette. 1982. "Performance and Theatricality: The Subject Demystified." Translated by Terese Lyons. *Modern Drama* 25.1: 170–81.

——. 1992. "What Is Left of Performance Art: Anatomy of a Function, Birth of a Genre." Translated by Carol Tennessen. *Discourse: Berkeley Journal for Theoretical Studies in Media and Culture* 14.2 (spring): 142–62.

Fernandez, Enrique. 1987. "Nuestro Teatro." *Village Voice,* May 12, 100.

Fernández Retamar, Roberto. 1972. *Calibán: Apuntes sobre la cultura en nuestra América.* Mexico City: Diógenes.

Ferreira, Ana Paula. 1994. " 'Los críticos (no) hacen falta': El crítico o la crítica como productores de significado." *Ollantay Theater Magazine* 2.1: 81–88.

Figueroa, Pablo. 1977. *Teatro: Hispanic Theatre in New York City, 1920–1976.* New York: El Museo del Barrio.

Flores, Arturo C. 1990. *El Teatro Campesino de Luis Valdez.* Madrid: Editorial Pliegos.

Flores, Yolanda. 1997. "Performing Difference: Intra-Ethnic Theatricalities." *Feministas Unidas Newsletter* 17.2: 10–16.

——. 2000a. *The Drama of Gender: Feminist Theater by Women of the Americas.* New York: Peter Lang.

——. 2000b. "Subverting Scripts: Identity and Performance in Plays by U.S. Latinas." In *Latinas on Stage,* edited by Alicia Arrizón and Lillian Manzor, 332–50. Berkeley: Third Woman.

Fornes, Maria Irene. 1988. Interview. In *In Their Own Words: Contemporary American Playwrights,* edited by David Sauran, 51–69. New York: Theatre Communications Group.

Forte, Jeanie. 1987. "Female Body as Text in Women's Performance Art." In *Women in American Theatre,* edited by Helen Krich Chinoy and Linda Walsh Jenkins, 378–80. 1981. Reprint. New York: Theatre Communications Group.

Foucault, Michel. 1972. *The Archeology of Knowledge and the Discourse on Language.* Translated by A. M. Sheridan Smith. New York: Pantheon.

Fox, Ofelia, and Rose Sánchez. 1994. "The Playwrights Speak: Sobre nuestra comedia 'S.I.D.A.' " *Ollantay Theater Magazine* 2.2: 34–36.

Fragoso, Victor. 1976. "Notas sobre la expresión teatral de la comunidad puertorriqueña de Nueva York." *Revista del I.C.P.* (Jan.–Mar.): 21–26.

Franco, Jean. 1984. "Ángel Rama y la transculturación narrativa en América Latina." *Sin Nombre* 14.3: 68–73.

Fregoso, Rosa Linda. 1993. *The Bronze Screen: Chicano and Chicana Film Culture.* Minneapolis: University of Minnesota Press.

Fricker, Karen. 1993. "The Challenge of a Monologue in the First Person." *New York Times,* Apr. 4, H10.

Frischmann, Donald. 1987. "Encuentro en Cuauhnáhuac, Aztlán: El XIII Festival Internacional de Teatro Chicano Latino del TENAZ." *Gestos* 3: 133–34.

Fuderer, Laura Sue. 1990. *The Female Bildungsroman in English: An Annotated Bibliography of Criticism.* New York: Modern Language Association of America.

Fusco, Coco. 1995. *English Is Broken Here: Notes on Cultural Fusion.* New York: New Press.

——. 2000. *Corpus Delecti: Performance of the Americas.* London, New York: Routledge.

Galeano, Eduardo. 1971. *Las venas abiertas de América Latina.* Mexico City: Siglo XXI.

Gallardo, Edward. 1989. *Simpson Street.* In *Simpson Street and Other Plays,* edited by John Antush, 15–73. Houston: Arte Público.

García, Cristina. 1992. *Dreaming in Cuban.* New York: Knopf.

García Canclini, Néstor. 1992. "Cultural Reconversion." In *On Edge: The Crisis of Contemporary Latin American Culture,* edited by George Yúdice, Jean Franco, and Juan Flores, 29–43. Minneapolis: University of Minnesota Press.

——. 1995a. "The Hybrid: A Conversation with Margarita Zires, Raymundo Mier, and Mabel Piccini." In *The Postmodernism Debate in Latin America,* edited by John Beverley and Michael Aronna, 77–92. Durham, N.C.: Duke University Press.

——. 1995b. *Hybrid Cultures: Strategies for Entering and Leaving Modernity.* Translated by Christopher L. Chiappari and Silvia L. López. Minneapolis: University of Minnesota Press.

García-Johnson, Ronie-Richele. 1993a. "Cherríe Moraga." In *Notable Hispanic American Women,* edited by Diane Telgen and Jim Kamp, 282–85. Detroit: Gale Research.

——. 1993b. "Josefina López." In *Notable Hispanic American Women,* edited by Diane Telgen and Jim Kamp, 232–33. Detroit: Gale Research.

——. 1993c. "María Irene Fornés." In *Notable Hispanic American Women,* edited by Diane Telgen and Jim Kamp, 160–63. Detroit: Gale Research.

García Romero, Anne. 1998. "The Playwrights Speak: Unearthing Cross-Cultural Terrain through My Plays." *Ollantay Theater Magazine* 6.10: 74–76.

García Vásquez, Guadalupe. 1995. "Hasta no verte, Aztlán!" *Women and Performance* 7.2–8.1: 141–49.

Garner, Stanton B., Jr. 1994. *Bodied Spaces: Phenomenology and Performance in Contemporary Drama.* Ithaca, N.Y.: Cornell University Press.

Geis, Deborah. 1990. "Wordscapes of the Body: Performative Language as *Gestus* in Maria Irene Fornes's Plays." *Theatre Journal* 42.3: 291–307. Also in *Postmodern Theatric(k)s: Monologue in Contemporary American Drama,* by Deborah Geis, 117–34. Ann Arbor: University of Michigan Press, 1995.

George, Rosemary Marangoly. 1996. *The Politics of Home: Postcolonial Relocations and Twentieth-Century Fiction.* Berkeley: University of California Press.

Ghandi, Leela. 1998. *Postcolonial Theory: A Critical Introduction.* New York and West Sussex: Columbia University Press.

Gilroy, Paul. 1990–91. "It Ain't Where You're from, It's Where You're At . . . : The Dialectics of Diasporic Identification." *Third Text* 13 (winter): 3–16.

Gimenez, Martha. 1989. "Latino/'Hispanic'—Who Needs a Name?: The Case against Standardized Terminology." *International Journal of Health Services* 19.3: 557–71.

Goldberg, RoseLee. 1988. *Performance Art: From Futurism to the Present.* Rev. ed. New York: Harry N. Abrams.

Goldman, Anne. 1992. " 'I Yam What I Yam': Cooking, Culture, and Colonialism." In

De/colonizing the Subject: The Politics of Gender in Women's Autobiography, edited by Sidonie Smith and Julia Watson, 169–95. Minneapolis: University of Minnesota Press.

Gómez, Alma, Cherríe Moraga, Mariana Romo-Carmona, and Myrtha Chabrán. 1983. *Cuentos: Stories by Latinas.* New York: Kitchen Table.

Gómez, Javier. 1997. "Actores latinos en Broadway." *Ollantay Theater Magazine* 5.1: 52–60.

Gómez, Magdalena. 2000. Personal correspondence to Alberto Sandoval-Sánchez. May 24.

Gomez, Marga. 1993. Interview by Nancy Saporta Sternbach. Smith College, November 3.

——. 2000. "Way Out Performance." Interview by Michelle Habell-Pallan. In *Latinas on Stage,* edited by Alicia Arrizón and Lillian Manzor, 164–90. Berkeley: Third Woman.

Gómez-Peña, Guillermo. 1992. *1992.* In *Walks on Water,* edited by Deborah Levy, 85–138. London: Methuen Drama.

Gonsior, Marian. 1993a. "Denise Chávez." In *Notable Hispanic American Women,* edited by Diane Telgen and Jim Kamp, 92–93. Detroit: Gale Research.

——. 1993b. "Estela Portillo Trambley." In *Notable Hispanic American Women,* edited by Diane Telgen and Jim Kamp, 323–24. Detroit: Gale Research.

Gonzalez, David. 1992. "What's the Problem with 'Hispanic'? Just Ask a 'Latino.'" *New York Times,* Nov. 15, 6E.

González, Mirza L. 1997. "La trayectoria dramática de María Irene Fornés." *Ollantay Theater Magazine* 5.1: 39–51.

González-Cruz, Luis F., and Francesca M. Colecchia, eds. and trans. 1992. *Cuban Theater in the United States: A Critical Anthology.* Tempe, Ariz.: Bilingual.

González–El Hilali, Anita. 2000. "Theater as Cultural Exchange: A Director's Perspective." In *Latinas on Stage,* edited by Alicia Arrizón and Lillian Manzor, 422–36. Berkeley: Third Woman.

Goodman, Lizbeth. 1993. *Contemporary Feminist Theatres: To Each Her Own.* London: Routledge.

Grandis, Rita de. 1997. "Incursiones en torno a hibridación: Una propuesta para discusión de la mediación lingüística de Bajtín a la mediación simbólica de García Canclini." *Revista de Crítica Literaria Latinoamericana* 23.46: 37–51.

Greenblatt, Stephen. 1991. *Marvelous Possessions: The Wonder of the New World.* Oxford: Oxford University Press; Chicago: University of Chicago Press.

Grewal, Inderpal. 1994. "The Postcolonial, Ethnic Studies, and the Diaspora: The Contexts of Ethnic, Immigrant/Migrant Cultural Studies in the U.S." *Socialist Review* 94.4: 45–74.

Grewal, Inderpal, and Caren Kaplan, eds. 1994. *Scattered Hegemonies: Post Moder-*

nity and Transnational Feminist Practices. Minneapolis: University of Minnesota Press.

Gruber, William E. 1994. *Missing Persons: Character and Characterization in Modern Drama.* London: University of Georgia Press.

Guillory–Brown, Elizabeth. 1996. *Women of Color: Mother-Daughter Relationships in Twentieth Century Literature.* Austin, Tex.: University of Texas Press.

Gupta, Akhil, and James Ferguson. 1992. "Beyond 'Culture': Space, Identity, and the Politics of Identity." *Cultural Anthropology* 7.1: 6–23.

Gussow, Mel. 1994. "Playwright's Tough Subject Draws Funny Offers." *New York Times,* Nov. 2, late ed., C13.

Gutiérrez, Ramón A., and Geneviève Fabre, eds. 1995. *Feasts and Celebrations in North American Ethnic Communities.* Albuquerque: University of New Mexico Press.

Guzman, Celeste. 2000. Personal correspondence with Alberto Sandoval-Sánchez, June 5.

Habell-Pallán, Michelle. 1996. "Family and Sexuality in Recent Chicano Performance: Luis Alfaro's Memory Plays." *Ollantay Theater Magazine* 4.1: 33–42.

Hall, Stuart. 1988. "New Ethnicities." In *Black Film, British Cinema,* edited by Kobeha Mercer, *ICA Documents* 7: 27–31.

Hart, Lynda. 1989. *Making a Spectacle: Feminist Essays on Contemporary Women's Theatre.* Ann Arbor: University of Michigan Press.

Hayes-Bautista, David E. 1980. "Identifying Hispanic Populations: The Influence of Research Methodology upon Public Policy." *American Journal of Public Health* 70.4: 353–56.

Hayes-Bautista, David E., and Jorge Chapa. 1987. "Latino Terminology: Conceptual Bases for Standardized Terminology." *American Journal of Public Health* 77.1: 61–72.

Hayward, Geoffrey D. 1975. "Home as an Environmental and Psychological Concept." *Landscape* 20.1: 2–9.

Heard, Martha. 1988. "The Theatre of Denise Chávez: Interior Landscapes with 'Sabor Nuevomexicano.'" *Americas Review* 16.2: 83–91.

Henry, William A., III. 1988. "Visions of the Past." *Time,* special issue, *¡Magnífico! Hispanic Culture Breaks out of El Barrio* (11 July): 82–83.

Herrera-Sobek, María. 1987. "El Teatro Chicano: Teatro en transición." *Gestos* 3: 135–36.

Heyck, Denis Lynn Daly. 1994. *Barrios and Borderlands: Cultures of Latinos and Latinas in the United States.* New York: Routledge.

Hicks, D. Emily. 1991. *Border Writing: The Multidimensional Text.* Oxford and Minneapolis: University of Minnesota Press.

Hirsch, Marianne. 1979. "The Novel of Formation as Genre: Between Great Expectations and Lost Illusions." *Genre* 12: 293–311.

"Hispanic Theater Discovers Strength in Ethnic Diversity." 1975. *New York Times,* Dec. 6, 31 and 35.

Hollander, John. 1993. "It All Depends." In *Home: A Place in the World,* edited by Arien Mack, 27–45. New York and London: New York University Press.

Honan, William B. 1992. "After State Cutbacks, What One Theater Is Doing to Survive." *New York Times,* July 14, C11.

hooks, bell. 1984. *Feminist Theory from Margin to Center.* Boston: South End.

———. 1990. *Yearning: Race, Gender, and Cultural Politics.* Boston: South End.

Horno-Delgado, Asunción, Eliana Ortega, Nina M. Scott, and Nancy Saporta Sternbach, eds. 1989. *Breaking Boundaries: Latina Writings and Critical Readings.* Amherst: University of Massachusetts Press.

Houston, Robert. 1994. *"Face of an Angel."* Review of *Face of an Angel,* by Denise Chávez. *New York Times,* Sept. 25, 20.

Huerta, Jorge. 1975. "Where Are Our Chicano Playwrights?" *Revista Chicano-Riqueña* 3.4: 32–42.

———. 1982. *Chicano Theater: Themes and Forms.* Ypsilanti, Mich.: Bilingual.

———. 1987. "Algunos pensamientos sobre El Teatro Hispánico en los Estados Unidos." *Gestos* 2.4: 143–45.

———. 1989a. "Developing the Hispanic American Play." *Los Angeles Theatre Center Quarterly* 1.2 (1988): 10–11. Reprinted in *Americas Review* 17.2: 84–91.

———. 1989b. "El Teatro de la Esperanza's *La Víctima*: A Historical Documentary." *Americas Review* 17.2: 93–99. Reprinted from *Centre Interdisciplinaire de Recherches Nord-Americaines International Symposium.* Paris: Centre Interdisciplinaire, 1987.

———. 1992a. "Moraga's *Heroes and Saints:* Chicano Theatre for the 90s." *Theatre-Forum* 1 (spring): 49–52.

———. 1992b. "Professionalizing Teatro: An Overview of Chicano Theatre during the 'Decade of the Hispanic.'" *Tonantzin* 8.3: 3–6.

———. 1994. "Looking for the Magic: Chicanos in the Mainstream." In *Negotiating Performance: Gender, Sexuality, and Theatricality in Latin/o America,* edited by Diana Taylor and Juan Villegas, 37–48. Durham, N.C.: Duke University Press.

———. 1996. "Professionalizing Teatro: An Overview of Chicano Dramaturgy Since *Zoot Suit." Ollantay Theater Magazine* 4.1: 91–102.

———. 1999. "Negotiating Borders in Three Latino Plays." In *Of Borders and Thresholds: Theatre History, Practice, and Theory,* edited by Michal Kobialka, 154–83. Minneapolis: University of Minnesota Press.

Huerta, Jorge, and Carlos Morton. 1993. "Chicano Theater in the Mainstream: Milwaukee Rep's Production of a Chicana Play." *Gestos* 8.16 (Nov.): 149–59.

Ibsen, Kristine. 1995. "On Recipes, Reading, and Revolution: Postboom Parody in *Como agua para chocolate.*" *Hispanic Review* 63 (spring): 133–46.

Jaffe, Janice. 1993. "Hispanic American Women Writer's Novel Recipes and Laura Esquivel's *Como agua para chocolate (Like Water for Chocolate).*" *Women's Studies* 22: 217–30.

Jameson, Fredric. 1990. "Modernism and Imperialism." In *Nationalism, Colonialism, and Literature,* by Terry Eagleton, Fredric Jameson, and Edward W. Said, 43–66. Minneapolis: University of Minnesota Press.

Jamison, Laura. 1991. "Mama's Girl." *San Francisco Weekly* 10.7 (Apr. 17): n.p.

Jones, Delmos. 1992. "Which Migrant? Temporary or Permanent?" In *Towards a Transnational Perspective on Migration: Race, Class, Ethnicity, and Nationalism Reconsidered,* edited by Nina Glick Schiller, Linda Basch, and Cristina Blanc-Szanton, 217–24. New York: Annals of the New York Academy of Sciences.

Joseph, May. 1995. "Diaspora, New Hybrid Identities, and the Performance of Citizenship." *Women and Performance* 7.2–8.1: 3–13.

Kanellos, Nicolás. 1980. "Chicano Theatre in the Seventies." *Theater* 12 (fall): 33–37.

——. 1983. "Two Centuries of Hispanic Theatre in the Southwest." In *Mexican American Theatre Then and Now,* 19–40. Houston: Arte Público.

——. 1984. "An Overview of Hispanic Theatre in the United States." In *Hispanic Theatre in the United States,* 7–13. Houston: Arte Público.

——. 1987. *Mexican-American Theatre: Legacy and Reality.* Pittsburgh: Latin American Literary Review.

——. 1990. *A History of Hispanic Theatre in the United States: Origins to 1940.* Austin: University of Texas Press.

——. 1992. "Hispanic Theatre in the United States: Post-War to the Present." *Latin American Theatre Review* 25.2 (spring): 197–209.

——. 1994. *The Hispanic Almanac: From Columbus to Corporate America.* Detroit: Visible Ink.

Kapchan, Deborah A. 1995. "Hybrid Genres, Performed Subjectivities: The Revoicing of Public Oratory in the Moroccan Marketplace." *Women and Performance* 7.2–8.1: 3–85.

Kaplan, Amy. 1993. "Left Alone with America: The Absence of Empire in the Study of American Culture." In *Cultures of United States Imperialism,* edited by Amy Kaplan and Donald E. Pease, 3–21. Durham, N.C.: Duke University Press.

Kaplan, Amy, and Donald E. Pease, eds. 1993. *Cultures of United States Imperialism.* Durham, N.C.: Duke University Press.

Kaplan, Caren. 1987. "Deterritorializations: The Rewriting of Home and Exile in Western Feminist Discourse." *Cultural Critique* 6: 187–98.

Keith, Michael, and Stephen Pile, eds. 1993. *Place and the Politics of Identity.* London and New York: Routledge.

Kellner, Elena. 1993. "Carmen Zapata." In *Notable Hispanic American Women,* edited by Diane Telgen and Jim Kamp, 423–25. Detroit: Gale Research.

Kent, Assunta Bartolomucci. 1996a. "Introducing 'Springtime' by Maria Irene Fornes." In *Amazon All Stars: Thirteen Lesbian Plays,* edited by Rosemary Keefe Curb, 97–98. New York: Applause Theatre.

——. 1996b. *Maria Irene Fornes and Her Critics.* Westport: Greenwood.

Keyssar, Helene. 1996. "Drama and the Dialogic Imagination: *The Heidi Chronicles* and *Fefu and Her Friends.*" In *Feminist Theatre and Theory,* edited by Helene Keyssar, 109–36. New York: St. Martin's.

Kintz, Linda. 1991. "Permeable Boundaries, Femininity, Fascism, and Violence: Fornes' *The Conduct of Life.*" *Gestos* 6.11 (Apr.): 79–89.

——. n.d. "The Purified Body, Femininity, and Violence: Adorno, Artaud, Kristeva, and Fornes." Unpublished manuscript.

Kirshenblatt-Gimblett, Barbara. 1987. "Recipes for Creating Community: The Jewish Charity Cookbook in America." *Jewish Folklore and Ethnology* 9.1: 8–12.

Kondo, Dorinne. 1997. "The Narrative Production of Home in Asian American Theater." In *About Face: Performing Race in Fashion and Theater,* 189–208. New York: Routledge.

Larsen, Neil. 1990. *Modernism and Hegemony: A Materialist Critique of Aesthetic Agencies.* Minneapolis: University of Minnesota Press.

——. 1995. *Reading North by South: On Latin American Literature, Culture, and Politics.* Minneapolis: University of Minnesota Press.

Laviera, Tato. 1985. "Nuyorican." In *AmeRícan,* 53. Houston: Arte Público.

Lawless, Cecelia. 1997. "Cooking, Community, Culture: A Reading of *Like Water for Chocolate.*" In *Recipes for Reading: Community Cookbooks, Stories, Histories,* edited by Anne L. Bower, 216–35. Amherst: University of Massachusetts Press.

Leal, Rine. 1993. "Asumir la totalidad del teatro cubano." *Ollantay Theater Magazine* 1.2: 26–32.

Lee, Josephine. 1997a. *Performing Asian America: Race and Ethnicity on the Contemporary Stage.* Philadelphia: Temple University Press.

——. 1997b. "Pity and Terror as Public Acts: Reading Feminist Politics in the Plays of Maria Irene Fornes." In *Staging Resistance: Essays on Theatre and Politics,* edited by Jeanne Colleran and Jenny S. Spencer, 166–85. Ann Arbor: University of Michigan Press.

Leonardi, Susan J. 1989. "Recipes for Reading: Summer Pasta, Lobster à la Riseholme, and Key Lime Pie." *PMLA* 104.3: 340–47.

LeSeur, Geta. 1986. "One Mother, Two Daughters: The Afro-Caribbean Female *Bildungsroman.*" *The Black Scholar* 17.2: 26–33.

Lessinger, Johanna. 1992. "Investing or Going Home? A Transnational Strategy among Indian Immigrants in the United States." *Annals of the New York Academy of Sciences* (July 6): 53–80.

Levy, Deborah, ed. 1992. *Walks on Water.* London: Methuen Drama.

Lionnet, Françoise. 1995. *Postcolonial Representations: Women, Literature, Identity.* Ithaca, N.Y.: Cornell University Press.

López, Josefina. 1993. "The Playwrights Speak: On Being a Playwright." *Ollantay Theater Magazine* 1.2: 43–46.

Lopez, Tiffany Ana. 2000. "Violent Inscriptions: Writing the Body and Making a Community in Four Plays by Migdalia Cruz." *Theatre Journal* 52.1: 51–66.

Lorde, Audre. 1994. *Zami: A New Spelling for My Name.* Freedom, Calif.: Crossing.

Lowe, Lisa. 1996. *Immigrant Acts: On Asian American Cultural Politics.* Durham, N.C.: Duke University Press.

La Lupe. n.d. "Puro teatro." In *Los mejores éxitos de La Lupe,* audiocassette. N.p.: n.p.

MacDonald, Erik. 1995. *Theater at the Margins: Text and the Post-Structured Stage.* Ann Arbor: University of Michigan Press.

Macdonell, Diane. 1986. *Theories of Discourse: An Introduction.* Oxford: Basil Blackwell.

Mack, Arien, ed. 1993. *Home: A Place in the World.* New York and London: New York University Press.

Malinowski, Bronislaw. 1973. "Prólogo." In *Contrapunteo cubano del tabaco y el azúcar,* by Fernando Ortiz, 5–15. Barcelona: Ariel.

Manzor-Coats, Lillian. 1991. "Who Are You, Anyways? Gender, Racial, and Linguistic Politics in U.S. Cuban Theater." *Gestos* 6.11: 163–74. Also in *Lo que no se ha dicho,* edited by Pedro Monge-Rafuls, 10–30. Jackson Heights: Ollantay, 1994.

——. 1994. "Too Spik or Too Dyke: Carmelita Tropicana." *Ollantay Theater Magazine* 2.1: 39–55.

—— (as Lillian Manzor). 2000. "From Minimalism to Performative Excess: The Two Tropicanas." In *Latinas on Stage,* edited by Alicia Arrizón and Lillian Manzor, 370–96. Berkeley, Calif.: Third Woman.

Markham, James M. 1971. "Street Theater Troupes Find the Play's Their Thing." *New York Times,* Aug. 6, 33+.

Marranca, Bonnie. 1992. "The State of Grace: Maria Irene Fornes at Sixty-Two." *Performing Arts Journal* 41 (May): 24–31.

Marrero, María Teresa. 1990. "1989 Hispanics Playwrights Project: The Issues, the Project, the Plays." *Gestos* 5.9: 147–53.

——. 1991. "Chicano-Latino Self-representation in Theater and Performance Art." *Gestos* 6.11: 147–62.

——. 1993. *"Real Women Have Curves:* The Articulation of Fat as a Cultural/Feminist Issue." *Ollantay Theater Magazine* 1.1: 61–70.

——. 1996. "In the Limelight: The Insertion of Latina Theater Entrepreneurs, Playwrights, and Directors into the Historical Record." *Ollantay Theater Magazine* 4.1: 74–90.

——. 1998. "Caridad Svich's *Brazo Gitano:* Cuban Women, Social Memory, and Identity through Afro-Cuban Ritual." *Ollantay Theater Magazine* 6.11: 143–50.

——. 2000a. "Latina Playwrights, Directors, and Entrepreneurs.: An Historical Perspective." In *Latinas on Stage,* edited by Alicia Arrizón and Lillian Manzor, 370–96. Berkeley: Third Woman.

——. 2000b. "Manifestations of Desires: A Critical Introduction." In *Out of the Fringe: Contemporary Latina/Latino Theatre and Performance,* edited by Caridad Svich and María Teresa Marrero, xvii–xxx. New York: Theatre Communications Group.

Martí, José. 1970. "Carta a Manuel Mercado." In *Nuestra América,* 177–81. Barcelona: Ariel.

Martin, Biddy, and Chandra Talpade Mohanty. 1986. "Feminist Politics: What's Home Got to Do with It?" In *Feminist Studies: Critical Studies,* edited by Teresa de Lauretis, 191–212. Bloomington: Indiana University Press.

Martín, Manuel, Jr. 1997. "The Development of Hispanic American Theater in New York City from 1960 to the Present." *Ollantay Theater Magazine* 5.2: 11–37.

Martínez, Marcos. 1998. "Community and the Sacred in Chicano Theater." *Ollantay Theater Magazine* 6.10: 103–13.

Martínez, Rubén. 1992. *The Other Side: Notes from the New L.A., Mexico City, and Beyond.* New York: Vintage.

Martínez-Jaramillo, Cleofas. 1939. *The Genuine New Mexico Tasty Recipes.* Santa Fe: Seton Village.

Massey, Doreen. 1994. *Space, Place, and Gender.* Minneapolis: University of Minnesota Press.

Maufort, Mark. 1995. *Staging Difference: Cultural Pluralism in American Theatre and Drama.* New York: Peter Lang.

McFerran, Virginia Derus. 1991. "Chicana Voices in American Drama: Silviana Wood, Estela Portillo Trambley, Cherríe Moraga, Milcha Sanchez-Scott, Josefina Lopez." Ph.D. diss., University of Minnesota.

McLane, Daisann. 1994. "The Havana Hat Trick." *New York Times Magazine,* Sunday, Apr. 24: 42–43.

Melville, Margarita B. 1988. "Hispanics: Race, Class, or Ethnicity?" *Journal of Ethnic Studies* 16.1 (spring): 67–83.

Mena, Alicia. 1994. "The Playwrights Speak: Was I on the Right Track?" *Ollantay Theater Magazine* 2.1: 56–58.

Mifflin, Margot. 1992. "Performance Art: What Is It and Where Is It Going?" *Art News* 91.4: 84–89.

Miller, John C. 1978. "Hispanic Theatre in New York, 1965–1977." *Revista Chicano-Riqueña* 7.1: 40–59.

Milleret, Margo. 1998. "Girls Growing Up, Cultural Norms Breaking Down in Two Plays by Josefina López." *Gestos* 13.26 (Nov.): 109–25.

Minh-ha, Trinh T. 1989. *Woman, Native, Other: Writing Postcoloniality and Feminism.* Bloomington: University of Indiana Press.

———. 1996. "An Acoustic Journey." In *Rethinking Borders,* edited by John Welchman, 1–17. London: Macmillan; Minneapolis: University of Minnesota Press.

Minich, Julie Avril. 1999. "The Space between the Borders: Strategies of Transculturation in U.S. Latina Lesbian Prose and Performance." Honors thesis, Smith College, April.

Miyoshi, Masao. 1993. "A Borderless World? From Colonialism to Transnationalism and the Decline of the Nation-State." *Critical Inquiry* 19 (summer): 726–51.

Mohr, Nicholasa. 1989. "Puerto Rican Writers in the U.S., Puerto Rican Writers in Puerto Rico: A Separation beyond Language." In *Breaking Boundaries: Latina Writing and Critical Readings,* edited by Asunción Horno-Delgado, Eliana Ortega, Nina M. Scott, and Nancy Saporta Sternbach, 111–16. Amherst: University of Massachusetts Press.

Monge-Rafus, Pedro R. 1990. *Noche de Ronda.* Unpublished manuscript.

Moore, Jim. 1976. "Minority Theatre Branching Out." *Los Angeles Times,* May 11, 2:3.

Moraga, Cherríe. 1983. *Loving in the War Years: Lo que nunca pasó por sus labios.* Boston: South End.

———. 1986a. "Interview with Cherríe Moraga." By Norma Alarcón. *Third Woman* 3.1–2 (1986): 127–34.

———. 1986b. "With Cherríe Moraga." Interview by Luz María Umpierre Herrera. *Americas Review* 14.2 (1986): 54–67.

———. 1993. "The Obedient Daughter." In *The Sexuality of Latinas,* edited by Norma Alarcón, Ana Castillo, and Cherrie Moraga, 157–62. Berkeley, Calif.: Third Woman, 1993.

———. 1996. "The Gaze of the Other." Interview by Ellie Hernández. *Ollantay Theater Magazine* 4.1: 58–65. Also in *Latinas on Stage,* edited by Alicia Arrizón and Lillian Manzor, 192–200. Berkeley: Third Woman, 2000.

———. 2000. "City of Desire." Interview by Bridget Kevane and Juanita Heredia. In *Latina Self-Portraits: Interviews with Contemporary Women Writers,* 97–108. Albuquerque: University of New Mexico Press.

Moraga, Cherríe, and Gloria Anzaldúa, eds. 1983. *This Bridge Called My Back: Writings by Radical Women of Color.* New York: Kitchen Table Women of Color.

Morales, Alejandro. 1988. "Notes from Southern California: South Coast Repertory's 1987 Hispanic Playwrights Project." *Gestos* 3.5: 125–28.

Morales, Aurora Levins, and Rosario Morales. 1986. *Getting Home Alive.* Ithaca, N.Y.: Firebrand.

Morales, Ed. 1992. "Valdez." *American Theatre* (Nov.): 14–19.

———. 1993. "Welcome to *Aztlan.*" *American Theatre* (Mar.): 38–40.

Moraña, Mabel, ed. 1997. *Ángel Rama y los estudios latinoamericanos.* Pittsburgh: Instituto Internacional de Literatura Iberoamericana.

Moreiras, Alberto. 1990. "Transculturación y pérdida del sentido: El diseño de la posmodernidad en América Latina." *Nuevo Texto Crítico* 3.6: 105–19.

Morejón, Nancy. 1982. *Nación y mestizaje en Nicolás Guillén.* La Habana: Unión de Escritores y Artistas de Cuba.

——. 1988. *Fundación de la imagen.* La Habana: Editorial Letras Cubanas.

Moroff, Diane Lynn. 1996. *Fornes: Theatre in the Present Tense.* Ann Arbor: University of Michigan Press.

Morse, Margaret. 1999. "Home: Smell, Taste, Posture, Gleam." In *Home, Exile, Homeland: Film, Media, and the Politics of Place,* edited by Hamid Naficy, 63–74. London: Routledge.

Morton, Carlos. 1974a. "Social Realism on Aston Place: The Latest Piñero Play." *Revista Chicano-Riqueña* 2.4: 33–34.

——. 1974b. "The Teatro Campesino." *The Drama Review* 18.4 (Dec.): 71–76.

——. 1976. "Nuyorican Theatre." *The Drama Review* 20.1: 43–49.

——. 1989. "Celebrating 500 Years of Mestizaje." *Melus* 16.3: 20–22.

Muñoz, Elías Miguel. 1990. *The Greatest Performance.* Unpublished manuscript.

Muñoz, José Esteban. 1995a. "Choteo/Camp Style Politics: Carmelita Tropicana's Performance of Self-Enactment." *Women and Performance* 7.2–8.1: 39–51.

——. 1995b. "No es fácil: Notes on the Negotiation of Cubanidad and Exilic Memory in Carmelita Tropicana's *Milk of Amnesia.*" *The Drama Review* 39.3 (fall): 76–82.

——. 1996a. "Ephemera as Evidence: Introductory Notes to *Queer Acts.*" *Women and Performance* 8.2 (1996): 5–16.

——. 1996b. "Flaming Latinas: Ela Troyano's *Carmelita Tropicana:* Your Kunst Is Your Waffen (1993)." In *The Ethnic Eye: Latino Media Arts,* edited by Chon A. Noriega and Ana M. López, 129–42. Minneapolis: University of Minnesota Press.

——. 1999. *Disidentifications: Queers of Color and the Performance of Politics.* Minneapolis: University of Minnesota Press.

Narvaez, Alfonso A. 1970. "Spanish Theater Seeking a Foothold." *New York Times,* Sept. 1, 30.

Negrón-Mutanar, Frances. 1995. "Beyond the Cinema of the Other or Towards Another Cinema." Unpublished manuscript.

Nelson, Candace, and Marta Tienda. 1985. "The Structuring of Hispanic Ethnicity: Historical and Contemporary Perspectives." *Ethnic and Racial Studies* 8.1 (Jan.): 49–74.

Neuwirth, Robert. 1993. "An Outsider Vows to 'Charm My Foes.'" *New York Newsday,* Apr. 29, n.p.

Newman, Harry. 1992. "The Promise of Multiculturalism." *Tonatzin* 8.3: 21–23.

Norrick, Neal R. 1982. "Recipes as Texts: Technical Language in the Kitchen." In *Sprache, Diskurs, und Text,* 173–83. Brüssels: Linguistische Kolloquiums.

Oboler, Suzanne. 1992. "The Politics of Labeling: Latino/a Cultural Identities of Self and Others." *Latin American Perspectives* 75.19 (fall): 18–36.

———. 1995. *Ethnic Labels, Latino Lives: Identity and the Politics of (Re)Presentation in the United States.* Minneapolis: University of Minnesota Press.

Olalquiaga, Celeste. 1996. "Vulture Culture." In *Rethinking Borders,* edited by John C. Welchman, 85–100. London: Macmillian; Minneapolis: University of Minnesota Press.

O'Neale, Sondra. 1982. "Race, Sex, and Self: Aspects of *Bildung* in Select Novels by Black American Women Novelists." *Melus* 9.4: 23–37.

Ortega, Eliana, and Nancy Saporta Sternbach. 1989. "At the Threshold of the Unnamed: Latina Literary Discourse in the Eighties." In *Breaking Boundaries: Latina Writings and Critical Readings,* edited by Asunción Horno-Delgado, Eliana Ortega, Nina M. Scott, and Nancy Saporta Sternbach, 2–23. Amherst: University of Massachusetts Press.

Ortiz, Altagracia, ed. 1996. *Puerto Rican Women and Work: Bridges in Transnational Labor.* Philadelphia: Temple University Press.

Ortiz, Fernando. 1940. "América es un ajiaco." *La Nueva Democracia* 21.11: 20–24.

———. 1947. *Cuban Counterpoint: Tobacco and Sugar.* Translated by Harriet de Onís. New York: Alfred A. Knopf.

———. 1973. *Contrapunteo cubano del tabaco y el azúcar.* 1940. Reprint. Barcelona: Ariel.

Osborn, Elizabeth M. 1987. *On New Ground: Contemporary Hispanic-American Plays.* New York: Theatre Communications Group.

Padilla, Felix M. 1984. "On the Nature of Latino Ethnicity." *Social Science Quarterly* 65.2 (June): 651–64.

Padilla, Genaro. 1991. "Imprisoned Narrative? Or Lies, Secrets, and Silence in New Mexico Women's Autobiography." In *Criticism in the Borderlands: Studies in Chicano Literature, Culture, and Ideology,* edited by Héctor Calderón and José David Saldívar, 43–60. Durham, N.C.: Duke University Press.

Padilla, Ivelyse. 1993. "Cultural Gentrification: Latino Theater Groups in New York." *Ollantay Theater Magazine* 1.2 (July): 50–53.

Palacios, Monica. 2000. "Dos lenguas listas." Interview by Antonia Villaseñor. In *Latinas on Stage,* edited by Alicia Arrizón and Lillian Manzor, 234–47. Berkeley: Third Woman.

Pavis, Patrice. 1982. *Languages of the Stage: Essays in the Semiology of Theatre.* New York: Performing Arts Journal.

Payán, Victor. 1992. "Gomez Rediscovers Mother, Self, in Funny, Touching 'Memory Tricks.'" *El Sol* (San Diego), Aug. 6., n.p.

Pease, Donald E. 1993. "New Perspectives on U.S. Culture and Imperialism." In *Cultures of United States Imperialism,* edited by Amy Kaplan and Donald E. Pease, 22–37. Durham, N.C.: Duke University Press.

Pêcheux, Michel. 1982. *Language, Semantics, and Ideology.* New York: St. Martin's.

Peden, Margaret Sayers. 1982. *A Woman of Genius.* Salisbury, Conn.: Limerock.

Pena, Silvia Novo. 1993. "Dolores Prida." In *Notable Hispanic American Women,* edited by Diane Telgen and Jim Kamp, 324–25. Detroit: Gale Research.

Peña, Terri de la. 1994. "Spoken Words." *off our backs* 24.6: 10–11.

Peres, Phyliss. 1997. *Transculturation and Resistance in Lusophone African Narrative.* Gainesville: University Press of Florida.

Pérez-Firmat, Gustavo. 1989. *The Cuban Condition: Translation and Identity in Modern Cuban Literature.* Cambridge: Cambridge University Press.

———. 1990. *Do the Americas Have a Common Literature?* Durham, N.C.: Duke University Press.

Perkins Kathy A., and Roberta Uno. 1996. *Contemporary Plays by Women of Color.* London: Routledge.

Perricelli, Antonio Lauria. 1992. "Towards a Transnational Perspective on Migration: Closing Remarks." In *Towards a Transnational Perspective on Migration: Race, Class, Ethnicity, and Nationalism Reconsidered,* edited by Nina Glick Schiller, Linda Basch, and Cristina Blanc-Szanton, 251–58. New York: Annals of the New York Academy of Sciences.

Pevitts, Beverley Byers. 1987. "Review of *Fefu and Her Friends.*" In *Women in American Theatre,* edited by Helen Krich Chinoy and Linda Walsh Jenkins, 314–17. New York: Theatre Communications Group.

Phelan, Peggy. 1993. *Unmarked: The Politics of Performance.* London: Routledge.

Phillips, Julie. 1993. "Her Mother's Voice." *Village Voice,* Apr. 13, 90.

Pilcher, Jeffrey M. 1998. *¡Que vivan los tamales! Food and the Making of Mexican Identity.* Albuquerque: University of New Mexico Press.

Piña, Jorge. 1992. "A Note from the Director." *Tonantzin* 8.3: 1.

Piña-Rosales, Gerardo. 1987. "Teatro Hispánico en Nueva York: El Décimo Festival Latino." *Gestos* 4: 146–49.

Pottlitzer, Joanne. 1988. "The Role of Women in U.S. Hispanic Theater." In *A Report to the Ford Foundation: Hispanic Theater in the United States and Puerto Rico,* 28–30. New York: Ford Foundation.

Pratt, Annis, with Barbara White. 1981. "The Novel of Development." In *Archetypal Patterns in Women's Fiction,* 13–39. Bloomington: Indiana University Press.

Pratt, Mary Louise. 1991. "Arts of the Contact Zone." In *Profession 91,* 33–40. New York: Modern Language Association, 1991.

———. 1992. *Imperial Eyes: Travel Writing and Transculturation.* London: Routledge.

Prida, Dolores. 1988. "Interview with Dolores Prida," by Luz Maria Umpierre. *Latin American Theater Review* 22.1 (fall): 81–85.

——. 1989. "The Show Does Go On." In *Breaking Boundaries: Latina Writing and Critical Readings,* edited by Asunción Horno-Delgado, Eliana Ortega, Nina M. Scott, and Nancy Saporta Sternbach, 181–88. Amherst: University of Massachusetts Press.

——. 1994. Telephone interview by Alberto Sandoval-Sánchez. August.

——. 1996. "Janis Astor del Valle: She Likes It Like That." In *Amazon All Stars: Thirteen Lesbian Plays,* edited by Rosemary Keefe Curb, 21–23. New York: Applause Theatre.

Pross, Edith E. 1986. "A Chicano Play and Its Audience." *The Americas Review* 14: 71–79.

Quintana, Alvina E. 1996. *Home Girls: Chicana Literary Voices.* Philadelphia: Temple University Press.

Rama, Angel. 1974. "Los procesos de transculturación en la narrativa latinoamericana." *Revista de Literatura Hispanoamericana* 5.

——. 1979. "El 'boom' en perspectiva." *Escritura* 4.7: 3–45.

——. 1982. *Transculturación narrativa en América Latina.* Mexico City: Siglo XXI.

——. 1984. *La ciudad letrada.* Hanover, N.H.: Ediciones del Norte.

Rebolledo, Tey Diana. 1987. "Tradition and Mythology: Signatures of Landscape in Chicana Literature." In *The Desert Is No Lady,* 96–124. New Haven, Conn.: Yale University Press.

——. 1995. *Women Singing in the Snow: A Cultural Analysis of Chicana Literature.* Tucson: University of Arizona Press.

Renan, Ernest. 1990. "What Is a Nation?" In *Nation and Narration,* edited by Homi K. Bhabha, 8–22. London and New York: Routledge.

Reser, Phil. 1988. "Marga Gomez Lifting Spirits, A Family Tradition." *San Francisco Hot Ticket* (September): n.p.

Rich, Adrienne. 1979. "When We Dead Awaken: Writing as Re-Vision." In *Lies, Secrets, and Silence: Selected Prose 1966–1978,* 33–49. New York: W. W. Norton.

——. 1986. "Notes toward a Politics of Location." In *Blood, Bread, and Poetry,* 210–31. New York: W. W. Norton.

Richard, Nelly. 1993. "Postmodernism and Periphery." Translated by Nick Caistor. In *Postmodernism: A Reader,* edited by Thomas Docherty, 463–70. New York: Columbia University Press.

——. 1996. "The Cultural Periphery and Postmodernism Decentering: Latin America's Reconversion of Borders." Translated by John Brotherton. In *Rethinking Borders,* edited by John C. Welchman, 71–84. London: Macmillan; Minneapolis: University of Minnesota Press.

Rivera, Carmen. 1995. "The Playwrights Speak: On Becoming a Playwright." *Ollantay Theater Magazine* 3.1: 79–81.

Rivera, José. 1987. *The House of Ramon Iglesia.* In *On New Ground: Contemporary*

Hispanic-American Plays, edited by Elizabeth M. Osborn, 192–242. New York: Theatre Communications Group.

Rivero, Eliana. 1989. "From Immigrants to Ethnics: Cuban Women Writers in the U.S." In *Breaking Boundaries: Latina Writing and Critical Readings,* edited by Asunción Horno-Delgado, Eliana Ortega, Nina M. Scott, and Nancy Saporta Sternbach, 189–200. Amherst: University of Massachusetts Press.

Rizk, Beatriz J. 1988. "El teatro hispano en Nueva York." In *Escenario de dos mundos: Inventario teatral de Iberoamérica,* vol. 2, 307–23. Madrid: Centro de Documentación Teatral, Ministerio de Cultura.

———. 1990. "El teatro latino de Estados Unidos." *Tramoya: Cuaderno de Teatro* 22 (January–March): 5–20.

———. 1991. "El teatro latino en los Estados Unidos." *Brújula/Compass* 11: 25–27.

———. 1993a. "Cuatro dramaurgos latinos: María Irene Fornés, Miguel Piñero, Tato Laviera, y Pedro Pietri." In *New Voices in Latin American Literature,* edited by Miguel Falques-Certain, 141–56. New York: Ollantay.

———. 1993b. "El Festival Internacional de Teatro Chicano Latino TENAZ XVI: La muestra de un teatro en transición." *Latin American Theater Review* 26.2: 187–90.

———. 1993c. "Haciendo historia: Multiculturalismo y el teatro latino en los Estados Unidos." *Ollantay Theater Magazine* 1.1: 9–18.

———. 1993d. "Logros de la literatura latina en Estados Unidos: El teatro." In *New Voices in Latin American Literature,* edited by Miguel Falques-Certain, 133–40. New York: Ollantay.

———. 1994. "El teatro latino de los Estados Unidos como discurso de resistencia posmodernista." *Ollantay Theater Magazine* 2.1: 114–24.

———. 1996. "Una mirada al teatro latino de los Estados Unidos." *Revista Teatro-CELTIT* 6.7: 52–55.

———. 1998. "Challenging Patriarchalism in Latino Women's Theater." *Ollantay Theater Magazine* 6.10: 90–102.

Robinson, Marc. 1994. *The Other American Drama.* New York: Cambridge University Press.

———, ed. 1999. *The Theater of Maria Irene Fornes.* Baltimore: Johns Hopkins University Press.

Rodríguez, Richard. 1982. *Hunger of Memory.* Boston: David R. Godine.

Roepke, Gabriela. 1993. "Three Playwrights in New York" *Ollantay Theater Magazine* 1.2: 70–88.

Román, David. 1994. "Review of *Memory Tricks.*" *Theatre Journal* 46 (Mar.): 135-37.

———. 1995a. "Carmelita Tropicana Unplugged." *The Drama Review* 39.3: 83–93.

———. 1995b. "Teatro VIVA! Latino Performance, Sexuality, and the Politics of AIDS in Los Angeles." In *Entiendes? Queer Readings, Hispanic Writings,* edited by

Emile Bergmann and Paul Julian Smith, 346–69. Durham, N.C.: Duke University Press.

——. 1997. "Latino Performance and Identity." *Aztlán* 22.2 (fall): 151–67.

——. 1998. *Acts of Intervention: Performance, Gay Culture, and AIDS.* Bloomington: Indiana University Press.

Román, David, and Holly Hughes, eds. 1998. *O Solo Homo: The New Queer Performance.* New York: Grove.

Romero, Elaine. 1996. "The Playwrights Speak: Finding My Voice." *Ollantay Theater Magazine* 4.1: 120–23.

Roosevelt, Franklin D. 1938–50. "The Year of Crisis: 1933." In *The Public Papers and Addresses of Franklin Delano Roosevelt,* vol. 2, 11–16. New York: Random House.

Rosaldo, Renato. 1989. *Culture and Truth: The Remaking of Social Analysis.* Boston: Beacon.

——. 1994. "Ideology, Place, and People without Culture." *Cultural Anthropology* 3: 77–87.

——. 1995. Foreword to *Hybrid Cultures: Strategies for Entering and Leaving Modernity,* by Néstor García Canclini, translated by Christopher L. Chiappari and Silvia L. López, xi–xvii. Minneapolis: University of Minnesota Press.

Rosenberg, Joe, ed. 1995. *APLAUSO: Hispanic Children's Theater.* Houston: Arte Público.

Rosenberg, Lou. 1993. "The House of Difference: Gender, Culture, and the Subject-in-Process on the American Stage." In *Critical Essays: Gay and Lesbian Writers of Color,* edited by Emmanuel S. Nelson, 97–110. New York: Harrington Park.

Rouse, Roger. 1991. "Mexican Migration and the Social Space of Postmodernism." *Diaspora* 1.1 (spring): 8–23.

——. 1992. "Making Sense of Settlement: Class Transformation, Cultural Struggle, and Transnationalism among Mexican Migrants in the United States." In *Towards a Transnational Perspective on Migration: Race, Class, Ethnicity, and Nationalsim Reconsidered,* edited by Nina Glick Schiller, Linda Basch, and Cristina Blanc-Szanton, 25–52. New York: Annals of the New York Academy of Sciences.

——. 1995. "Questions of Identity: Personhood and Collectivity in Transnational Migration to the United States." *Critique of Anthropology* 15.4: 351–80.

Ruffinelli, Jorge. 1983. "Angel Rama: La carrera del crítico de fondo." *Escritura* 8.15 (Jan.–June): 123–31.

Rykwert, Joseph. 1993. "House and Home." In *Home: A Place in the World,* edited by Arien Mack, 47–58. New York and London: New York University Press.

Sachs, Susan. 1999. "Boy's Kin Say That His Story of Solo Woe Is Contrived." *New York Times,* June 30, A21.

Safran, William. 1991. "Diasporas in Modern Societies: Myths of Homeland and Return." *Diaspora* 1.1: 83–99.

Sahagún, Fray Bernardino de. 1961. *The People.* Book 10, vol. 14.11 of *General History of the Things of New Spain.* Santa Fe: University of New Mexico, School of American Research.

Said, Edward W. 1983. *The World, the Text, and the Critic.* Cambridge, Mass.: Harvard University Press.

Saldívar, José David. 1991a. "Chicano Border Narratives as Cultural Critique." In *Criticism in the Borderlands: Studies in Chicano Literature, Culture, and Ideology,* edited by Héctor Calderón and José David Saldívar, 167–80. Durham, N.C.: Duke University Press.

——. 1991b. *The Dialectics of Our America: Genealogy, Cultural Critique, and Literary History.* Durham, N.C.: Duke University Press.

——. 1997. *Border Matters: Remapping American Cultural Studies.* Berkeley: University of California Press.

Sánchez, Edwin. 1996. *Unmerciful Good Fortune.* New York: Broadway Play Publishing.

Sánchez-Scott, Milcha. 1990. "Language as a Cure: An Interview with Milcha Sanchez-Scott." By Jon Bouknight. *Latin American Theater Review* 23.2: 63–74.

Sandla, Robert. 1991. "Downtown: Not Dead Yet." *Dance Magazine* 65 (Mar.): 70–71.

Sandoval, Chela. 1991. "U.S. Third World Feminism: The Theory and Method of Oppositional Consciousness." *Genders* 10 (spring): 1–24.

Sandoval-Sánchez, Alberto. 1990. "*Coser y cantar* de Dolores Prida." *Tramoya* 22: 111–15.

——. 1993. "La puesta en escena de la familia puertorriqueña." *Revista Iberoamericana* 162–63 (Jan.–June): 345–59.

——. 1994. "Staging AIDS: What's Latinos Got to Do with It?" In *Negotiating Performance: Gender, Sexuality, and Theatricality in Latin/o America,* edited by Diana Taylor and Juan Villegas, 49–66. Durham, N.C.: Duke University Press.

——. 1999. *José, Can You See? Latinos on and off Broadway.* Madison: University of Wisconsin Press.

——. 2000. "No More 'Beautiful Señoritas': U.S. Latina Playwrights' Deconstruction of Beauty Myths and Gender Stereotypes." In *Latinas on Stage,* edited by Alicia Arrizón and Lillian Manzor, 304–31. Berkeley: Third Woman.

Sandoval-Sánchez, Alberto, and Nancy Saporta Sternbach. 1996. "Rehearsing in Front of the Mirror: Marga Gomez' Lesbian Subjectivity as a Work-in-Progress." *Women and Performance* 8.2 (April): 205–23.

——. 1999. "Performing and Constructing Hybrid Identities in U.S. Latina Theatre."

Paper presented at the New Immigrants of the United States Conference, November, Huelva, Spain.

——, eds. 2000. *Puro Teatro: A Latina Anthology.* Tucson: University of Arizona Press.

——. Forthcoming. "Revisiting Chicana Cultural Icons: From Sor Juana to Frida." In *The State of Latino Theater in the U.S.: Mexican-American, Cuban-American, Puerto Rican, and Other Hispanic Voices of the Diaspora,* edited by Luis A. Ramos-García. Minneapolis, Minn.: Hispanic Issues.

Santeiro, Luis. 1994. *The Rooster and the Egg.* Unpublished manuscript.

Sarup, Madan. 1994. "Home and Identity." In *Travellers' Tales: Narratives of Home and Displacement,* edited by George Robertson, Melinda Mash, Lisa Tickner, Jon Bird, Barry Curtis, and Tim Punam, 93–104. New York and London: Routledge.

Schiller, Nina Glick, Linda Basch, and Cristina Blanc-Szanton. 1992a. "Towards a Definition of Transnationalism: Introductory Remarks and Research Questions." Introduction to *Towards a Transnational Perspective on Migration: Race, Class, Ethnicity, and Nationalism Reconsidered,* edited by Nina Glick Schiller, Linda Basch, and Cristina Blanc-Szanton, ix–xiv. New York: Annals of the New York Academy of Sciences.

——. 1992b. "Transnationalism: A New Analytic Framework for Understanding Migration." In *Towards a Transnational Perspective on Migration: Race, Class, Ethnicity, and Nationalism Reconsidered,* edited by Nina Glick Schiller, Linda Basch, and Cristina Blanc-Szanton, 1–24. New York: Annals of the New York Academy of Sciences.

Schmidt, Friedheim. 1994. "¿Literaturas heterogéneas o literatura de la transculturación?" *Nuevo Texto Crítico* 7.14–15 (July): 193–99.

Schuler, Catherine A. 1990. "Gender Perspective and Violence in the Plays of Maria Irene Fornes and Sam Shepard." In *Modern American Drama: The Female Canon,* edited by June Schlueter, 218–28. Toronto: Associated University Press.

Scott, Nina M. 1992. "Juana Manuela Gorriti's *Cocina ecléctica:* Recipes as Feminine Discourse." *Hispania* 75.2: 310–14.

Serematakis, C. Nadia, ed. 1996. *The Senses Still: Perception and Memory as Material Culture in Modernity.* Chicago: University of Chicago Press.

Sheffer, Gabriel, ed. 1986. *Modern Diasporas in International Politics.* New York: St. Martin's.

Shigley, Sally Bishop. 1997. "Empathy, Energy, and Eating: Politics and Power in *The Black Family Dinner Quilt Cookbook.*" In *Recipes for Reading: Community, Cookbooks, Stories, Histories,* edited by Anne L. Bower, 118–31. Amherst: University Press of Massachusetts.

Shirakawa, Sam H. 1988. "Beyond the Ghetto Mentality." *TheaterWeek* (May 16–22): 33–37.

Shohat, Ella. 1992. "Notes on the Post-Colonial." *Social Text* 10.2–3: 99–113.

Shohat, Ella, and Robert Stam. 1994. *Unthinking Eurocentrism: Multiculturalism and the Media.* New York and London: Routledge.

Shorris, Earl. 1992. "Latino, Sí. Hispanic, No." *New York Times,* Oct. 28, A21.

Sider, Gerald. 1992. "The Contradictions of Transnational Migration: A Discussion." In *Towards a Transnational Perspective on Migration: Race, Class, Ethnicity, and Nationalism Reconsidered,* edited by Nina Glick Schiller, Linda Basch, and Cristina Blanc-Szanton, 231–40. New York: Annals of the New York Academy of Sciences.

Smith, Barbara. 1989. "A Press of Our Own. Kitchen Table: Women of Color Press." *Frontiers* 10.3: 11–13.

Smith, John H. 1987. "Cultivating Gender: Sexual Difference, Bildung, and the Bildungsroman." *Michigan Germanic Studies* 13.2: 206–25.

Sommers, Joseph. 1977. "From the Critical Premise to the Product: Critical Modes and Their Applications to a Chicano Literary Text." *New Scholar* 6: 51–80.

Sommers, Joseph, and Tomas Ybarra-Frausto, eds. 1979. *Modern Chicano Writers: A Collection of Critical Essays.* Englewood, N.J.: Prentice Hall.

Sopher, David E. 1979. "The Landscape of Home." In *The Interpretation of Ordinary Landscapes: Geographical Essays,* 129–49. New York and Oxford: Oxford University Press.

Spitta, Silvia. 1995. *Between Two Waters: Transculturation and the Ambiguity of Signs in Latin America.* Houston: Rice University Press.

——. 1997. "The Spice of Life, the Taste of Diversity: Latin American Poetic Recipes and Iconoclastic Prayers." *Americas Review* 24.1–2: 197–226.

——. n.d. "Theories of Colonialism in/of the Americas: Towards a Post-Colonial American Imagery." Unpublished manuscript.

Svich, Caridad. 1998. "The Playwrights Speak." Interview by Pedro Monge-Rafuls. *Ollantay Theater Magazine* 6.11: 132–42.

——. 2000. "In Defense of Beauty." In *Out of the Fringe: Contemporary Latina/Latino Theatre and Performance,* edited by Caridad Svich and María Teresa Marrero, ix–xvi. New York: Theatre Communications Group.

Swales, Martin. 1978. *The German Bildungsroman from Wieland to Hesse.* Princeton, N.J.: Princeton University Press.

Tamblyn, Christine. 1990. "Hybridized Art." *Artweek* 21.1 (May): 18–19.

Taylor, Diana. 1991a. "La representación de la otredad en el teatro y cine latinoamericano y chicano." *Gestos* 6.11: 7–10.

——. 1991b. *Theatre of Crisis: Drama and Politics in Latin America.* Lexington: University of Kentucky Press.

——. 1991c. "Transculturating Transculturation." In *Interculturalism and Performance,* edited by Bonnie Marranca and Gautam Dasgupta, 60–74. New York: PAJ.

——. 1998. "A Savage Performance: 'The Couple in the Cage.'" *The Drama Review* 42.2 (summer): 160–75.

Taylor, Diana, and Juan Villegas, eds. 1994. *Negotiating Performance: Gender, Sexuality, and Theatricality in Latin/o America.* Durham, N.C.: Duke University Press.

Telgen, Diane, and Jim Kamp, eds. 1993. *Notable Hispanic American Women.* Detroit: Gale Research.

Tienda, Marta, and Vilma Ortíz. 1986. " 'Hispanicity' and the 1980 Census." *Social Science Quarterly* 67 (Mar.): 3–20.

Turner, Joseph. 1979. "The Kinds of Historical Fiction: An Essay in Definition and Methodology." *Genre* 13 (fall): 333–55.

Turner, Victor. 1982. *From Ritual to Theatre: The Human Seriousness of Play.* New York: Performing Arts Journal.

——. 1983. *Drama, Fields, and Metaphors: Symbolic Action in Human Society.* Ithaca, N.Y.: Cornell University Press.

Uno, Roberta. 1994. "Marga Gomez: Resistance from the Periphery." *International Theatre Forum* 4: 4–10.

Valdez, Luis. 1971. "Notes on Chicano Theater." *Latin American Theatre Review* 4.2: 52–55.

——. 1990. *Luis Valdez—Early Works: Actos, Bernabé, and Pensamiento Serpentino.* Houston: Arte Público.

——. 1992. *I Don't Have to Show You No Stinking Badges.* In *Zoot Suit and Other Plays,* 155–214. Houston: Arte Público.

van Gennep, Arnold. 1993. *The Rites of Passage.* 1960. Reprint. Chicago: University of Chicago Press.

Vasconcelos, José. 1942. *La raza cósmica.* In *Vasconcelos,* edited by Genaro Fernández MacGregor, 87–130. Mexico City: Ediciones de la Secretaría de Educación Pública.

Villarreal, Edit. 1989. "El Teatro Ensemble de UCSD: First International Tour." *Americas Review* 17.2: 73–83.

Villegas, Juan. 1988. "La estrategia llamada transculturación." *Conjunto* (July–September): 3–7.

Wald, Priscilla. 1993. "Terms of Assimilation: Legislating Subjectivity in the Emerging Nation." In *Cultures of United States Imperialism,* edited by Amy Kaplan and Donald E. Pease, 59–84. Durham, N.C.: Duke University Press.

Waller, Marguerite. 1994. "Border Boda or Divorce Fronterizo." In *Negotiating Performance: Gender, Sexuality, and Theatricality in Latin/o America,* edited by Diana Taylor and Juan Villegas, 67–87. Durham, N.C.: Duke University Press.

Ward, Skye. 1993. "Cherríe Moraga." In *Contemporary Lesbian Writers of the United States: A Bio-Bibliographical Critical Sourcebook,* edited by Sandra Pollack and Denise D. Knight, 379–83. Westport, Conn.: Greenwood.

Watson, Maida. 1988. "Teatro, mujeres hispanas, e identidad." In *Hispanos en los Estados Unidos,* edited by Rodolfo J. Cortina and Alberto Moncada, 287–

96. Madrid: Ediciones de Cultura Hispánica, Instituto de Cooperación Ibero-americana.

———. 1991. "The Search for Identity in the Theater of Three Cuban American Female Dramatists." *Bilingual Review* (Revista Bilingüe) 16.2–3: 188–96.

Welchman, John C. 1996. "The Philosophical Brothel." In *Rethinking Borders,* edited by John C. Welchman, 160–86. London: Macmillan; Minneapolis: University of Minnesota Press.

Weiss, Judith. 1981. " 'Broadway es sólo una calle': Dolores Prida y el teatro hispano de Nueva York." *Areíto* 7.28: 51–53.

———. 1994. "Mainstreaming Traditional Culture: Luis Valdez's Television Adaptation of the Pastorela." *Ollantay Theater Magazine* 2.1: 31–38.

West, Cornel. 1990. "The New Cultural Politics of Difference." In *Out There: Marginalization and Contemporary Cultures,* edited by Russell Ferguson, Martha Gever, Trinh T. Minh-ha, and Cornel West, 19–36. New York: New Museum of Contemporary Art; Cambridge, Mass.: MIT Press.

Weston, Kath. 1991. *Families We Choose: Lesbians, Gays, and Kinship.* New York: Columbia University Press.

Wetzsteon, Ross. 1992. "A Different Light." *Village Voice,* Aug. 11, 99–100.

Williams, Brett. 1997. "Why Migrant Women Feed Their Husbands Tamales: Foodways as a Basis for a Revisionist View of Tejano Family Life." 1984. Reprinted in *Ethnic and Regional Foodways in the United States: The Performance of Group Identity,* edited by Linda Keller Brown and Kay Mussell, 113–26. Knoxville: University of Tennessee Press.

Williams, Patrick, and Laura Chrisman, eds. 1994. *Colonial Discourse and Postcolonial Theory: A Reader.* New York: Columbia University Press.

Wilmoth, Charles. 1992. "A Review of Gomez." *San Diego Gay and Lesbian Times* (Jan.): n.p.

Wood, Daniel B. 1989. " 'Magic Realism' and the Latino Theatre Lab." *Christian Science Monitor,* Jan. 3, 10.

Worthen, W. B. 1997. "Staging América: The Subject of History in Chicano/a Theatre." *Theatre Journal* 49: 101–20.

———. 1998. "Drama, Performativity, and Performance." *PMLA* 113.5 (Oct.): 1093–107.

Yankauer, Alfred. 1987. "Hispanic/Latino—What's in a Name?" *American Journal of Public Health* 77.1 (Jan.): 15–17.

Yarbro Bejarano, Yvonne. 1981. "El papel de la mujer en organizaciones de Teatro Chicano" (The Role of Women in Chicano Theater Organizations). *Revista Literaria de el Tecolote* 2.3–4: 7.

———. 1983. "Teatropoesía by Chicanas in the Bay Area: Tongues of Fire." *Revista Chicano-Riqueña* 11.1: 78–94.

———. 1984. "The Image of the Chicana in Teatro." In *Gathering Ground: New Writing* and Art by Northwest Women of Color, edited by Jo Cochran, J. T. Stewart, and Mayumi Tsutakawa, 90–96. Seattle: Seal.

——. 1985. "Chicanas' Experience in Collective Theatre: Ideology and Form." Women and Performance 2.2: 45–58.

——. 1986a. "Cherríe Moraga's Giving Up the Ghost: The Representation of Female Desire." Third Woman 3.1: 113–20.

——. 1986b. "The Female Subject in Chicano Theatre: Sexuality, 'Race,' and Class." Theater of Color 38.4: 389–407. Also in Performing Feminisms: Feminist Critical Theory and Theatre, edited by Sue Ellen Case, 131–49. Baltimore: Johns Hopkins University Press, 1990.

——. 1988. "The Politics of Rape: Sexual Transgression in Chicana Fiction." In Chicana Creativity and Criticism: New Frontiers in American Literature, edited by María Herrera-Sobek and Helena María Viramontes, 245–56. Albuquerque: University of New Mexico Press.

——. 1993. "Cherríe Moraga's Shadow of a Man: Touching the Wound in Order to Heal." In Acting Out: Feminist Performances, edited by Lynda Hart and Peggy Phelan, 85–104. Michigan: University of Michigan Press.

——. 1995. "The Lesbian Body in Latina Cultural Production." In Entiendes? Queer Readings, Hispanic Writings, edited by Emilie L. Bergmann and Paul Julian Smith, 181–97. Durham, N.C.: Duke University Press.

Ybarra-Frausto, Tomás. 1983. "La Chata Noloesca: Figura del Donaire." In Mexican-American Theater Then and Now, edited by Nicolás Kanellos, 41–51. Houston: Arte Público.

——. 1984. "I Can Still Hear the Applause. La Farándula Chicana: Carpas y tandas de variedad." In Hispanic Theater in the United States, edited by Nicolás Kanellos, 45–60. Houston: Arte Público.

Young, Iris Marion. 1990. "The Ideal of Community and the Politics of Difference." In Feminism/Postmodernism, edited by Linda J. Nicholson, 300–302. London: Routledge.

Young, Robert. 1990. White Mythologies: Writing History and the West. London: Routledge.

——. 1995. Colonial Desire: Hybridity in Theory, Culture, and Race. London: Routledge.

Yúdice, George. 1988. "Marginality and the Ethics of Survival." In Universal Abandon? The Politics of Postmodernism, edited by Andrew Ross, 214–36. Minneapolis: University of Minnesota Press.

——. 1992a. "Postmodernity and Transnational Capitalism in Latin America." On Edge: The Crisis of Contemporary Latin American Culture, edited by George Yúdice, Jean Franco, and Juan Flores, 1–28. Minneapolis: University of Minnesota Press.

——. 1992b. "We Are Not the World." Social Text 10.2–3: 202–16.

Yúdice, George, Jean Franco, and Juan Flores. 1992a. "Interview with Tomás Ybarra-Frausto: The Chicano Movement in a Multicultural/Multinational Society." In *On Edge: The Crisis of Contemporary Latin American Culture,* edited by George Yúdice, Jean Franco, and Juan Flores, 207–15. Minneapolis: University of Minnesota Press.

———. 1992b. Introduction to *On Edge: The Crisis of Contemporary Latin American Culture,* edited by George Yúdice, Jean Franco, and Juan Flores, vii–xix. Minneapolis: University of Minnesota Press.

Zimmer, Elizabeth. 1995. "Has Performance Art Lost Its Edge?" *Ms.* 5.5: 78–83.

INDEX

Actos (Teatro Campesino), 98

African Caribbean Poetry Theatre, 61

AIDS, 5, 52–53

ajiaco, 128–29

Alabau, Magali, 62, 198n. 10

Alan, Juan Shamsul, 47

Alicia in Wonder Tierra (Gonzalez S.), 37, 159; discussion of, 179–84

Alvarez, Julia, 49

Alvarez, Lynn, 35, 65, 198n. 10, 199n. 14

Another Part of the House (Cruz), 52, 158; discussion of, 162–67

anthologies, 8, 65, 66, 200n. 16

Anzaldúa, Gloria, 18, 21, 49, 58, 158–59, 175; on borders, 29, 30, 31, 49; and new mestiza consciousness, 70–71, 201n. 21

Appadurai, Arjun, 28–29, 193n. 17

Argüedas, José María, 23

Arizmendi, Yareli, 64, 98

assimilation, 47, 103, 107–8, 130, 131, 149, 180

Astor del Valle, Janis, 53, 62, 157; *I'll be Home para la Navidad,* 5, 35, 159, 171–79

Atracciones Noalesca, Variedades Mexicanas, 100

Aztlán, 29, 48, 136, 146, 155, 159, 184, 185

Bamba, La (Valdez), 46

Barbers and Other Men, Of (Fox and Sánchez), 50, 52, 69, 136

Beautiful Señoritas (Prida), 4, 50, 52, 70, 71, 77, 93; discussion of, 83–91

Belsey, Catherine, 82

Between Two Waters (Spitta), 24

Bhabha, Homi, 26, 154, 194nn. 22, 23

biculturalism, 25, 172

bildungsroman, 168; as theme, 66–70

bilingualism, 34, 61

Bilingual Theatre Foundation of the Arts, 62

Blahnik, Jeremy, 77, 91–92

Blood Speaks (Las Hermanas Colorado), 23

body, 95–96, 194–95n. 26

Bonet, Wilma, 98

Border Book Festival, 63

Borderlands (Anzaldúa), 49

borders, borderlands, 6, 14, 16, 155, 193nn. 18, 20; anthropology of, 30–31; hybridity and, 31–32; liminality of, 184–85; U.S.–Mexico, 25, 29

Botánica (Prida), 35, 36, 50, 52, 69, 70, 136, 171

Brava! For Women in the Arts Theatre, 63

Brito, Sylvia, 62, 198n. 10

Café con leche (González), 61

Cantinflas (Mario Moreno), 99, 204n. 9

Cantú, Norma: *Canícula,* 98

Cara Mia Theatre Company, 63

Caribbean, 15, 17–18, 19–20. *See also* Cuba; Puerto Rico

carpas (tent shows), 59, 99, 203n. 6

casa de Bernarda Alba, La (Lorca), 80, 81, 162, 202n. 5

Castillo, Ana, 175

Catholic Church, 51, 81–82

Causa, La (Rodríguez), 58

Celaya, Gloria, 62

Cervantes, Lorna Dee, 49

Chata Noalesca, La (Beatriz Escalona), 59, 99–100, 203–4n. 8

Chávez, Denise, 29, 44, 54, 63, 65, 98, 102, 197n. 5, 198n. 10; *Novena narrativas,* 50, 58, 71, 77, 90–91, 93, 151–52

Chevalier, Willie, 120, 122, 124, 125

Chicanas/os, 42, 44, 48, 57, 58, 76, 129, 132, 155, 185; food and, 130–31, 136–37; lesbianism and, 113–18; performance by, 99–100; stereotyping, 181–82

chisme, 133, 134, 135, 139–40, 149–50

chiste, 133, 134, 135

Cigarettes and Moby Dick, 52

code-switching, 34, 194n. 25

Colón, Miriam, 62, 198n. 10

colonialism, 15, 26, 194n. 22

Comadres, Las, 62

community, 5, 136–37, 204n. 10

Conboy, Roy, 50

Conduct of Life, The (Fornes), 52

conscientización, 59, 159

Contrapunteo cubano del tabaco y del azúcar (Ortiz), 16

Coser y cantar (Prida), 34, 37

Couple in the Cage, The (Fusco and Gómez-Peña), 23, 98, 192–93n. 13

Crow, Amparo García, 63

Cruz, Migdalia, 44, 53, 54, 58, 63, 64, 65, 68, 87, 157; *Another Part of the House,* 52, 158, 162–67; *The Have-*

Little, 37, 50, 69, 70, 72, 158, 159–62, 164, 166–67

Cruz, Nilo, 48

Cuba, 15, 16, 17–18, 106–7, 109–10, 128–29, 192nn. 5, 7, 9

Cuban Americans, 42, 47, 48, 84, 196n. 14

Cubanidad, 103

Cuban Revolution, 22

Cubans, 42, 47, 132, 193n. 16, 196n. 14; as exiles, 48, 110–11

Cuban theater, 44, 47–48

culture(s), 13, 96; borders and, 30–31; food and, 130–35, 136–41, 147–48; hybridity and, 31–32, 192n. 8; icons of, 179–81; material, 34–35; memory and, 143, 144–45; mythologizing of, 181–82; stereotyping of, 108–9

Darío, Rubén, 14

Day of the Swallows, The (Portillo), 66, 77, 79, 80–82, 83, 91

desire: 115, 116–17

deterritorialization, 28, 47

Doña Rosita's Jalapeño Kitchen (Duarte Clark and Pérez), 130, 134, 135, 136, 138, 140–42, 148–49, 150–151, 206n. 2; discussion of, 140–42, 148–51

DramaDIVAS, 63

Dreaming in Cuban and Other Works (García), 102

Dream of Canaries, A (Saénz), 52

Duarte Clark, Rodrigo: *Doña Rosita's Jalapeño Kitchen,* 130, 134, 135, 136, 138, 140–49, 150–51, 206n. 2

education, 34, 69–70; and culture, 143–44, 145, 146; and home, 162, 167; and identity, 49–50; and patriarchy, 168–69

Emigración (Rodríguez), 52

Escalera, Brenda Cotto, 63
Escalona, Beatriz (La Chata Noalesca), 59, 99–100, 203–4n. 8
Escarlata, Estela, 62
Esparza, Laura, 62, 64
El Espejo, 66
Esteves, Sandra Maria, 60
ethnicity, 20, 48, 100, 115–16, 129, 174–75, 179–80
ethnoscapes, 28, 30
exiles, 104, 106, 110–11, 112, 167

Face of an Angel (Chávez), 102
familia: food and, 136–38, 146–47, 148–49; and home, 159, 161; identity and, 176–77, 178, 179
Farmworkers Union, 46
Fat-Free Chicana and the Snow Cap Queen, The (Romero), 35, 50, 69, 171; discussion of, 130-38, 142–49
Fefu and Her Friends (Fornes), 77, 88, 91, 93, 200n. 15; discussion of, 83–88
female impersonation: lesbian, 123–24
femininity: as subtext, 124–25
feminism, 10, 78, 83, 84, 185; Fornes', 86–87; home and, 167–68, 170–71; lesbianism and, 79–80; Alina Troyano's, 108–9
Fernández Retamar, Roberto, 18, 19–20, 193n. 18
food, foodways: and culture, 132–35, 140–41, 143–49, 206n. 7; Cuban, 128–29; gender and, 136–37; memories of, 130–31; politics of, 150–51; semiotics of, 127–28; and sexuality, 107–8, 115–16, 117; as social code, 136–38; symbolism of, 104, 106, 138–40
Fornes, Maria Irene, 7, 52, 54, 63,

198n. 10, 199n. 14; *Fefu and Her Friends, 77,* 83, 84, 85–86, 87–88, 91, 93, 200n. 15; as mentor, 86–87; other works by, 64, 65, 70, 85, 199–200nn. 14, 15
Fox, Ofelia, 48, 53; *Of Barbers and Other Men,* 50, 52, 69, 136
Franco, Jean, 22
frontera, la, 14, 19, 155
fruit: symbolism of, 107–8
Fuchsia (Astor del Valle), 53
Fusco, Coco: *The Couple in the Cage,* 23, 98, 192–93n. 13

Gallardo, Edward: *Simpson Street,* 47
Galván, Margarita, 62
García, Cristina, 49, 102
García Canclini, Néstor, 31, 32, 33
García Lorca, Federico: *La casa de Bernarda Alba,* 80, 81, 162, 202n. 5
gender, gender roles: and behavior, 120, 124–25, 159, 161; and meal preparation, 127, 136–37; and transculturation, 20, 111
geopolitics, 36–37
Giving Up the Ghost (Moraga), 5, 36, 52, 72, 90, 91, 202n. 3; discussion of, 77–79, 81, 82, 93
Gleaning (Svich), 50
globalization, 28, 153
God Smells Like a Roast Pig (M. López), 48
Gómez, Magdalena, 60, 63
Gomez, Marga, 7, 8, 44, 101, 126, 204–5nn. 18, 19, 20, 21, 22; *A Line around the Block,* 99, 102, 118, 120–24; *Marga Gomez is Pretty, Witty, and Gay,* 52, 102, 118, 119(fig.), 122; *Memory Tricks,* 98, 118, 120, 124
Gómez-Peña, Guillermo, 29, 97; *The*

Couple in the Cage, 23, 98, 192–93n. 13
Gonzalez, Amy, 62
González, Gloria: *Café con leche,* 61
Gonzalez S., Silvia, 157; *Alicia in Wonder Tierra,* 37, 159, 179–84
Good Grief, Lolita! (Bonet), 98
Good Neighbor Policy, 21–22, 192n. 10
gossip. *See* chisme
Greetings from a Queer Señorita (Palacios), 36, 98; discussion of 113–18
Gringa, La (Rivera), 61
Guillén, Nicolás, 20

Hall, Stuart, 26
The Have-Little (Cruz), 37, 50, 69, 70, 72, 164, 166; discussion of, 158–62
Heart of the Earth (Moraga), 44, 45(fig.), 54
Henry Street Settlement House, 60, 62
Las Hermanas Colorado, 198n. 9; *1992: Blood Speaks,* 23
Heroes and Saints (Moraga), 5, 52, 53, 72
heterosexuality, 123–24; compulsory, 77, 78, 79, 85, 113, 115. *See also* sexuality
Hispanic Playwrights-in-Residence Laboratory, 61
hispanidad, 43, 195n. 5
home, homeland, 8, 36, 48–49, 50, 146, 196–97n. 20; concepts of, 153, 158–59; defining, 154–55; and identity, 167–68, 171–79; memories of, 155–56; as myth, 179–90; patriarchy and, 168–70; as prison, 159, 161–64, 166–67; transcultural, 37–38, 156–57
home plays, 157–58
homophobia, 113, 115, 178; and sexuality, 79, 80, 81, 172; as subtext, 5, 52, 69, 82, 176–77
homosexuality, 80, 81, 123. *See also* sexuality
House of Ramón Iglesia, The (Rivera), 47, 50
humor, 54. *See also* chisme
hybridity, hybridization: cultural, 6, 31–32, 102, 194n. 22

identity, 78; border, 29–30, 33; cultural, 18, 129, 130–31, 146; education and, 49–50; ethnic, 179–80, 196n. 16; feminist, 167–68; food and, 139–40, 141–42; formation of, 118, 143, 168–69, 182–84, 187–90; home and, 167–68; Latino/a, 44, 91–92, 193–94n. 21; location and, 8–9, 36–37; marginalization and, 35–36; of place, 153–54; politics of, 20, 54–55, 80, 171–79; race and, 177, 178, 195n. 27; sexual, 83, 120, 122–24; subject formation and, 5–6; transcultural, 48, 69, 70, 71–72, 107–8, 111, 125, 170–71; transnational, 109–10
I'll Be Home para la Navidad (Astor del Valle), 5, 35, 159; discussion of, 171–79
Immigrant Acts (Lowe), 32
immigration. *See* migration(s)
Immigration and Naturalization Service (INS), 16, 92, 150, 151
imperialism: U.S., 14, 15–16
independence: social, 168, 169
indigenous peoples, 17, 18, 23, 98
International Arts Relations (INTAR), 60, 61

Joseph Papp Public Theatre, 61
Juana Inés de la Cruz (Sor Juana), 58, 205n. 1

Kahlo, Frida, 58
Kaplan, Amy, 14, 15–16
kitchen, 8, 36, 129, 205–6n. 1; cultural transmission in, 148–49; as restaurant, 130, 135–36, 141–42; space definition in, 145–46, 150–51, 206nn. 3, 6

language policy: of theaters, 60–61
lard, 137–38, 143–44, 147–48
Latina (Sánchez-Scott and Blahnik), 52, 77, 91–92
Latina/o, 42–43, 44, 195nn. 3, 5, 6
Latin America, 18, 192nn. 11, 12, 193–94n. 21; migrations in, 26, 27; transculturation in, 20–21; and U.S. and, 15–16, 21–22, 192n. 10
Latinidad, 35, 101
Latino Playwrights Lab, 61
Latino Theatre Initiative, 62
Leguizamo, John, 101
lesbians, lesbianism, 5, 62, 80, 91, 102–3, 159; Chicana, 77, 83, 113–18; Cuban Americans and, 84, 106, 108, 112; and identity formation, 122–24, 171–79; liminality in, 184–85; and sexuality, 77–82, 85–86, 204n. 15
Line around the Block, A (Gomez), 99, 102, 118, 205n. 22; discussion of, 120–24
literature, 13–14, 101–2
Living Dolls (Romero), 68
Lolita (Cruz), 58
Loomer, Lisa: *The Waiting Room,* 52
López, Josefina, 62, 64, 65, 71, 87, 157; *Real Women Have Curves,* 36, 51(fig.), 52, 58, 61, 68, 69, 72, 92, 171; *Simply Maria or The American Dream,* 5, 50, 70, 72, 158, 167–71, 206n. 3
López, Melinda, 48

Los Angeles, 46, 62, 198n. 10
Lowe, Lisa, 32
Lucy Loves Me (Cruz), 52, 68

Malinche, La, 58
Mar, María, 62
Marga Gomez Is Pretty, Witty, and Gay (Gomez), 52, 102, 118, 119(fig.), 122, 205n. 22
marginalization, marginality, 6, 19, 35–36, 67–68, 83, 93, 98, 196n. 14
Mark Taper Forum, 62
marriage, 51, 160–61, 166–67, 168, 169
Martí, José, 14, 107, 167, 191n. 1
masculinity, 106, 107, 124; and public space, 145–46. *See also* patriarchy
meals, meal preparation, 127, 130, 205n. 1, 206n. 6; culture and, 136–38; as oral tradition, 148–49; as sharing, 131–32; social setting of, 139–41; transculturation and, 128–29, 143–44, 145
Medusa's Revenge, 62
Memories of the Revolution (Tropicana), 112
memory, 48, 111; cultural, 143, 144–45; and desire, 116–17; food, 130–31; of home, 155–56; transcultural, 38–39, 104
Memory Tricks (Gomez), 98, 118, 120, 124
Mena, Alicia: *Las nuevas tamaleras,* 34, 50, 70, 130, 136–40, 147–50
Menchú, Rigoberta, 23, 24
mestizaje, 17, 18–19, 25, 35, 49, 129, 184, 189
Mexicans, 43, 44, 179–80, 185
Mexico, 15, 16, 25, 29, 180–81
Migra, La. *See* Immigration and Naturalization Service

migration(s), 17, 26, 27, 28, 46, 48, 52, 193n. 16. *See also* immigration
Milk of Amnesia (Tropicana), 5, 36, 48, 98; discussion of, 103–12
Miranda, Carmen, 109, 110
Mitchell, Ana, 54
Moraga, Cherríe, 7, 58, 62, 63, 64, 65, 133, 175; *Giving Up the Ghost,* 5, 36, 52, 72, 77–79, 81, 82, 90, 91, 93, 202n. 3; *Heart of the Earth,* 44, 45(fig.), 54; *Heroes and Saints,* 5, 52, 53, 72
Morales, Aurora Levins, 49
Morales, Rosario, 49
Morejón, Nancy, 17–18, 19, 20, 21, 22, 49
Moreno, Mario (Cantinflas), 99, 204n. 9
Muñoz, Elías Miguel, 48
mural art, 145, 197–98n. 6
My Art Belongs to Daddy (Gomez), 124
mythologizing, 54, 181–82, 197–98n. 6; of borders, 184–85; identity and, 187–90
My Visits with MGM, 69, 70

nation: and transculturation, 26–27
new mestiza consciousness, 70–71, 201n. 21
newsletters, 62–63
New York City, 46, 47, 60–61, 120; Latino arts and culture in, 62–63, 198n. 10
Niggli, Josefina, 59
1992 (Gómez-Peña), 23
nostalgia, 48, 155–56
Nostalgia Maldita: 1-900-Mexico (Arizmendi), 98
novena narrativa, 54
Novena narrativas (Chávez), 50, 58, 71, 77, 90–91, 93, 151–52
nuevas tamaleras, Las (Mena), 34, 50,

70, 130; discussion of, 136–40, 147–50
Nuyorican Poets' Cafe, 61

oral tradition, 99, 133–34
Ortiz, Fernando, 16, 17, 21, 22, 26; on ajiaco, 128–29
Ortiz Cofer, Judith, 102
Ortiz Cortés, Noelia, 63
Our Lady of the Tortilla (Santeiro), 50

Pagán, Irma, 122–24
Palacios, Monica, 8, 64, 102, 126; *Greetings from a Queer Señorita,* 36, 98, 113–18
Papp, Joseph, 60
Path to Divadom, The (Rodriguez), 130, 133, 138, 147–48
patriarchy, 84, 88–89; dismantling, 51–52, 85, 135; home and, 159, 168–70
Payán, Ilka Tanya, 62, 198n. 10
pelado, peladita, 100, 204n. 9
Pérez, Ruby Nelda: and *Doña Rosita's Jalapeño Kitchen,* 130, 138, 140–42, 148–49, 150–51, 206n. 2
performance, 128, 202–3nn. 1, 2, 7; poetry as, 57–58, 60, 98; and reality, 122, 123. *See also* solo performance
performance art, 97, 98–99, 203nn. 3, 6, 204n. 11
Pilcher, Jeffrey, 132
Pilgrim Woman (Palacios), 102
Piñero, Miguel, 47
Pinza, Carla, 62
place: identities of, 153–54
plovel, 54
poetry, 4, 54, 197–98n. 6; Nuyorican, 60, 98, 194n. 25; and performance, 57–58, 117
politics, 71, 83, 87, 93, 151, 158, 201nn. 22, 23
politics of affinity, 5, 189–90

politics of identity, 5, 54–55, 112; in *Beautiful Señoritas,* 89–90; in *I'll be Home para la Navidad,* 175–76, 177–78; sexuality and, 80, 83
politics of location, 5, 36–37
politics of representation, 4
politics of resistance, 6–7, 150–51
Portillo Trambley, Estela, 59, 65, 93, 198n. 10; *The Day of the Swallows,* 66, 77, 79, 80–82, 83, 91; other works by, 66, 202n. 4
postcolonialism, 24–26, 32, 194n. 23
postmodernism, 31, 87, 97–98
Prida, Dolores, 7, 34, 37, 44, 48, 55, 61, 62, 63, 64, 65, 198n. 10; *Beautiful Señoritas,* 4, 50, 52, 70, 71, 72, 77, 83, 84–85, 87–90, 91, 93; *Botánica,* 35, 36, 44, 50, 52, 69, 70, 136, 171
prison: home as, 159, 161–64, 166–67, 170
proverbs, 133, 134–35
publication: of plays, 64–65, 75
Puente, El, 61
Puerto Ricans, 15, 43, 47, 48, 100, 132, 197n. 4; defining, 173–75; U.S., 42, 44
Puerto Rican Traveling Theatre, 60, 61, 62, 198n. 10

queer agenda, 106, 108, 113, 115, 116. *See also* lesbians, lesbianism
Que vivan los tamales (Pilcher), 132
quincentenary, 23–24

race, 20, 129, 192n. 7; categorization of, 18, 192n. 10; and identity, 177–78, 195n. 27, 201n. 22; and Puerto Ricanness, 173–75
racism, 5, 106–7, 176, 177, 192n. 7
Rama, Angel: on transculturation, 17, 20, 21, 22–23, 31, 37
raza cósmica, 18

Real Women Have Curves (J. López), 36, 51(fig.), 52, 58, 61, 68, 69, 72, 92, 171
Rebolledo, Tey Diana, 132
recipes, 129; and culture, 130, 137, 141–42; as oral tradition, 133–34, 148–49; as sharing, 131–32
reconversion, 31, 32–33, 193n. 19, 194n. 24
resistance, 97; politics of, 6–7; social setting of, 139–40, 141–42, 150–51, 178
restaurant: as cultural space, 141–47; kitchen as, 130, 135–36
Revista Chicano-Riqueña, 66
Rhythm, Rum, Café con Leche, and Nuestros Abuelos (García), 102
rites of passage, 143, 200–201n. 20; food preparation and, 139–40, 141, 147; identity formation and, 168, 182–84; theater and, 38–39
Rivera, Carmen, 61
Rivera, José, 47, 50
Rodriguez, Diane, 62; *The Path to Divadom,* 130, 133, 138, 147–48
Rodríguez, Yolanda, 52, 58
Rolón, Rosalba, 62
Romero, Elaine, 64, 157; *The Fat-Free Chicana,* 35, 50, 69, 130–31, 133, 134, 135, 136, 137–38, 142–47, 148, 149, 171; *Living Dolls,* 68; *Walking Home,* 58, 159, 179, 184–90
Roosevelt, Franklin, 22
Roosters (Sánchez-Scott), 52, 53(fig.)
Rosaldo, Renato, 30–31

Sáenz, Diana, 44, 52, 65
Saldívar, José David, 21, 29, 30
Salt (Cruz), 52
Sanchez, Eddie, 50

Sánchez, George Emilio, 61

Sánchez, Rose, 48, 53; *Of Barbers and Other Men,* 50, 52, 69, 136

Sánchez-Scott, Milcha, 7, 63, 64, 198n. 10; *Latina,* 52, 77, 91–92; *Roosters,* 52, 53(fig.), 77

Sandoval, Chela, 5, 153

Santeiro, Luis, 48, 50

Sarita (Fornes), 70, 85, 198n. 14

Savings (Prida), 52

schools of performance art, 63–64

self, selfhood, 54, 71, 78, 98, 135, 155–56

Serrano-Bonaparte, LynNette, 62

sexual abuse, 77

sexuality, 17, 69, 95, 120, 163; lesbian, 77–82, 115–18, 122–23, 172, 175, 204n. 15; politics of, 83, 110, 123, 177–78; repressed, 162–63; as subtext, 85–86, 88

Shakespeare Festival Hispanic Writer's Unit, 60

Shattering the Myth (Feyder), 65, 66

Short Eyes (Piñero), 47

Siempre Intenté Decirte Algo (SIDA) (Fox and Sánchez), 53

Silent Dancing (Cofer), 102

Simo, Ana María, 62, 64, 198n. 10

Simplemente María, 170

Simply Maria or The American Dream (López), 5, 50, 70, 72, 158, 206n. 3; identity formation in, 167–71

Simpson Street (Gallardo), 47

Sisters on Stage, 62

So . . . (Cruz), 53

social action, 5, 58–59, 157–58

social code, 163–64

solo performance, 8, 36, 95–96, 98, 197n. 24; La Chata's, 99–100; by lesbians, 102–3; space and, 100–101

song lyrics: recitation of, 98-99

Sor Juana and Other Plays (Portillo), 66, 202n. 4

South Coast Repertory Hispanic Playwrights Project, 61

space, 5; constructing, 52, 67–68; cultural, 34–35, 132, 135–36, 137; defining, 154–55; public vs. private, 130, 142–43, 144, 145–46; and solo performance, 100–101; as territory, 139–40, 141, 146–47

Spitta, Sylvia, 16, 24

stereotyping, 108–9, 110, 113, 132, 181–82

Sun Images (Portillo), 66

Svich, Caridad, 35, 50, 63, 64, 65, 87

tamalada, tamales, 133, 149–50; and chisme, 139–40; culture and, 136–39, 206n. 7

Taylor, Diana, 96

Teatro Campesino, El, 7, 46, 57, 62, 99, 195n. 2; *Actos,* 98, 206n. 2

Teatro Duo, 60, 62

teatromentira, 54

Teatro Nacional de Aztlán (TENAZ), 59

teatropoesía, 57–58

Teatro Pregones, 61, 102

Teatro Repertorio Español, El, 60, 61

Teatro Thalia, 62

Tejada, Celia, 100

TENAZ. *See* Teatro Nacional de Aztlán

tent shows (carpas), 59, 99, 203n. 6

territory, 52, 139–40, 141, 142–43, 146–47

theater(s), 57, 191n. 2, 197n. 2, 198–99nn. 7, 8, 10; Chicana, 46–47, 58–59; language policies of, 60–61; locations of, 36–37; rites of passage in, 38–39; and transculturation, 33–36

This Bridge Called My Back (Anzaldúa and Moraga), 58

Tierra, Tatiana de la, 102
Tijuana, 31
Tongues of Fire, 58, 98
Transculturación narrativa en América Latina (Rama), 17, 20, 21, 22–23
transculturation, 4–5, 7, 15, 26–27, 94, 135, 143, 192nn. 5, 6; borders and, 29, 155; in Caribbean, 18, 19–20; discursive, 37–38, 187–88, 202n. 2; education and, 49–50; food and, 128–29, 133, 147–48; home and, 156–57; homosexuality and, 113, 115, 123–24; identity and, 8, 48, 69, 70, 71–72, 107–8, 111, 125, 170–71; in Latin America, 20–21; as performance, 96–97; postcolonialism and, 24–25; quincentennary, 23–24; theater and, 33–36; theory of, 16–17, 22–23; in U.S., 103–4
transfrontera, 19, 24, 30, 155
transnationalism, 28, 31, 109–10, 111, 193n. 171
Tropicana, Carmelita (Alina Troyano), 7, 8, 65, 97, 102, 112, 126, 202–3n. 2; *Milk of Amnesia,* 5, 36, 48, 98, 103–12
Tubert, Susana, 62, 64

United States, 25, 27, 29; and Latin America, 14, 15–16, 21–22
Unmerciful Good Fortune (Sanchez), 50
urban settings, 5, 27, 47

Valdez, Luis, 46, 47, 57
Vasconcelos, José, 18
Moreno Vega, Marta, 62, 198n. 10
Villarreal, Edit, 63, 64, 65, 198n. 10
Virgin of Guadalupe, 58, 91, 139

Waiting Room, The (Loomer), 52
Walking Home (Romero), 58, 159, 179; discussion of, 184–90
Watsonville (Moraga), 58
Wedding March, The (Teatro Pregones), 102
When El Cucui Walks (Conboy), 50
Women in the State of Grace (Chávez), 44, 90
Women of Ill Repute: REFUTE!, 63, 64(fig.)

Yarbro-Bejarano, Yvonne, 57, 71
You Don't Look Like It (Gómez), 60
Zapata, Carmen, 62
Zoot Suit (Valdez), 46, 47

ABOUT THE AUTHORS

ALBERTO SANDOVAL-SÁNCHEZ is Professor of Spanish and U.S. Latino literature at Mount Holyoke College. He received his Ph.D. in 1983 at the University of Minnesota. He is both a creative writer and a cultural critic. His bilingual book of poetry, *New York Backstage/Nueva York tras bastidores* (1993), was published in Chile. In 1993, Mount Holyoke College produced his theatrical piece *Side Effects,* based on his personal experiences with AIDS. He has edited a special issue of *Ollantay Theater Magazine* on U.S. Latino theater and AIDS (1994). He has published numerous articles on U.S. Latino theater, Latin American colonial theater and colonial identity formation, Spanish baroque theater, Puerto Rican migration, images of Latinos in film and Broadway, Latino theater on AIDS, and Latina theater. He is the author of *José, Can You See? Latinos on and off Broadway* (University of Wisconsin Press, 1999) and the coeditor of *Puro Teatro: A Latina Anthology* (University of Arizona Press, 2000), with Nancy Saporta Sternbach.

NANCY SAPORTA STERNBACH is Professor of Spanish and Women's Studies at Smith College, where she teaches courses on Latina and Latin American literature. She is coeditor of *Breaking Boundaries: Latina Writing and Critical Readings* (University of Massachusetts Press, 1989) and *Puro Teatro: A Latina Anthology.* She has published widely on Latina and Latin American women's literature and feminist movements. Currently she is completing a book about women and representation in Latin American modernismo entitled *The Death of a Beautiful Woman.*